*Jen,
Always wish
upon a star —
dreams do come
Best Always
Carolyn "C"*

WISHING ON A STAR

Wishing on a Star: The Life of Eddie Carroll
© 2013 Carolyn Carroll and Brad Strickland. All Rights Reserved.

No part of this book may be reproduced in any form or by any means, electronic, mechanical, digital, photocopying or recording, except for the inclusion in a review, without permission in writing from the publisher.

Published in the USA by:
BearManor Media
PO Box 1129
Duncan, Oklahoma 73534-1129
www.bearmanormedia.com

ISBN 978-1-59393-242-8

Printed in the United States of America.
Book design by Brian Pearce | Red Jacket Press.

WISHING ON A STAR:
THE LIFE OF EDDIE CARROLL

BY **CAROLYN CARROLL** AND **BRAD STRICKLAND**

WITH A FOREWORD BY **JAMIE FARR**

Table of Contents

Foreword by Jamie Farr 9

The Warm-Up 13

Entrances 19

Raising the Curtain 35

Hollywood and Bust? 45

Eddie Makes a Name for Himself 55

Stage and Screen and Jamie 65

Carolyn 73

Crushing the Grapes, Sipping the Wine 87

Ready for his Close-up 99

Mr. Cricket Enters 111

"Happy and Fulfilling Years" 121

"Hello again, this is Jack Benny talking…" 131

Eddie and a Small Eternity 143

Lucy and Later 153

Private Moments 167

Jiminy, Jack, and the Curse of Goofy 173

Jiminy Does Japan, Benny Does Cucamonga........................ 185
Upheavals Good and Bad — or Shake, Rattle and Roll...... 195
Jack and Groucho, Together Again.. 205
Always Something New.. 219
Life on the Road.. 235
New Places, New Faces.. 249
Clubs, Recognitions, and Awards.. 261
The Shining Star Begins to Dim.. 273
Eddie's Farewell... 293
Index.. 295
Acknowledgements... 307
About the Authors.. 311

For all of Eddie's family, friends, and fans.

Foreword by Jamie Farr

I don't remember the number on the door, but it was a patient's room at the Motion Picture Hospital in Woodland Hills, California. He was lying in the twin-sized hospital bed — you know, the kind that can raise and lower the head and foot of the bed and that has those awful egg-crate pads that are supposed to stop your body from getting bed sores. *Supposed to.* He wore a stocking cap on the top of his head. I believe that was to cover the incisions that had been made to cut out some of those malignant brain tumors. And a couple of machines were connected to his body, one monitoring his vital signs and one running a tube to his arm and feeding him painkillers. The room had that familiar hospital smell of ozone, and the machine made a typical hospital-machine noise when it emitted its measured dose of medicine.

Eddie was never a dark-complexioned individual, but against the pillow his skin looked even lighter than usual and his face had the coloring of a Dresden doll. His eyes would look up at you and sometimes you got the feeling he was smiling at you and was aware of what was going on all around him. He couldn't speak, but he tried to talk with his eyes.

Keeping Eddie company were my wife Joy, Eddie's daughter Tina, and Eddie's wife, Carolyn. She was sitting on the right side of the bed and clutching Eddie's hand in hers, the picture of a comforting angel, patting his hand, saying encouraging, loving words to her still husband. She was the author of hope.

A doctor came into the room and said quietly, "I need to speak to someone in the family about these last tests." Apparently he didn't want Eddie to overhear the news. My wife Joy has always been considered part of the family, and she, Tina, and Carolyn left with the doctor.

I told Carolyn I would stay in the room with Eddie and take her place, sitting by the bedside and holding his hand. It was an awkward moment for me. Here was my dear friend of so many years incapacitated, lying there in front of me motionless with the exception of the few times he would bolt and groan and almost pull the IV needle out of his arm. I would have to calm him, tell him he had to lie still so the medication could keep him out of pain. And to my surprise, each time I did, Eddie, thinking that it was still his wife Carolyn clutching his hand, would in a weak voice say, "Yes dear."

He made me laugh.

Eddie and Jamie Farr, friends, business partners, and brothers forever.
PHOTO BY ROGER KARNBAD

This moment reminded me of the old joke of the actor on his deathbed. When someone asks him what it feels like to die, the old trouper replies, "Comedy is harder."

Eddie dozed a bit and I looked at him, and just like a movie I saw in my mind an overlap of dissolves in our lives. The first time we met: A charity event hosted by actors Doug McClure and Burt Reynolds. Eddie performed and I did a comedy routine with another actor friend. Eddie and I talked and were amazed at how much our lives seemed to parallel. We exchanged phone numbers. We met again and again and eventually decided to team up with ideas for scripts and game shows. We became close friends, business partners, family friends and finally brothers. I won't go into details because this book will tell the whole story.

Eddie and I would spend anywhere from eight to ten hours a day working on a script for a television series, or a script for a Hanna-Barbera cartoon, or an idea for a new game show. And we would talk and talk and talk. After we both went to our respective homes for dinner, we would get on the phone — and talk and talk and talk. We never got bored with each other. Our conversations covered just about any and every subject: Show business, family, childhood, jokes, you name it and we talked about it. We'd say goodnight and be up early the next morning at the office talking again. And no conversation was ever a rehash. Always something new. We'd solve a problem in a script, or we'd hash out the details of a game-show scoring system. We'd puzzle over how to provide a contestant who looked to be losing the game a chance to make a spectacular comeback with the last question.

It sounds like, and was, a lot of work, but it was such a joy. Being with Eddie was a treat. He and I always got along. I can't remember our ever having the smallest argument. I guess we just had too much respect for each other.

And now I miss our talks, our exchanges, our friendship. He had such positivity. Even in his last difficult days he kept a positive attitude. I was not with Eddie at the very last moment, but that is okay by me because Eddie is still with me. I am still talking to him. I sense his presence backstage just before I have to make my first entrance in one of the many live theatre shows I've been doing. I feel secure knowing he is next to me and encouraging me to be the very best as we always tried to be when we worked together.

Certainly Eddie and I are still talking. What's more, we've still not run out of things to say. Excuse me…

"Yes Eddie. I'll be right with you."

I have to go. I believe Eddie and I are about to have a conversation.

Love,
Jamie Farr
March 12, 2012

CHAPTER 1

The Warm-Up

EDDIE CARROLL: When I was five years old, my mother took me to see a movie called *Pinocchio*. I loved it. The story moved me, the colors, the characters. But the one character in the movie that I fell in love with was Jiminy Cricket, because any five-year-old would love to have a friend so small that you could put him in your pocket to carry around and talk to. The concept just blew my mind.

So when I got home that night, and for the next couple of weeks, I drove my mother crazy. I couldn't keep myself from raving about Jiminy Cricket. She finally said, "Eddie, please give me a break! Stop talking about Jiminy. You're driving me nuts."

So as a typical five-year-old, I said, "Okay, but one day I'll meet Jiminy and he'll be my friend."

I had no idea how prophetic that was.

Years went by, and I became an actor in Hollywood. I did television work, voice-over work, commercials, whatever. And one day in 1973 my voice-over agent, Herb Tannen, called me and said, "Eddie, Cliff Edwards, the original voice of Jiminy Cricket, passed away two years ago and Disney has been spending all that time auditioning all kinds of people to replace him, and they just can't find someone who gets the character exactly. So," he said, "do you think you could do it?"

Being an actor, what was I going to say, "No"? I said, "Oh, yeah, of course!" I hung up the phone and said, "Oh, God, tell me what Jiminy sounds like, please." Because it had been years since I'd heard him.

Luckily my children at that time were young enough that we had some children's albums, excerpts from movies and things, and there was one cut from *Pinocchio*, a bit from the movie, that had the character in it. And Jiminy is saying, "Now, remember, Pinoke, always tell the truth because if ya tell a lie, your nose is gonna grow and grow," and there were a few other lines. So I looked into the attitude, the behavior, and all that, and then I rehearsed Cliff's Midwest drawl, that little twang in his voice, his dropping the g's, and the study became a very, very rarefied thing, to make sure that all of that character, the warmth, the quality, was always there.

Anyway, I auditioned for it. Weeks went by. Months went by. The suspense was driving me nuts.

And finally they came in one day and said, "We want to try you on two new sections of something they're working on right now." Anyway, I went in, we did it, and then Herb Tannen called me to tell me it was official, and then I re-voiced the character for the stereo version of the film, and that led to more and more assignments to play Jiminy.

What most people don't realize is that the character Jiminy, being such an attractive, lovable human being, so wise, gave audiences such a feeling of kindness that eventually he became the ultimate spokesman for anything Disney did. I played Jiminy in sing-along things, instructional tapes, safety films, and educational films. I even traveled to Japan and learned to speak some of his lines in Japanese!

Jiminy and Eddie whose dream did come true. PHOTO BY ROGER KARNBAD

Because I spoke for Jiminy, I spent time in Japan helping them put a program together, teaching little Japanese children how to speak English at an early age so they could get rid of that "rotsa ruck" *r* and *l* symptom that forms on their palate while still young. So later, when they went to college, they learned English and became salesmen for Toyota and Sony, they went out and spoke perfect English, confident and successful, and those people started with this program. Being part of that, I feel proud knowing that there are Japanese walking around today who practiced their English with Jiminy's help, and in some small way I was able to be a part of their getting a better education.

So the fulfillment that I've had through this character over the years has just been absolutely super, and I don't mind telling you that when I get up in the morning and say I'm the happiest man in the world, I mean it sincerely. For me to have seen something on the screen all those years ago and put into a fantasy and then be able to have that kind of longevity means so much.

So, "When you wish upon a star your dreams do come true." I'm a living example. I said, "One day I'll meet Jiminy Cricket, and he'll be my friend," and it happened, and I did become the very character I fell in love with.

Eddie Carroll as beloved Jack Benny.

Eddie Carroll always enjoyed telling that story. He also would add that Herb Tannen, his voice-over agent, seemed so elated when Eddie landed the role of Jiminy that it puzzled him. Eddie asked why he should get so excited about another voice-over job, even if it was as Jiminy, and Tannen responded, "Eddie, this isn't just a job. It's a *career*."

And so it was. From that audition in 1973 until his death in 2010, Eddie Carroll did indeed enjoy a rich, busy, and full professional career as the voice of Disney's beloved little "conscience," Jiminy Cricket. If you've seen any of the later cartoons featuring Jiminy, if you've played the video game *Kingdom Hearts* in any of its incarnations, or if you've ever visited one of the Disney parks and watched a parade or the fireworks show, you have heard the voice of Eddie Carroll.

Not many people outside the business or Disney fandom know that, but in fact Eddie is probably the most widely-heard star that most people have never seen. It was a role he dearly loved, a personality he always protected and respected, and a character to whom he brought the skills, talent, and dedication of a fine actor.

But Eddie Carroll had a wonderful life outside his role as Jiminy. It was a life filled with challenges, with courage, with humor, with a dazzling talent, with a zest for living, with faith, and with a deep and abiding love for his friends and his family: his wife and partner Carolyn and their children Leland and Tina. By turns demanding and rewarding, serious and funny, Eddie's life, and his philosophy, are — to use a term he probably would be too modest to admit — an inspiration.

Along the way, both in and out of his role as Jiminy, Eddie acted with a whole galaxy of stars: Jack Benny, Lucille Ball, Andy Griffith and Don Knotts, and even — in a way, as you will see — with that old rapscallion Groucho Marx. Eddie also developed a major second career as the embodiment of the universally beloved comedian Jack Benny, touring the continent for decades with a brilliantly hilarious and touching one-man show, *Laughter in Bloom,* that Eddie himself wrote. The stage show brought Benny back to life in an unforgettable and uncanny performance that stunned and delighted audiences. And oh, the stories he told! Eddie collected wonderful anecdotes about himself, his friends, and the actors, directors, and other people he befriended and with whom he loved to spin yarns.

We have tried to put all of these into this book to give you a sense of Eddie as we knew and loved him. Still, we feel that Eddie's life and personality overflow the pages. Though he has passed from our presence, Eddie still seems here with us, vital and energetic and overflowing with life and humor and the urge to speak straight from his heart and straight to you.

So we have decided to let him have his say. In the following pages, we'll include the stories that Eddie so enjoyed telling, and we give them to you as he gave them to his listeners, in his own words. We'll fill in the gaps with the facts and the chronology, and we'll tell the story of his life, but try to hear his voice as you read. It is an experience you will never forget. Eddie was a real storyteller, a born raconteur, gifted with a brilliant sense of timing and a twinkle in his eye that no one else could match, and this is your chance to enjoy his gift.

Ladies and gentlemen, meet Eddie Carroll.

Eddie Eleniak aka Eddie Carroll.

CHAPTER 2

Entrances

Before the turn of the twentieth century, Ukrainian farmers found it increasingly hard to scratch a living out of their small farms. Centuries of agriculture had left the soil depleted of nutrients and generations of dividing up land among heirs had left the farms inadequately small to support a family. The rich farmlands of North America offered one avenue of escape and along with many others from the Ukraine, the Eleniak family looked westward and across the Atlantic.

True, the great land-rush days of the United States had ended, and it was no longer possible for an aspiring farmer or rancher to gallop in a desperate race to claim free acreage in Oklahoma. However, the United States wasn't the only country with wide expanses of abundant, productive, and available land. There was also Canada.

North of Calgary, which had been established in the province of Alberta as Fort Calgary in 1876, and beyond the foothills of the Canadian Rockies, stretched the broad prairies. In the early days bison still roamed freely there, though already the agricultural and economic potential of the land was beginning to be recognized. Not only did the prairie offer immense possibilities for wheat farmers, but it also held vast reserves of oil and natural gas. The Canadian government offered good land at irresistible prices (often for free, providing the homesteaders would settle on and improve the acreage), and the Eleniaks were among thousands of immigrant families who responded.

Wasyl Eleniak was born on December 22, 1859, at Nebyliv, district of Kalush in Western Ukraine. Wasyl had heard tales of Canada, where the settlers could receive 160 acres of land for nothing. With only dim prospects in Ukraine, Wasyl determined to make a better life in the New World. Soon Ivan Pylypow and Yurko Panischak, two friends and fellow villagers, joined him, and all three young men left their homeland to travel to Hamburg, Germany, the city from which they planned to set sail to Canada in the summer of 1891. Unfortunately, before he could arrange passage Yurko ran short of money and had to turn back.

Wasyl and Ivan (John) made the crossing together, though. It almost exhausted their funds, so the two of them went to work in Manitoba to earn enough money for Wasyl to return to Ukraine to bring six family members with him back to Canada. After more years of working and saving money in Manitoba, Wasyl and his family moved to Alberta in 1898, where they settled a homestead later called Chipman, Alberta. Wasyl, the

Left: Wasyl Eleniak will be Eddie's great uncle. Right: Ukrainian Culture Center monument dedicated to Wasyl Eleniak and Ivan Pylypiw First Ukrainian settlers in Canada.

patriarch of the Canadian Eleniak clan, became a very successful farmer and lived to the age of 97. Three sons, four daughters, 51 grandchildren, 62 great-grandchildren and many, many great-great-grandchildren survived him. More, Wasyl blazed the trail for a huge, extended family of Eleniaks to make their way to Canada, including his brother Ivan (John), who would be Eddie Carroll's grandfather.

When the Eleniaks first arrived in Alberta, Edmonton was a fairly new settlement. Small at first, it steadily grew until it incorporated as a city in 1904, with a population just over 8,000. Then, the next year, the Canadian Northern Railway connected with the town and, like the wheat on the prairie, Edmonton burgeoned, becoming the capital of the province. Today the city boasts a population of over a million and is a thriving center of commerce, economic development, and culture.

According to family historian Steven Eleniak (Eddie's cousin), the growing Eleniak family settled the prairies around Edmonton, becoming wheat farmers for the most part. They prospered, raised their families, and enjoyed their new lives in Canada. Eddie's father, Peter Eleniak, was part of the generation growing up and getting his start in the years just prior to the Great Depression. Peter was a versatile man who in his younger

Eddie as a child with his parents, Peter and Marie.

days had many different occupations. According to the stories the family still tells, he also had a fairly wicked sense of humor.

"Eleniak" is not a common Ukrainian name. Once Peter got into a serious poker game with some Ukrainian railroad workers, and they decided to take advantage of this naïve young fellow. As they played, one of them murmured in Ukrainian, "Let's clean this guy out." The others silently nodded agreement.

From then on they began to drop little bits of Ukrainian into their conversation as they played, tipping each other off when they had good hands. Eddie's father played poker-faced and lost a little, won a little, lost it again. Finally the railroad workers decided the time had come to relieve the young stranger of his money. One had a good hand, and the others agreed to bluff along to encourage Peter to bet it all.

Except he had an even better hand, and they didn't know that. He played his part well, hesitating, looking at his cards, grimacing, taking deep breaths, squirming. The pot grew bigger and bigger until Peter went all in, and the others matched him. In the end, of course, Peter won the pot, a considerable sum. He raked it in, pocketed it, stood up casually, headed for the door, and — in perfect Ukrainian — said, "Thank you for the game." Then he got out of there, fast.

Peter Eleniak married Marie Starcheski on June 7, 1928. They had four children who survived to adulthood: Edward, Jerry, Bob, and Dale. Although he didn't know it until years later, Eddie shared something with Abraham Lincoln: He was born in a log cabin. It wasn't supposed to be that way, but his parents were visiting relatives in Smokey Lake, Alberta, when Marie went into labor. With little time for Peter to summon a doctor and no time for Marie to get to a hospital from the relatives' log cabin, Edward Eleniak arrived in the world on September 5, 1933. Evidently Marie and Peter didn't consider the sudden birth a big deal — like everything else, they simply took it in stride. Maybe it's typical of his parents that they never mentioned the circumstances of Eddie's birth to him until many years later, after he had grown up, moved out, married, and started his own family.

Eddie's family remembers that he was a delicate child, whom his parents worried about and protected as much as they could. In fact, he was the third child born to the Eleniaks, but only the first to survive infancy. Having lost two babies, Marie fretted about Eddie's health and coddled him a great deal. Maybe she was also a little overly protective of him. Once she took him out with her as she went shopping on a cold winter day, and as usual she had bundled him up warmly. On the trip back home, they rode the streetcar as far as they could and then got off for a long walk home in the snow. Marie didn't notice when Eddie kicked off the blanket covering his leg and foot.

When they arrived home, Eddie's mom saw that her son's leg had turned blue from the cold. She panicked and spent a long time gradually warming him up, first massaging and rubbing the area and then very slowly immersing his leg in warm water, gradually adding warmer and warmer water until Eddie's skin regained its normal pink tone. Perhaps partly because Marie worried so much and looked for any little symptom of illness, Eddie always seemed to be coming down with something. However, Marie's concerns were not just a typical fretful mom's anxieties: her next child, like the first two, died very young.

Eddie certainly didn't seem to be bothered by his sometimes fragile health, and he had a good childhood, even though his enjoyment of it was often interrupted by bouts of serious illness. His family recalls that Eddie had the normal childhood diseases like measles and chicken pox, and also several much more serious ailments: yellow jaundice (we call it hepatitis today), whooping cough, and rheumatic fever, all very grave in an era that had not yet developed much in the way of effective antibiotics. The diseases he suffered didn't seem to slow Eddie down much, though — like his mother, Eddie had resilience and a sense of humor that helped him adapt and cope. He was a survivor.

As if illness were not enough to drive Marie frantic, the occasional accident could panic her as well. In the early 1930s, as the Great Depression hit Canada, Eddie's father Peter managed to get a job working on the railroad. Times were tough, and Peter was grateful to have the position, which involved long, exhausting days and thousands of miles of rail travel. Still, Peter had a railroad car to live and work in, and it was rent-free. Even though it was against company policy, family man Peter let his wife and son join him aboard the train. Eddie once met a friend whose father was also a railroad worker. The two boys played together on the train — after all, they were mobile, and there were no athletic fields or playgrounds handy — and as they ran along the roofs of the cars, Eddie slipped, fell, and broke his arm.

Then there was the trip that Eddie made with his mother to visit Eddie's Grandma Starcheski out on her farm. Marie dressed him in short pants, a shirt, and a vest. Why the vest? Peter had recently given Eddie his first pocket watch, and Eddie had to have a place to keep it! The little boy was so proud of his watch that he seemed to check the time every two minutes. On the trip to the farm, Eddie also was fascinated by the water cooler on the train and took a couple of the small cone-shaped paper drinking cups when he and his mom reached the station and disembarked.

At the farm, Marie and her mother chatted…and chatted…and chatted. Eddie grew bored and finally broke into the conversation to ask if he could go outside to play. "Yes," Marie told him, "but stay close to the house." Eddie went out exploring and soon discovered the huge rain barrel at the corner of the house. Because he still had the paper cups he had picked up on the train, drinking a cupful of rainwater seemed like a good idea to him at the time. Unfortunately, the barrel was a big one, and Eddie wasn't very tall.

He was resourceful, though, and he soon found a wooden plug jutting out from the side of the barrel where a knothole had been stopped up. Eddie found a toe-hold on the plug, grasped the rim of the barrel, and leveraged himself up. He balanced on the edge, bending way over and reaching down with his cup, but the water level was just a little out of his reach. Teetering, he reached farther…and farther…and felt himself slip. As he lost his balance, Eddie let go of the cup and made a frantic grab for his watch. He'd be in a lot of trouble if he ruined it!

However, he had another small problem. Although Eddie managed to grab onto his watch and hold it above the surface, his head and shoulders were underwater, and he couldn't hold his breath forever. Bending his knees to keep his legs and feet on the dry side of the barrel, Eddie flailed around with his free hand until he found the part of the plug that projected inside. He pushed and braced his knees against the side and squirmed and finally managed to get his head out of the water, just in time to take a desperate gasp of air.

At that point Marie and Mrs. Starcheski, who had heard the splashing, came out to see what was going on. Eddie's grandmother helped him out of the barrel. He was soaked from the chest up and dry from there down. And even though her son showed her he had managed to save his pocket watch, at the thought of how close he had come to drowning in the farmyard, Marie Eleniak fainted dead away.

The Starcheski farm could be hazardous to a boy's health. About a year later, on another visit to his grandmother, Eddie asked if he could go play in the barn, and Grandma Starcheski said he could, but gave him another warning: "The plow is out there, and it's really sharp. Stay away from it." Eddie promised that he would. Now, when it hangs on the wall, a plow is stored with the sharp cutting blade of the plowshare pointing upwards. As he had promised, Eddie gave the implement a wide berth and instead climbed up into the hayloft to play. This time he was wearing overalls that closed with snaps. He didn't weigh very much, but maybe he jumped a little too hard, or maybe the barn was just old, but however it happened, one of the dry floorboards gave way beneath Eddie's feet, and he plunged through the hayloft floor.

The plowshare caught him — luckily just by snagging the back of his overalls. It cut through the denim, but only scratched his back. For some time Eddie dangled there until he finally realized that he could free himself by unsnapping his overalls. He did, dropped to the ground, retrieved his ripped overalls, and got dressed again. Then, with his clothes torn and his back scratched and bloody, he went back into the farmhouse. Marie looked up at him as he came in, saw the state of his clothes and back, and once again fainted.

Eddie took the accidents much as he took the illnesses, never letting them scare him too much or hold him back. There were many times, though, that Peter and Marie wondered if their son was going to make it out of childhood at all.

In February, 1940, the Walt Disney animated film *Pinocchio* was released, and, as Eddie enjoyed explaining, his parents took him to see it in Edmonton. It was the first movie he had ever seen, and it affected him powerfully. Eddie's memory played a little trick on him — he was actually six, not five, when he first saw *Pinocchio* — but the rest of his story is accurate. The character Jiminy Cricket simply enthralled him, and Eddie daydreamed about the idea of having a tiny friend like Pinocchio's buddy Jiminy. Then, too, there was just something about Jiminy Cricket's appearance and personality that appealed to Eddie tremendously. He didn't know it at the time, but part of the magic was casting, and part of it was Walt Disney's savvy.

The original voice actor for Jiminy was Cliff Edwards, a popular entertainer also known as "Ukulele Ike." A Vaudeville star and novelty singer, Edwards had made a name for himself playing the ukulele and singing jazzy renditions of popular songs like "California, Here I Come," "Hard-Hearted Hannah," "Paddlin' Madelin' Home," and especially "Singin' in the Rain," a huge hit for him in 1929. In one of those six-degree coincidences that are so common in Hollywood, Edwards sang that tune in a film called *Hollywood Revue of 1929*, a variety-show movie that had as its master of ceremonies a newcomer to film, a dapper young fellow named Jack Benny.

Edwards had a pleasant tenor voice that could effortlessly slide way up into a comic falsetto, and his jazzy scat-singing took on the timbre of musical instruments. If you listen to one of his recorded songs, say "It's Only a Paper Moon," pay close attention to the horn solo. It's not a horn — it's Edwards imitating a horn. He does the same thing in *Pinocchio* in the "Give a Little Whistle" number. His natural speaking voice was a little breathy, and it had a pleasantly flat Midwestern tone that came from his native Hannibal, Missouri. It was a very American voice, laid-back, amiable, and casual.

And that voice landed him the role of Jiminy Cricket in the Disney film *Pinocchio*. As Eddie tells the story, "Walt Disney was simply a genius. He always knew just what he wanted up there on the screen, from the look of the characters to the sound of their voices. When Cliff Edwards was chosen to do the role of Jiminy Cricket, Walt coached and advised him. He said, 'Now, Cliff, here are pictures of Jiminy. He's just a little guy, and I know the audience is going to expect him to be comic relief because of his size, but I don't want that. You see, Jiminy is Pinocchio's conscience, and he takes his job seriously. This picture just won't work if you do a silly cartoon voice. I want the audience to understand that Jiminy is Pinocchio's true friend as well as his conscience, so as small as he is, he has to come across as a father-like character. He cares about Pinocchio, and he's gentle, and he gives him good advice.' When Edwards asked exactly what Walt expected, Walt said simply, 'Use your own voice, Cliff, but speak as if you're talking to a little boy who looks on you as his best friend.'" It was an inspired decision of Walt's that paid off over the years in ways not even dreamed of when the film was being made.

As Eddie always told the story, he drove his mother crazy over the next few weeks by raving about Jiminy Cricket and about wanting to have him as a friend one day. Marie, exasperated, tried to tell her son that Jiminy wasn't real, but Eddie insisted that one day he would have Jiminy as a friend, and he must have wished hard on that star, because one day much later in Eddie's life, he really did.

Early on in his childhood Eddie developed a love of music, and his father wanted to encourage that. A musician himself who played the violin, Peter was not only an expert carpenter, but also an accomplished cabinetmaker and woodworker, and as a surprise he crafted a home-made guitar for Eddie when the boy was only six and in first grade. Eddie began playing with it and learning by ear to accompany himself as he sang "You Are My Sunshine." Then his first break as a performer came. Eddie tells the story best:

EDDIE CARROLL: The teachers decided to have a little concert after a PTA meeting and asked the kids if we'd like to do something, or perform. My father had made me, actually hand-crafted for me, my first guitar, and I had taught myself to play it. My father was a genius with his hands. Every house we lived in, he built from the ground up, including everything inside, and he also hand-crafted both guitars and violins.

I started taking violin lessons a couple of years later, though I eventually gave that up, but that's another story. Anyway, when the teacher asked, I had agreed that I would play the guitar and sing a song at the school that evening. The PTA meeting came, and the kids assembled in the cloakroom, a little hallway behind the wall with the blackboard, where in the winter time we hung our coats. We waited there for the meeting to end so we could perform.

Well, the teacher finished talking to the parents about the curriculum, and now she said, "We're going to have a little concert, a little show for you." So a little girl went out and did a tap-dance routine, and someone else did a recitation, and so forth. And then she said, "Now Eddie's going to come out with his guitar and sing a song."

I'd been practicing this at home all week and telling my folks how I was going to sing, and my mom and dad were out there waiting to hear me. I got up to play that guitar — and my feet froze to the ground. I got hit with such fear I couldn't move, I simply could not move to go past that doorway and out to where the audience, the people were. I didn't know what to do. It was like my feet were nailed to the floor from fear. At the same time, I knew my folks were out there expecting me to perform. With tears pouring down my cheeks, I took my guitar and sang my song as loud as I could behind that wall — that's the only thing I could think of doing. I could hear the audience, the parents, sort of tittering and chuckling out there because they knew what had happened.

Well, thank God my folks didn't say anything negative at all — they told me, "Don't worry, it's okay, it happens," and they didn't try to make me feel bad about it. But even as young child, I was so angry at my inability to have the courage to go out and perform that I promised myself that was never, ever going to happen to me again. After that, for the next few years at school I got into every play I could, every local show I could, everything I could think of to get over that stage fright, and eventually I began to realize what fun being up in front of people and amusing them could be. I went through the strain of forcing myself to go out and do my best in front of audiences to conquer my fear, and in the process I gained such a love of performing in the next few years that I knew it was what I wanted to do.

As he progressed through elementary school, Eddie gradually outgrew his fascination with Jiminy Cricket, at least on the surface, and he even forgot about the details of the film. After all, in the 1940s there were no DVDs of movies that a kid could see over and over again until he had learned every line by heart. However, he clearly had taken something away from his experience of seeing *Pinocchio*, because even then he was developing a kind of offhand, casual charm, a winning stage presence that was so laid-back and confident that no one could guess that he had started off with a feeling of overwhelming anxiety. It was the same kind of optimistic, cheerful approach that Jiminy showed in the film.

Eventually Eddie's younger brothers came along, but Jerry, Bob, and Dale were respectively eight, ten, and twelve years younger than Eddie. The age gap was so great that Bob and Dale's main memories of Eddie are of him being a kind of babysitter-second-father to them. Jerry, sadly, died some years before his big brother realized his dream of becoming a successful performer.

As in all families, Jerry, Bob, and Dale had their share of disagreements with big brother Eddie, but they got along well — and, speaking to Bob and Dale today, one learns that they looked up to him as an inspiration. By the time they were born, as Eddie mentioned in his story, their father Peter had found a new calling, one at which he excelled: he was a genius at building homes. Peter would build a house, the family would live in it for a while, and then he would sell it for a profit, enabling him to build a somewhat better one. The family would move on, and the process would be repeated.

The boys found the constant moving a little tough on them, though Peter and Marie gave them as stable a home life as they could manage. Eddie's brothers remember especially one house that Peter built: it was a two-story home with a basement. The Eleniaks lived on the second floor; a small mom-and-pop store occupied the first floor. They rented the store to a Chinese gentleman named Tom Wong.

The immediate Eleniak family. Top row: Eddie and his Dad, (Peter). Bottom row: Jerry, Bob, Marie (Mother) and Dale.

Eddie always remembered Mr. Wong as one of his favorite characters. Mr. Wong spoke English imperfectly, because he had only recently arrived in Edmonton from China, and in addition to tending the store, he also was willing to keep an eye on Jerry, Bob, and Dale whenever Peter and Marie were out of town, nominally leaving Eddie in charge. Peter and Marie trusted Eddie — but they also knew what boys, and especially their boys, were like. Mr. Wong's oversight helped to reassure them that things would not get too far out of hand when they were away.

Once when their parents were on a trip to British Columbia, Bob and Dale decided to act out the meeting of Robin Hood and Little John on a single-log bridge crossing a stream. They set up two chairs and laid a plank between them to represent the log, and then they chose sticks to be their swords.

Everything went according to the script until Bob thwacked Dale a little harder than he intended. Dale fell off the plank and cracked his head hard, and as even minor scalp wounds will do, it bled a lot. Fortunately, Mr. Wong had heard the ruckus upstairs and rushed in. He cleaned the cut, applied a poultice of herbs, and wrapped Dale's head in a towel. It looked like a turban. When the boys' parents returned, of course Marie panicked, though by this time she seems to have been a little more used to these scenes and no one remembers her fainting.

Tom Wong's Chinese herbs did the trick, and Dale healed quickly and completely. The Eleniak boys learned that Mr. Wong had a deep knowledge of Chinese medicine and of the healing powers of plants and herbs, and they grew to respect him. For birthdays and Peter and Marie's anniversaries, Tom would always cook banquets of Chinese food for the family, and he became an honorary Eleniak.

Eddie's favorite story about Tom went back to a time when Eddie was helping in the store. Eddie stocked the shelves, helped clean, and ran errands, and did other little chores, and one day Mr. Wong "sent me down into the basement. He said, 'I want you bring up my cheese.' Well, I went down to the basement where everything was stored and found the dairy supplies. I could find jack cheese, cheddar cheese, blue cheese, Swiss cheese, and even limburger cheese, but I didn't know which one of these Tom wanted. None of them was labeled 'my cheese!' I even wondered if it might be some weird kind of Chinese dairy product — *Mai* Cheese, maybe — but I couldn't find anything that might be what Tom wanted.

"So I went back upstairs and told Tom, 'I looked all through the basement, but I couldn't find it.'

"'No my cheese?' Tom asked, sounding a bit irritable and a bit astounded. 'No my cheese? Geezie Christ, we got patch yesterday!'

"So he led me down to the basement to show me, but he didn't go to the dairy products at all. Instead he went to where the cigarettes were stored, and beside them he pointed at a big batch of kitchen matches. Tom picked up a box of them and rattled it in front of me, saying 'My cheese! My cheese!'"

Whenever he told this story, Eddie always brought gales of laughter — not only from whomever he was talking to, but also from himself. His warm memories of Tom Wong were apparent, and it was obvious that to the Eleniaks, Mr. Wong was a shining star and an important part of the family.

Eddie's battles with illness caused him to miss a lot of school, but even so, he was a good scholar and maintained a respectable academic record. More than that, he was well-liked by his teachers and classmates. When the time came for high school, instead of continuing in the public system Eddie went to St. Joseph, at that time an all-boy Catholic institution that had been established in Edmonton in 1931. From its inception, St. Joe's offered its students unusual freedom in choosing their studies and their school activities, and it provided the teen-aged Eddie far more scope for developing his musical and stage talents than elementary school had done. He entered St. Joe in 1949 and found surroundings that offered support and encouragement for his developing talents. He also formed a firm friendship with another young man who was to go on to win some fame in show business: Robert Goulet.

Orion Musical Theater program cover, 1956.

Eddie and Robert were the same age and had some striking similarities in their backgrounds. Robert Goulet was the son of French-Canadian parents, although he was born in Lawrence, Massachusetts, so technically he was an American, not a Canadian. Like Eddie, Robert had begun to entertain while still just a boy — and like Eddie, Robert had gone through a traumatic performance that had given him a terrible case of stage fright that he had to deal with as he matured.

Robert's father had passed away when Robert was thirteen, and he and his mother moved to Edmonton. Again like Eddie, Robert worked on his stage nerves by performing and in fact made his first-ever professional appearance singing with the Orion Musical Theatre at the age of sixteen. Even then Goulet was a much better singer, but Eddie had a good voice, too, and the two of them often appeared together on stage in musical performances sponsored by the school.

Perhaps as a way of compensating for his frail constitution, Eddie also went out for football and made the team, playing tackle. Goulet was a running back. The two of them hit it off and became buddies, although occasionally Eddie envied Robert's good looks and charm. Robert seemed to be able to get away with anything and be able to talk himself out of any consequences. Eddie also claimed that he enjoyed hanging out with Goulet because "I had the chance to comfort the girls that really would have preferred dating him."

St. Joe's football, Bob Goulet, bottom row, second from left. Eddie middle row, third from right.

Eddie and Robert became pals on and off stage, on and off the football field, and together they dreamed and planned for the future. Neither was quite sure yet how to go about realizing those dreams, but both of them knew they wanted to go into performance as a career. They received a boost from another young friend, Tommy Banks, today the Senator representing Alberta in the Canadian Senate. Banks himself was musically talented and went on from high school to carve out a career as a performer, producer, and radio and television personality before going into politics, and even though he is today an immensely successful statesman, Tommy Banks still leads his orchestra in special engagements.

Banks transferred to St. Joe in 1949 when his family moved to Edmonton from his native Calgary. He speaks warmly of the friendships he made at St. Joe's and remembers Goulet as a very polished singer already, with a voice that could fill an auditorium, and Eddie as a charming and versatile performer who could do a little of everything — singing, dancing, stand-up comedy, acting, you name it. By then Eddie had developed a nickname, "Sach," which his high school friends remembered for years afterward, though no one could quite recall what it meant or how he got it.

It's a show-biz explanation: From 1937 to 1958, a comedy team variously known as the Dead End Kids, the Little Tough Guys, the East Side Kids, and the Bowery Boys had made a series of mostly low-budget

Orion Drama Club. In the top row, Robert Goulet is second from left, and Eddie is last on the right.

films that featured slapstick comedy (although the first movie the core of the group appeared in, *Dead End*, was a serious drama of delinquency featuring Humphrey Bogart and Claire Trevor as leads). Leo Gorcey was the group's leader for most of these films, playing a warm-hearted wise-guy character called "Slip" Mahoney. His right-hand man, played by the actor Huntz Hall, was a skinny, gawky, amiably dim fellow with a screwball delivery and a precise sense of comic timing. The character's name? Horace Debussey Jones, better known as "Sach."

And the goofy, gangly Sach was one of the many movie characters that Eddie Eleniak could flawlessly mimic — so flawlessly that he gained the nickname himself. Eddie's comic gifts already included a sharp ear for voices and dialects, and he could act or sing in styles ranging from the serious to the flat-out silly. Senator Banks also remembers Eddie as having a dead-on sense of timing with a gag even when he as a teen, and he recalls St. Joe's generally as overflowing with talent.

More than just appearing on stage, at St. Joe's Eddie developed an abiding interest in other aspects of show business, including production, directing, and writing. Even in high school he started to create his own material for stand-up comedy bits and began to write music, including parody take-offs of popular songs for himself or Robert to sing. As the years went by, Eddie blossomed, becoming an entertainer who could do just about everything required, from singing to acting, from dancing to stand-up, from producing and directing to writing. This versatility stood him in good stead, and it blossomed, really, at a very special community theater in Edmonton.

Hollywood Plaza Hotel in 1956.

Just out of high school, Tommy Banks became the musical director of a legendary venue in Edmonton, the Orion Theater (pronounced with the accent on the first, not the second, syllable). A home for young talent, it became the place where Eddie got a real grounding in being a pro onstage, beginning while he was still in school — but more about that later.

It was perhaps inevitable that even before his high-school career ended, Eddie had started to look beyond the stage and to the screen. In the summer of 1950, he and Tommy Banks scratched up enough money to fly to Hollywood. Banks chuckled as he remembered, "We booked air passage and reserved rooms at the Hollywood Plaza Hotel, which was very close to the intersection of Hollywood and Vine. What did we know? It sounded pretty posh and exotic. It…wasn't. We wound up staying there anyway."

Over the next week the two boys made the rounds, visiting jazz clubs, dropping in at movie studios, and catching some stage shows, one at the Huntington Hartford Theatre, close to the Hollywood Plaza. It wasn't actually a professional visit, though, and the two were really doing little more than sight-seeing. They had not come prepared to audition and in fact weren't quite sure how to go about doing that even if they had wanted to.

They rented a car and one day Banks was driving, even though he didn't have a driver's license — not for Alberta, and certainly not for California. "On a left turn near the Beverly Hills Hotel I smashed into a car being driven by a very pretty girl." How pretty? "Well," Banks says, "she was pretty *mad*, anyway!"

A policeman came, and because this was back in the days before the L.A cops had gained a reputation for being hard on suspects, the officer listened patiently to the story, surveyed the dents, then spoke sternly to the two teen-agers, who were visibly frightened. When he found out they were from Edmonton, and that Edmonton was in a whole different country, the policeman evidently decided that it would be wisest not to create an international incident. He let Eddie and Tommy off with a warning: "Just take care of getting this fixed up and be more careful next time."

The two boys had to scrape together enough money to pay the woman for the dent they had put in her car, and then they also had to pay for the scratches and dings they had inflicted on the rental. Senator Banks remembers, "The car rental guy was perfectly happy to accept $200.00 from us." Actually, that was quite a lot of money at the time, probably much more than was needed to repair the minor damages.

What with one thing and another, Eddie and Tommy economized in other ways and wrapped up their week-long stay glad that they had come out of the experience with nothing more serious to show for it than an embarrassing moment and seriously flattened wallets. Even though the visit had had its down moments, Eddie felt elated and oddly at home in Hollywood. As the two prepared to return to Edmonton, Eddie announced to Tommy Banks, "I'm coming back here just as soon as I can. This is it. This is where I need to be."

CHAPTER 3

Raising the Curtain

Edmonton's Orion Musical Theatre was a dream of founder Dasha Shaw Goody (1922-2001). Born in Winnipeg, Dasha had begun her musical career at the age of fourteen as a vocalist, and as an adult she moved to Edmonton after marrying Joe Goody. There she became a local celebrity as a revered teacher and inspiration — her motto was "Those who can, do. Those who CAN, teach!" Dasha Goody not only taught, but she sought out others who could both teach and do and nurtured their talents and careers. All of her life she remained a tireless and much-beloved force for the arts, always on the lookout for young talent and always planning ways to enrich the artistic community of Edmonton.

In 1952, Dasha Goody teamed with the young Tommy Banks to establish the Orion Musical Theatre, with Banks acting as the Musical Director. It was an inspired beginning, and Dr. Goody would continue to be active in the theatre and musical world of Edmonton up to her death at the age of 81: she founded the Second Generation outfit in 1973 and the Edmonton Musical Theatre in 1977. She worked in radio, taught audio-visual arts, and won an honorary doctorate and scads of awards for her achievements as a director and promoter of musical theatre. Today a major financial educational award, the Dasha Shaw Goody Memorial Scholarship, perpetuates her name and continues her work of encouraging young people to practice their art and apply their talents.

The Orion began with the goal of offering young performers the chance to perform at a professional level, gaining experience and confidence as they polished their skills. Senator Tommy Banks remembers that in the early days the group leaned heavily on revues and variety-style shows — "An Evening of Broadway Hits," for example — but that it soon went on to produce full-fledged versions of musicals. Eddie Eleniak and his high-school buddy Robert Goulet were among the first generation of young performers at the Orion.

About that name…of course, the whole concept of the theater was all about a constellation, a group of stars. However, you might not realize that if you just heard it spoken. Senator Banks maintains, with something of a twinkle, that the offbeat pronunciation was planned: "We decided that if we called it Orion and pronounced it the same way the constellation is pronounced, people in Edmonton would think it was an Irish place — O'Ryan's." However, others are convinced that no one in the group had ever actually heard the name of the constellation spoken aloud, so they simply said it the way they thought it looked and changed the accent without realizing they were placing it on the wrong syllable. The Orion became such an institution in Edmonton that eventually no one would think of changing it. And after all, they had some literary precedent: Samuel Clemens's older brother was named Orion, and the family pronounced his name "OR-ion," too.

Eddie Eleniak steadily gained experience and confidence as a writer and performer at the Orion. He remembered the first year of the Orion's existence as "semi-professional theater. We did comedy bits, musical bits — it was sort of like an early stage version, a Canadian version, of *Saturday Night Live*." Blossoming in the friendly surroundings, Eddie served as emcee of many of the revues and he regularly performed in them, sometimes teaming with his buddy Robert Goulet, sometimes doing solo bits. Robert Goulet, with his already impressive singing voice, became one of the regular leads in the Orion stage productions.

Marilyn Dingle was also a member of the group, and she has fond memories of singing, dancing, and acting onstage: "As kids, we thought we were a bunch of stars. I was 14, Eddie about 16. Bob Goulet was Eddie's age, I believe. Our favorite name for Eddie was 'Sach.'" And as long as she knew Eddie, he was always "Sach" to her.

In the Orion productions, Eddie was variously a musician, a dancer, a singer, an actor, and a comedian — really, whatever the role or the production needed. "He already had developed a kind of stand-up act," Senator Tommy Banks recalls, and from time to time he emceed the revues, sometimes doing comic bits in between musical numbers. Eddie liked to do dialect characters — a form of comedy that today may not be politically correct, but which was very popular in the mid-twentieth century. And even given today's standards, the accents Eddie did probably would never have been taken as an affront, because Eddie's brand of humor was never mean or insulting and his comedy was already the warm kind that encouraged the audience to recognize and laugh at the foibles and weaknesses that we all share, no matter what our ethnic or social backgrounds might be.

Eddie began to develop another facet of his talents with the Orion Musical Theatre: writing. His comic routines as emcee were ones he wrote himself, and he began to learn the fine points of the art of timing and delivery. If a joke fell flat, he'd either toss it out or tinker with it, sometimes discovering that a well-placed pause or even a throwaway gesture or facial expression would pull a laugh from the audience and save the moment. Like all young performers, though, Eddie observed and borrowed. Later, Senator Tommy Banks recalls, Eddie developed a stand-up act delivered in a Mexican accent. "He was basically performing the same kind of comedy as Bill Dana, who later, in 1959, created José Jimenez as a comic persona," Banks remembers. However, Eddie emphatically did not steal Dana's act, which debuted a few years later on the *Steve Allen Show*. Eddie also wrote his own scripts and tailored his presentation to the local audience.

Meanwhile, Eddie was busy finishing high school. In 1953, having established a good academic record, Eddie graduated and decided he needed more training before struggling to establish himself as a performer. He applied to and was accepted by the Radio College of Canada, where he would spend the next two years.

Headquartered in Toronto, the Radio College of Canada (today the RCC Institute of Technology) was founded in 1928 as one of the earliest educational institutions in the Americas to concentrate on teaching the skills required for broadcast media. The main emphasis at the college was initially not on performance, but technology — but already Eddie knew that he had to have skills to fall back on in between his efforts to find work as a singer or actor. He wasn't completely on his own in Toronto, either, because his high-school pal Robert Goulet was there, too, studying music at the Royal Conservatory of Music. At the Radio College of Canada, Eddie concentrated on theater studies, looking ahead to the time when he would become a true professional. In addition to the technical classes, he developed a familiarity and ease with performing to a radio microphone.

In 1955, Eddie moved back home to Edmonton. By then, Robert Goulet had already made a few television appearances, and eventually he co-starred (with a young man named William Shatner) in a Canadian version of the American puppet show *Howdy Doody*. That was simply a beginning, though, and Goulet had talked to Eddie about his bigger dreams of Broadway (they would be realized in 1960 when Goulet was cast as Lancelot in Lerner and Lowe's *Camelot*).

As for Eddie, he had told Tommy Banks that one day he would return to Hollywood, but now he thought instead of New York, where he hoped to study with the famous Lee Strasberg and find a place on the Broadway stage. While it may be true that anyone who can make it in New York can make it anywhere, there is also the little matter of getting to New York first — and having enough money to sustain you while you struggle to make it there. Eddie needed money, but that was not really an overwhelming problem. He had never been afraid of hard work, and he knew that sometimes it's a challenge to follow your star.

So in preparation for his big move, Eddie looked around for a job and found one that paid well, but was also fairly grueling and demanding. He went to work for Western Geophysical Oil, a petrochemical exploration company that helped to locate spots to drill for oil in the northern fields of Canada. The process they used was reflection seismology, which is just about as technical as it sounds. Using some of the skills he had gained at the Radio College of Canada with instruments and machinery, Eddie worked in oil exploration.

Basically he drove a truck to a prospective oil-well field, set explosive charges in pods buried in the earth in a carefully worked-out pattern of depths and distances, detonated them, and then recorded and measured the resulting seismic waves with equipment in the truck. The instruments indicated whether the field held oil, the approximate depth if oil was present, and the best places to drill to extract it.

The task could be repetitive and routine, and up in the north fields of Canada, it demanded lots of travel, skill, and determination. Because it dealt with explosives, it also called for a measure of close attention and care. Eddie soon discovered that it wasn't just a forty-hour-a week job. In fact, he had to work steadily for three entire months before taking three weeks off — and at times he was pretty far away from civilization. When he completed a three-month stint, though, he considered himself very well paid, and no wonder: the job called for considerable expertise and the rewards reflected that. When his three-week vacation finally arrived, Eddie gladly planned to return home.

And then, the morning he was to return, he woke up feeling ill. At first he thought he might have picked up a virus. His throat was sore, and as he got out of bed, "the floor came up and hit me in the face." He had fainted dead away, and when he finally came to, he felt as sick as he had ever felt in his life: "my whole scalp was itching and it felt like my skin was melting." Though he didn't realize it immediately, Eddie was running a dangerously high fever. He also found himself in a strange place. Gradually he realized that he was lying in a hospital bed, but he couldn't even get up, because "I couldn't move my left leg at all." He was at first too disoriented to realize it, but in fact Eddie was seriously ill.

Nurses and doctors came by, and to his horror, Eddie learned that he had polio and was in a polio ward in the hospital. The news came as a terrible shock. His first thought was not of the life-threatening danger he was in, but rather that "there was going to be no show-biz career for me." He quickly sank into depression as the star he had wished on seemed to have winked out permanently. He had worked, he had learned, he had planned, and now nothing was going to come of all his dreams. Then something happened that helped Eddie begin to pull out of his dejection and bitter disappointment.

"I kept hearing a continuous gulping sound," he recalled. "I looked around and finally saw that in a bed not far away was a man who must have been in his eighties. He was chewing and trying to swallow with enormous difficulty." From the nurses Eddie learned that the old man had polio-induced paralysis of the throat. Over the next few days, with little else to do, Eddie watched as the old man gamely fought his disability: "He could eat, but it was terribly hard for him to swallow and it took him a long time to do it. But he kept at it. They would bring his breakfast tray, and he would slowly begin to eat, chewing and then fighting hard to swallow the food down. Every bite was a battle. It took him hours to make the attempt, because he would have to gather his strength after every swallow before going on to the next bite. He never finished his breakfast until just before lunch arrived, but he would force himself to eat lunch, too, finally getting it down about the time dinner came."

Eddie's depression slowly began to lift as he compared himself to the old man. He thought, "This man is trying to get his muscles working again. He's not giving up. And here I am just feeling sorry for myself." That marked a turning point, a moment when Eddie decided that he would follow his star, after all. One day, he promised himself, he would appear again on stage — and he would walk on, not roll in sitting in a wheelchair or helping himself along on crutches. He began to cooperate with the physical therapists and even forced himself to go beyond the standard exercises. If his therapist would be satisfied with ten repetitions of a given exercise, Eddie would make himself do fifteen.

Little by little the muscles in his leg began to respond until eventually he was able to walk again, though he limped. But at least Eddie had made it back to his feet, and he didn't plan to stop there. He was determined to find a way to recover his full abilities. Once he was back home and able to get around a little, Eddie thought about his problem and came up with a challenging way to gain back more muscle tone and strength.

"I enrolled in a ballet class," he said. That seems an unlikely form of therapy, but it offered regular exercise, stretching, and movements that would help him recover flexibility. He was the only man in the class, and though at first his weak leg made him clumsy, he fiercely concentrated on improving, and he became one of the hardest-working students the teacher had ever seen. The stretching, dancing, and exercises took hold, and gradually Eddie was able to dance again. More important, he regained his ability to walk without a limp. In fact, when the ballet class performed a recital, Eddie reportedly was the star of the show.

Then as soon as he was able, Eddie returned to the Orion and auditioned for a role. It might have been the best idea he had ever had, both because Tommy Banks and Dasha Goody knew him so well and because the Orion performers were like a huge supportive family. They were in his corner and rooting for him to succeed, and even more, Eddie had proved to them that he had the kind of determination that would, time and time again, see him through such challenges. However, at the moment he needed something to restore his confidence in himself.

Musical director Tommy Banks was happy to see Eddie up and around, and fortunately he could offer just the kind of opportunities Eddie was looking for. The Orion group was like another family to Eddie — they knew him, appreciated his talents, and loved him, and that encouraging environment was perfect for his stage comeback.

As the Orion Musical Theatre branched out from revues to full-fledged productions, Eddie and his fellow Orion performers took to the stage not in individual variety-show turns, but in regular roles that called for acting, singing, and dancing. One production in which the recuperating Eddie performed was Rodgers and Hammerstein's ground-breaking first collaboration, *Oklahoma!*

It had debuted on Broadway in 1943, and by the mid-1950s it had become a theatrical warhorse, popular all over the country. Because the production seamlessly integrated the songs and musical numbers into the plots, unlike earlier musicals in which the characters' action came to a standstill while the actors sang their specialty numbers and did their dances, *Oklahoma!* seemed fresh, new, and exciting when it first opened on Broadway. In the years since its first production, the play had not gone stale or lost its luster, because by the 1950s the songs had become well-loved standards, and in both professional and amateur productions the colorful costumes, dances, and sets regularly bewitched audiences.

Oklahoma! still had that magical cachet in 1955, when the Orion mounted its own ambitious production. Based on a 1931 stage play by

Executive

Tommy Banks

Richard Keraack

Jimmy Richards

Dasha Goody

Larry Arcand

Colleen Bennett

Mickey Bricker

Tommy Banks was an Executive in the Orion Drama Club.

Lynn Riggs, *Green Grow the Lilacs,* Rodgers and Hammerstein's musical takes place on ranches and farms near Claremore, Oklahoma. At curtain rise, the year is 1906, and Oklahoma is still a territory, though statehood is looming.

The plot is both melodramatic and romantic: Cowboy Curly McLain is in love with a farmer's daughter, Laurey Williams, but there are three problems that complicate their romance. First, ranchers and farmers are at each other's throats, both parties convinced that their approach makes the best use of the land. The farmers grow crops that have to be cultivated in carefully fenced-in acreage; but the ranchers need vast expanses of grassland for grazing their herds and despise fences that keep their cattle out.

Second, Laurey has grown tired of Curly's shy and hesitant wooing, and she plays hard to get, teasing him by refusing to go to a big dance as his date. And finally, brutish and dangerous farmhand Jud Fry, the kind of man who today would be called a stalker, wants Laurey for himself and will stop at nothing to get her.

Other characters include Laurey's friend Ado Annie Carnes, who is sort of inclined to marry Will Parker, a plain-spoken, naïve, and even faintly goofy cowboy who has recently returned from visiting the bustling metropolis of Kansas City, where, as he sings in a rousing number, everything is up to date. Will is eager to get hitched to Annie, though first he has to prove to her father that he is a responsible prospect by coming up with a huge amount of money (for him, anyway). Unfortunately for Will's hopes and dreams, an itinerant peddler, Ali Hakim (he is, or at least says he is, Persian) has been seeing her, too, and as Ado Annie confesses, she is a gal who "cain't say no" when a feller comes courtin'.

The feud between the ranchers and farmers, Oklahoma's imminent achievement of statehood, the love stories of Laurey and Curly and Annie and Will, and the violent and ultimately deadly confrontation of Jud Fry and Curly are all acted out to Rodgers and Hammerstein's high-spirited tunes and energetic choreography. The musical signs off with its rousing title song, and by then audiences are practically on their feet from laughter and the sheer energy and excitement of the spectacle.

In the Orion Musical Theatre production, Eddie had an exceptionally well-received comic role as cowboy Will Parker, who works hard and scares up the fifty-dollar stake that Mr. Carnes demands and finally succeeds in winning Ado Annie from Ali Hakim. In the role of lanky, skinny Will, Eddie sang the show-stopping "Kansas City," and he squaredanced with the best of them. No one in the audience would even have suspected that not long before he had been flat on his back with polio, confined to a hospital bed with a paralyzed left leg. Then too, Eddie deftly got all the laughs the part called for, receiving a huge reaction with each funny line. Senator Banks remembers the show as "Outstanding. Eddie was still just a young man, but he was already performing on a professional level." Audiences were enthralled and appreciative, and to many of them it was obvious that the Orion would not hold onto such a talent for very long.

Eddie was still pegging away at earning money to go back to the U.S. and on the side had begun writing copy for the radio (although that was not as lucrative as his oil-exploration job had been). To help him out, and as a reward for his perseverance, courage, and dedication — and of course for his talent — the Orion Musical Theatre provided Eddie with a precious chance. In 1956, he learned that he had won a scholarship, not to college, but to the place he once visited and ever since had dreamed of, the city where everyone wished on stars, or at least wished to be stars.

Eddie Eleniak was going to work for NBC in Hollywood, California.

CHAPTER 4

Hollywood and *Bust?*

Not yet 22, young Eddie Eleniak set about getting ready for his trip to Hollywood, potentially his big break. His family all wished him well, of course, but his father in particular wasn't at all sure about the move. "Dad always wanted me to learn how to be a salesman," Eddie recalled later. "He didn't trust show business, and he thought I should always have something to fall back on."

Of course, in many ways Eddie had already followed Peter's advice: he had studied not only theater arts, but also the technical end of radio production at the Radio College of Canada, he had worked in the field as an oil seismologist, and he was perfectly willing to do whatever it might take to support his dream. Becoming a successful performer, Peter Eleniak thought, was the longest of long shots, and he kept advising his son to find "a real job" that he could do just in case things didn't pan out. Eddie, though, was confident, even if he secretly fought down the fluttering butterflies in his stomach at the vast changes that he knew lay ahead. He had trained himself not to be afraid in front of audiences, and now he worked on not showing any anxieties he might have felt on the verge of the biggest challenge of his life.

Part of that challenge, he soon learned, lay just in the preparations for leaving Canada and moving to Hollywood. This time Eddie wasn't traveling to the United States as a tourist or visitor, but as a "resident alien," which meant he had expressed a wish to live and work in the U.S.A. and that he presumably planned to become a citizen sometime in the future. And it also meant a snowstorm of paperwork, as Eddie explained:

EDDIE CARROLL: I came [to the U.S.] as a resident alien, and because of that, before I got here I couldn't just climb aboard the plane. I had to get all sorts of papers filled out, I had to have clearance from the local police and the federal police to show that I was a respectable citizen, I had to prove that I had a certain amount of money in the bank, I had to prove that I had the background to fulfill the scholarship — just a staggering amount of red tape and paperwork. What I had to go through was enormous just to arrive here. And I came to Hollywood right at the end of 1956.

I had the scholarship to the NBC talent program, back when NBC was still on the corner of Sunset and Vine. Now, I had really amassed a

NBC Studios at Hollywood and Vine, 1956.

lot of stage experience with the Orion back then — I had appeared in stage productions including the first Canadian productions of *Brigadoon, Finian's Rainbow,* and *Oklahoma!,* I could sing and dance, I had studied writing and directing and so forth, and of course I had written songs and sketches and all sorts of things. I had also worked for CHED Radio as a copywriter. In my own mind, I had done everything that I could to prepare, and now I was going through the NBC talent program, and naturally after that would end, I hoped to find some performing or writing field I could work in that would let me remain there in Hollywood.

Of course I was most interested in performance, but at NBC they put me to work as a page, and because I had the scholarship, they kept putting me in all sorts of different divisions — that was the way the scholarship worked. I mean, I didn't get to act at all, but I was inside the studios, behind the scenes, and I did get to assist in small ways in the production division, the writing division, and so on. I didn't resent not being able to act and I didn't mind that at all because it was all a creative outlet for me, and that's just what I wanted. NBC was a fantastic training place for someone like me, and I was very happy to be there.

The mid-1950s were a kind of golden age for NBC television shows, which boasted big-name talent, and as a page Eddie worked for some world-famous personalities, including two other Eddies: Eddie Cantor and Eddie Fisher, who both appeared regularly on NBC TV. Young Eddie Eleniak was thrilled to be working with both men, one a veteran comic and musical star whose career on Broadway, in movies, and on radio and TV went back to the 1930s, one a young teen heartthrob. And the talent at NBC, of course, attracted fans. "You know," Eddie said, "as much as I enjoyed my work, it was also such fun just walk *out* of the studio back in those days. Girls would stop me and ask for my autograph, and when I gave it to them, they'd stare at it and ask me, 'Are you anybody?'"

Well, maybe he wasn't, not yet, but during his months at NBC, Eddie was setting his sights on *becoming* somebody. In addition to Cantor and Fisher, Eddie worked on the Dinah Shore, Groucho Marx, and *Queen for a Day* shows, a heady line-up for a young man from Edmonton. He threw himself into the job with all his enthusiasm and his usual adaptability and cheerfulness.

Though his family might have worried about him, Eddie was having the time of his life in California. He had arrived in Los Angeles not knowing a soul there, but he kept so busy he didn't have time to be lonely. And who knew? This was Hollywood! This was the place where stars were born. His big break might come just any day like a bolt out of the blue.

And then an unforseen development arose. Eddie had been working at NBC for about eleven months when, in November, 1956, he received an official-looking envelope from the United States Government. Thinking it might have something to do with his resident alien status, he opened it up to read the surprising header: From The President of the United States to Edward Eleniak. In a terse line or two, he was directed to report to a U.S. Army Induction Center for a physical.

Eddie had just been drafted.

The next day, Eddie took the notification in with him to work and showed it to his supervisor at NBC, explaining why he needed to take a little time off to go over to the nearby induction center and take care of this obvious mistake. "Don't worry," he said. "I'm a Canadian citizen, I'm not an American. I'll straighten this out and I'll be back in just a few minutes."

He underestimated the time he needed. As it turned out, it wasn't a few minutes, but two years. Eddie went over to the Induction Center, showed the notice, and instead of being given the chance to explain why it had been sent in error, he was herded into a room with a lot of other young men. They were instructed to stand and recite the Pledge of Allegiance to the flag, and Eddie didn't. A sergeant came over to bawl him out, and Eddie politely replied, "But it's not my flag —"

Before he could get further into the explanation, he found himself face-down on the floor giving the sergeant twenty-five push-ups. The staff hustled him through the physical exam, he passed (he was so flustered that he didn't even mention his bout with polio), and almost before he knew it, Eddie had been inducted into the United States Army.

At first he was absolutely stunned by this turn of events — even before his scholarship had run out, here he was sidetracked again by forces he couldn't control. However, the more Eddie thought about his situation, the less terrible it seemed: "We were in between wars — Korea had ended a few years before, and Viet Nam hadn't started, so combat seemed unlikely. Now, this was also about the time, almost the same years, when stars like Elvis Presley were being drafted. If Elvis's career couldn't keep *him* out of the service, what chance did I have? And I realized that if I did serve in the United States Army, that it would be a definite plus for me if I wanted to apply for U.S. citizenship in the future."

Eddie Eleniak, Protector of the USA.

As he always did, Eddie found the silver lining and went through basic training in a mood that might not have been completely cheerful, but that was at least cheerfully resigned to making the best of the situation. He was up to the physical rigors of training, and he was a bright young man who had no problems with the educational side.

After completing his training, Eddie found himself stationed at Ford Ord, on Monterey Bay, about a hundred miles south of San Francisco and 330 miles north of Hollywood. Established in 1917 as an artillery-training field, it had become Camp Ord in 1933 and then Fort Ord in 1940, the home of the 7th Infantry Division. By 1957 it had also become the home base of the 4th Replacement Training Center and would serve as the staging ground for troops heading out for foreign parts for the next fifteen years or so. At Fort Ord, the newly-minted Private Eleniak soon met a guy who had a similar background in theater and who would become a close friend: Ben Cooper.

Like Eddie, Ben had started in show business early, joining the cast of a Broadway smash hit, Harold Lindsay's and Russel Crouse's *Life with Father*, a comedy that they adapted from Clarence Day's comic-autobiographical book of the same title. Both play and book told of Day's autocratic stockbroker father and the amusing scrapes he ran into with his large family in the New York City of the 1890s. The play became a phenomenon, opening in 1939 and running for eight solid years, establishing box-office records. One serious problem faced the production, though: many of the cast members were children or adolescents, and young folks have the habit of growing visibly older and taller, so the children's roles tended to rotate among new crops of actors every few years.

Cooper recalls, "My parents had learned from a friend of the family that there was an opening in the cast of the show, and they asked if I'd like to audition. I thought it would be a day off from school, and I said, 'Sure!' At the audition call there must have been 5,000 kids. I made it to the call-backs and they gave us all a page of dialogue to practice for the second round of auditions." He took it home, quickly learned the lines with his father's help, went on to memorize the entire part, and then went back to the theater with his mother for the next step of the process. As they listened to the others reciting the same lines from scripts, Cooper whispered to his mother, "They don't sound like they're really talking to anyone." She reassured him, "I know, dear. Just do it the way you think you should."

Ben blew away the professionals when he did the passage off-book without even a glance at the script. Then he told the casting directors that he had memorized the rest of the part, and they heard him perform that, and then they tried giving him directions, which he followed beautifully. He was the right age and size, he had the right look for the role, and he landed it. He enjoyed acting the part and liked the other actors in the play, including the script's co-author Harold Lindsay, who starred as the fussy, demanding, and repeatedly deflated Father.

Ben recalls, "So I started on Broadway in New York when I was eight years old, in 1942, in that wonderful play called *Life with Father*. I joined it after it had been running about three years through kind of a crazy fluke, and I replaced the original actor who played the youngest son in the family. Then I played the youngest boy for a year and three months, and then the next-to-youngest for a year and nine months, so I spent three years all told on Broadway in the very first play I had ever been in. Oh, God, I had such fun! When I auditioned I had never acted at all. My mom and dad gave me the best advice ever. My dad went to MIT and taught there — he was an automotive engineer — and my mom was a registered nurse from Canada, and they told me, 'You listen to the man who is called the director, and you do whatever he tells you to do.' That was the best advice I ever got."

Eddie and Ben in their stint in the Army in Fort Ord.

Ben's great stage gift was an extremely open and natural approach to acting. "My mom and dad didn't make a big deal out of my being on Broadway," he says, "so I didn't, either. And the fact is that I was just too young to be afraid of it." He was never full of himself, never resistant to direction, and on stage he sounded both relaxed and believable, all without visible effort.

Like the other kids in the play, Ben eventually grew out of his roles, but "after that I went into radio." He remembers that when he auditioned for an early radio role he asked the director how to play a certain line. The director wanted to know why Ben hadn't asked for advice from his mother, who was in the studio, and Ben replied, "My mother told me never to ask her. She said I should ask the director and do whatever he tells me."

Ben laughs and adds, "I think he got on the phone and called every director he knew at every radio studio and told them, 'Listen, I've found a young man who's got a great voice, is a good actor, and whose parents don't interfere.' And because of that I went on to appear about 3,500 times on different radio shows."

Among his radio credits is a well-remembered program, *The FBI in Peace and War*. Ben's acting credentials grew, and by the early 1950s he had begun to appear on TV and in films as well: TV's *Armstrong Circle Theater*, the movies *Thunderbirds*, *Flight Nurse*, *Sea of Lost Ships*, *Johnny Guitar*, *The Rose Tattoo*, and *Duel at Apache Wells*, among others. Cooper's lean good looks and easy, natural manner of acting meant that he found ready employment, and he had begun to settle comfortably in as a screen actor with a solid career in action films and Westerns. Then, like Eddie, he

Entertainers in USO shows. Dear friend David Hammond is in the middle row on far left, and Eddie is in the bottom row, far right.

was drafted into the Army and was stationed at Fort Ord. He says that he and Eddie met and liked each other right off the bat. "We were very similar in our backgrounds and our attitudes. You know, I don't recall either one of us ever bitching about being in the Army. In fact, we had a ball."

As for Eddie, "he was one of the most fun people I ever knew. Just a terrific guy." By the time they met, both Eddie and Ben were seasoned performers, both of them ambitious to get ahead in show business. Unfortunately their first assignments in the Army as infantrymen didn't offer much promise of this, and they found participating in war games not much of a creative outlet.

Luckily for the two young men, they quickly discovered that even in the Army they had opportunities to practice their profession. With his training and background in radio, Eddie secured an assignment with the Armed Forces Radio Service, both on microphone and doing writing and production chores. Eddie also sang with the 6th Army Chorus, and before long he and Ben began to appear in USO shows.

"We really didn't have an act as such," Ben remembers, "but we did comedy routines in between the main acts. I was usually the straight man. I remember that Eddie had this bit that he did in a Mexican accent, sort of a Bill Dana thing, and he was the funniest guy I had ever seen." But Cooper was also impressed with Eddie's versatility and energy. Ben remembers, "Eddie was doing everything he could. He was directing and singing and acting and writing, just a little of everything. On the base, we were in so many things together, and being in the Army, and having to do these things on short notice, we frankly would steal little bits from comics." Well, maybe not steal exactly, but the two would at least adapt the material for an Army audience.

As a part of the Army entertainment services, Ben had assignments similar to Eddie's, and he had received permission to live off-base: "I had a little apartment up in Carmel, and on the weekends it became Eddie's home away from home." As for Eddie, his favorite job with the Army was with the Motion Picture Department, where he wrote and directed instructional movies. Eddie would chuckle as he talked about this: "We made training films, and for a young guy in the service, it was a dream job. I got to tell the generals what to do!"

In the midst of his Army stint, though, Eddie fell ill yet again, this time with serious abdominal pains. He checked into the base hospital. After examining him, an Army surgeon decided to operate, and Eddie went under the anesthetic. "When I woke up," he remembered, "the Army doctor came into the room and he was lugging this huge, thick book under his arm. Well, I thought this guy is a real professional. Then I saw that the book he was carrying wasn't a medical volume at all, but a *Peanuts* collection by Charles Shultz!"

The surgeon casually told Eddie, "We took out your appendix."

"Thank goodness that's all it was to it," Eddie murmured, still a little groggy from the anesthetic.

The doctor shrugged and said, "Well, yeah, but it turned out not to be your appendix, though. It's a kidney stone that's too big to pass."

Eddie blinked. "Then why did you remove my appendix?"

The doctor bristled at that and snapped, "You got the operation for nothing, so why are you complaining?"

Eddie replied in a hurt tone, "Because it was *my* appendix!"

To add insult to injury, when Eddie was up and around again, he discovered that above his appendectomy scar was another, smaller scar. The Army "expert" had begun to operate in the wrong place! "It could be the plot of a comedy," Eddie said. "Except that it wasn't all that funny when it happened to me."

Eddie's Army service passed quickly enough, and in November, 1958, after two years in uniform, he was mustered out (in those days a draftee served two years active duty, two years active reserve, and then a final two years of inactive reserve). Ben Cooper re-joined civilian life at the same time, and both of the young men decided to set about re-establishing their careers. Eddie had not yet broken in to performing in Hollywood in any professional way, and as for Ben, "I'd had a contract with Republic Studios, but during my time in the Army that division had gone out of business." Both of them were at loose ends and eager to get back into their professions again.

The U.S. Army pay was not generous, and Eddie left the service practically broke. With him the trip so far had not been a case of "Hollywood or bust," but "Hollywood *and* bust." Relying only on his meager savings, Eddie moved into the spare bedroom in Ben Cooper's apartment to keep his expenses to a minimum. Having gained more experience and polish in acting, performing, directing, and writing for the Army, and having lost his appendix., Eddie now set out to find himself a niche in the difficult world of Hollywood show business.

CHAPTER 5

Eddie Makes a Name for Himself

Like all young men fresh out of the Army, Eddie and Ben wanted to unwind. Both of them started to date — California has never had a shortage of pretty girls — and they enjoyed themselves as much as their frugal budgets allowed. Working out of the apartment they shared, both of them began to seek employment in Hollywood. Before being drafted, Ben had been appearing in a string of Westerns, not all of them prestige films, but steady work. He had played Turkey Ralston in *Johnny Guitar*, a quirky Western that starred Joan Crawford and Sterling Hayden and featured two other familiar character actors, Royal Dano and Ernest Borgnine.

"Dano had the longest legs of anybody I've ever seen," Cooper remembers. "I think his waist was about up to my shoulder level." He remembers one scene as his rite of passage and true initiation into Westerns: "There was a scene where Dano and Borgnine and I had to sort of leap into the saddle and go galloping off. Well, the horses sensed that something was coming up, they got nervous and a little wild, and when I jumped into the saddle, I couldn't stay there. The horse threw me and I came down on my back so hard that I passed out for a few seconds. I came to with the director, Nicholas Ray, leaning over me and asking, 'Can you move your arms and legs?'

"Instead of answering him, I asked him, 'What's that sound?'" It was a harsh, rasping noise, and Ray said, "That's you." Cooper was fighting hard to breathe, and even in his dazed state he noticed that the struggle was to exhale. "You'd think you'd be trying to pull air in, but I was fighting hard to push it out. And even though I was lying there kind of dazed, I thought, huh, I have to remember that in case I ever have to play a scene where I get the wind knocked out of me." After a minute or so, Ben managed to get his breathing re-established, and then he stood up, dusted himself off and said, "Are we ready to do it again?"

"That night," he recalls, "we went back to the camp where Ernie Borgnine I were rooming together — they were little cabins like the old motels, two to a cabin. They told us that after we cleaned up there was a meeting. I thought they were going to tell us what we were going to shoot the next day, but when we walked in, there were all the wranglers and stunt men. I thought I was in trouble, but then one of the stunt men

Eddie in western wardrobe.

poured a tumbler of bourbon all the way up to the top and handed it to me and said, 'Welcome to the club.' I was in — a nineteen-year-old kid, and I had made it." He laughs. "The hard part was the day after that, when I woke up feeling the effects. And after I sobered up the next day, I think I'd become a pretty good cowboy actor."

That was the field that Cooper now set out to re-enter, and he saw no reason why Eddie, trim and handsome as he was, couldn't also find a place in Westerns. In the 1950s, Western films were still good box-office for theaters, and even better, TV had discovered that Western series were a top ratings draw. Cooper gave Eddie some lessons in handling a six-gun, and with his usual dedication, Eddie was a good study. "Eddie was left-handed, so he just followed my instructions like a mirror image. Well, Eddie would practice at anything until he was the best he could be. And teaching him sharpened me up, too. In the end, we both became pretty good at quick draws," Ben remembers.

Actors seeking roles stand in need of many things, and one of these — the number-one tool of the aspiring actor, in fact — is a set of photos: head shots, medium shots, full-body shots, shots in various costumes, all of these are a vital part of the actor's portfolio. His or her look is what will get the actor auditions, call-backs, and — as every actor hopes — good roles. Because Westerns were so hot, Eddie needed some costume shots that might get his foot in the door at a movie or TV studio interested in casting horse operas.

Eddie remembered, "Ben had all this stuff, and he was willing to let me borrow it for a photo shoot. Now, he had this beautiful Stetson hat, really top of the line, and he volunteered to lend it to me. It didn't quite fit me, but Ben explained that the beauty of a Stetson is that it can be re-shaped. You just have to get it good and wet and then you can remold it to fit your face and head and suit your general look. Once it looks good, you put it in a low, warm oven to dry, and it sets its shape. And he gave me permission to do that."

Scraping together the money for a set of publicity photos, Eddie made an appointment with a photographer and the day before he got his gear ready and wet down the hat in the shower. He shaped it, then put it in the oven, turned to a very low temperature, and left it to "cure" overnight. He showered and went to bed. "Then the next morning I got up and started to get ready for the day. I went into the kitchen and turned the oven onto 'broil' because I was going to use it to make toast. As I waited for it to warm up, I went and dressed. And then I smelled smoke. In fact, I *saw* smoke, and I remembered the hat."

Rushing back into the kitchen, Eddie yanked the oven door open. "Smoke billowed out, and when it cleared, all that was left of the hat was a crumbled hat-shaped ashy thing and a charred headband. It was gone. I was so ashamed of myself that it took me two days to tell Ben what had happened, to apologize, and to promise that one day I would replace the hat with one just as good." Eddie always chuckled. "It took me *thirty years* before I did replace it!"

As for Ben, he was — well, he wasn't happy. "It was my best hat," he remembers. "It was that nice tan color and looked really sharp, and by the time Eddie took it out of the oven, it was a little, crumpled, black thing, very, very small. He waited to tell me until the second night after it happened. He came to the door of my bedroom — I was already in bed, I suppose he thought that I wouldn't jump up and take a swing at him — and said, 'I've got something to tell you,' sounding as if he was going to talk about someone who had just died, and then he told me about the hat. Well, what are you going to do? I couldn't get mad at him — I mean, what the hell, it was just a hat! But I could tell that Eddie really felt bad about it. What could I say? Anything I could have told him would only have made it worse."

So fortunately Ben accepted Eddie's apology, and even through that tough time the two of them remained buddies. As for Ben, he soon began to find employment as an actor again. Just before going into the Army he had landed a role in *Dick Powell's Zane Grey Theater*, the first Western anthology show on American television. Anthology shows weren't episodic series like *Star Trek* or *Gunsmoke*, with the same cast continuing in the same roles week after week, but rather collections of individual shows, each with a different cast (even if the same actor might be selected to play three or four different roles over time).

Zane Grey, which at first offered stories at least loosely adapted from the writer Zane Grey's well-known series of Western novels, was a top-ten success when it had debuted, in 1958 it was still going strong, and Ben soon racked up four appearances in episodes of the show, each time playing a different character. Eddie was not so lucky. "I don't know what it was," Ben says, "but directors just didn't want to give Eddie a chance at a Western. You'd think it would be a natural for him — he had the look and the skills, but somehow he just couldn't click with the casting directors."

On one occasion, Eddie went with Ben to Republic Studios for a casting call. As usual, it was "thanks but no thanks" for Eddie's audition, but as they were about to leave the lot, they saw a familiar tall figure coming toward them: screen icon Gary Cooper (no relation to Ben). Ben said, "I met him once. I'll introduce you."

When Gary Cooper ambled close enough Ben said, "Mr. Cooper, you won't remember me, but we met once. Back in 1943, you came backstage in New York when I was in *Life with Father* and shook hands with all of us. I was playing the youngest son."

The laconic star widened his eyes and looked up and down the tall adult Ben Cooper, dressed in cowboy garb. Poker-faced he replied in his famous slow drawl, "Shit! Time sure flies, don't it?"

Eddie always thought, "In anybody else, that would have sounded rude, but coming from Gary Cooper, it was like a warm greeting."

Ben and Eddie worked even more on the fast draw, and as Ben said, Eddie gradually became quite good at it. Ben recalls, "I got him to go with me down to Midland, Texas, and we did a telethon down there to raise money for charity. Eddie wore his left-handed gun, and I wore my right-handed gun. They sent some performers, re-enactors over from one of their western towns where they did gunfights for tourists, and these guys wanted to draw against us. Four o'clock in the morning. I said, 'Okay, but we start without our hands on the guns, and we'll have a kid say *go!* Not '1-2-3,' but just *go!* We set it up so we weren't facing each other, but the cameras, so the viewers of the telethon could see who won. We got the signal, and it was *bam-bam-bam!* Eddie and I won hands down, against these guys that did this every day. I don't think he ever got a real Western role, but that just goes to show that when he decided he was going to do something, that was the end of the discussion. He was going to do it and get good at it. He was an amazing man."

Eddie remembered this period of intense auditioning as occasionally frustrating, but occasionally fun. "When you're an aspiring actor," he would say, "you're like a boy scout, always prepared. I mean, I'd line up two or three auditions a day when I could, for anything and everything: voice-over work, radio and TV commercials, small roles in TV shows, stage work, just the whole gamut.

"A young would-be actor in Hollywood needed transportation, so you'd buy a used car — a *well*-used car — and make your rounds in that. Because I was going to so many different studios, I'd pile the trunk full of three or four changes of clothes, a suit for radio and voice-over auditions, maybe a sort of makeshift costume for a stage or TV role, and I'd just rush from one casting director to the next, each time running into the studio carrying a change of clothes on a hanger, and I'd change in the men's room, wash my face in the sink and pat it dry so they couldn't tell

I'd been running, and then come in to the receptionist trying to look calm and collected and just as professional as Sir Laurence Olivier. I probably did some of my best acting for receptionists."

Small jobs, especially radio commercials for local businesses, brought in a certain level of income, but Eddie wasn't feeling particularly flush with cash. He found time to date, and as a matter of fact he and Ben squired a parade of pretty girls around town. Often, of course, the dates had to be on the economical side. Eddie would sometimes laugh at the recollection and say, "Well, you know, it turned out to be good training for playing that cheapskate Jack Benny."

Eddie was beginning to establish a toehold in the business, but as 1959 went on, once more ill health ambushed him. The kidney stone that the Army surgeon had told him was "too large to pass" decided to force its way out anyway, but it lodged and caused Eddie excruciating pain. Sick and suffering, he visited a doctor who diagnosed the problem accurately. Eddie, he said, needed to go into the hospital immediately. He had to have surgery — the kidney stone could actually cause a life-threatening infection unless it was taken care of. Eddie attempted to arrange for the surgery with his insurance company.

"So I checked with my health insurance company," he recalled, "but the insurance people said that the kidney stone had been diagnosed while I was in service, so it was a pre-existing condition and they weren't responsible."

The hospital could only suggest that Eddie call the Army and see if he could get treatment from an Army doctor. Feeling worse and worse, Eddie got on the phone and tried that approach, only to be stonewalled there, too. Even though technically, he was still on active reserve, the Army washed its hands of him. "You're a civilian now," they told him flatly. "It's not the Army's responsibility once you're out of service."

However, insurance or no, Eddie's pain was cripplingly intense. Eddie tried the Veteran's Hospital — he certainly was a veteran — but they refused him admission because he had not been in a foreign war. He went to the Emergency Room of Doctors Hospital, and in considerable agony he asked to be admitted and treated. He ran into yet more red tape: He could not be admitted without a doctor's orders. He had no insurance coverage for the condition, they told him, and they would not treat him.

"I felt like I was on my last legs," Eddie confessed. "I didn't know what to do, but I knew I had to do *something*. I could barely stand up because of the pain. But I walked out of the hospital and saw a pay phone across the street. I did a John Wayne and forced myself to cross the street and get down the Yellow Pages and begin looking up urologists and calling them, one after the other."

Fortunately he found one who was willing to admit him, and after an examination, the doctor made sure that he was admitted quickly into that hospital for the operation. By then it was literally a question of life and death: Eddie was hemorrhaging inside. "They wheeled me back into the operating room and put me out, and that was the first relief I had from that awful pain for what seemed like weeks."

The emergency surgery was a success. Eddie recalled waking up with everything fuzzy from the anesthetic, feeling horrible but not in intense pain any more. Someone was sitting beside his bed, and he struggled to focus and see who it was.

"Eddie," the person said, and he recognized his mother's voice.

"I couldn't quite grasp at first how she got there," Eddie would say. "I hadn't even called my parents, because I knew they weren't financially able to help me out. Ben had phoned them, though, and told them how ill I was, and Mom took the first plane she could get into Los Angeles. She knew I needed her, and she wasn't about to leave me on my own so far away from home."

Eddie murmured something, but Marie interrupted him: "Eddie," she said, "you have to change your name."

To a woozy, sick guy this seemed like a strange kind of greeting. "What?" Eddie asked.

Firmly, Marie said, "You have to change your name. I've been in this hospital for hours and I just now managed to find you. Nobody here knows how to say 'Eleniak.'"

As Eddie recuperated, he thought about that. Maybe Marie was right. "Eleniak" does have a somewhat exotic look to it, at least to most Americans, and Eddie had heard it mispronounced many times: *EElennie-ak*, *El-EH-nay-ak*, what have you. He thought of his favorite aunt, his mom's sister Carol, and a little later he asked his mother, "If I change my name, what do you think of Eddie Carol?"

His mom liked it a lot, and Eddie made just one small change, adding an *l* so his last name would be Carroll. "So I went into the hospital as Eddie Eleniak and came out as Eddie Carroll," he would say. "And at least along with my last name I lost that kidney stone for good."

Eddie had often proved his resilience over the years, and again his positive attitude and his love of performance let him bulldoze his way through difficulties and obstacles to get back on path. Once he had hoped to go to New York to study with legendary acting coach Lee Strasberg, but polio had sidetracked that goal. Now, though, out of the hospital and mending, Eddie decided to sharpen his skills and take acting lessons with drama coach Jack Kosslyn, who was about thirteen years older than Eddie and who would go on to work closely with Clint Eastwood's production company. As always, Eddie's openness, ambition, and good nature made him not only a student, but a good friend of Kosslyn's.

Eddie Eleniak becomes Eddie Carroll.

Another accomplishment: Eddie had begun, once more, to find employment. In fact, Eddie had used the time when he was still recovering from his ordeal to work on an idea that wouldn't be too physically demanding, but that might get his name — his *new* name, of course — out before the public.

Eddie wrote and polished some monologues and worked on some songs. In the end, he put together a comedy album, its theme college days and girls — a topic that he knew well, or thought he did! He wrote some of the music and found some musicians to perform it. The album was titled *On Fraternity Row*, starring Eddie Carroll and the Kidney Stone Trio. The name of the group is not only a takeoff on the Kingston Trio, one of the most popular acts among college-age students of the day, but also shows that Eddie began working on the concept while still healing from his very unpleasant hospital stay.

The punning title also hints at the good humor he managed to hang on to. The Kidney Stone Trio (actually three of the Four Preps, a group that had already had a hit with the million-selling tune "26 Miles") provided music and back-up, and Eddie himself contributed his singing voice and comedy bits. Eddie and the Kidney Stones practiced the songs and the comedy bits, and they recorded the album in live performance. The album was a thoroughly professional production, released nationally by Duo Records. The front liner of the LP advertised "A Delirious Dissertation and Divey-Jivey from the Halls of Ivy!"

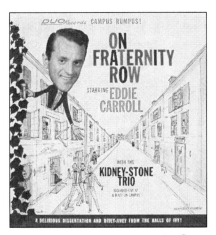

Eddie's comedy album cover for On Fraternity Row.

A *Billboard* ad pictured the album jacket, with Eddie's face prominently featured, and offered this enticing come-on: "Have you ever been to a real campus rumpus? If you haven't, you've missed a wild blend of laughs, songs, and intoxicatingly interesting conversation. Eddie Carroll and the Trio kick off a blast "*ON FRATERNITY ROW*" that will warm the hearts of every guy and gal who ever lifted a cold stein of beer in good company." Who could resist?

Indeed, the album included some funny songs and bits: "The Election Song," "I Hate Banjoes," and "100 Years from Today" (a prophecy on what we can expect if we all go on lousing up the world). However, to tell the truth, *many* people could resist, and *On Fraternity Row* wasn't a big hit — though it sold a respectable number of copies. Today it has become a collector's item, still available on eBay and elsewhere at prices up to seventy or a hundred dollars. Though it didn't set sales records, the album was another good credit, and probably more important for Eddie, it featured his photo on the jacket and it prominently billed him under his new stage name, which he had received courtesy of a kidney stone (the stone, not the Trio).

It was a beginning. With the release of *On Fraternity Row in* 1960, Eddie Carroll had at last made a mark in show business.

CHAPTER 6

Stage and Screen and Jamie

About the same time Eddie's record album was released to a gigantic wave of public apathy, Ben Cooper met a beautiful lady, dated her, and fell in love with her. They had first run into each other on the set of *Wagon Train*, the classic Western series, for which Ben had twice performed (once in a leading role as the title character in the episode "The Tom Tuckett Story"). Ben proposed, Pamela accepted, and then Ben asked Eddie if he would serve as the best man at their wedding. Of course Eddie would do anything for his great friend Ben. He was honored and was pleased to agree.

The match was a beautiful one, by the way. Ben and Pamela remained deeply in love and stayed together for close to fifty years before she passed away. It's unusual (maybe especially in Hollywood) to find a couple like that, but their marriage was solid as Gibraltar. When Ben first introduced Eddie to Pamela, Eddie had immediately liked her and of course as Ben's good buddy he wanted to make the very finest impression in this new real-life role of best man. The happy couple completed their planning and Ben told Eddie that the wedding was to be performed on May 13, 1960, in Valencia, north of Hollywood, with a reception following about fifty miles to the south in the Malibu home of Ben's sister Bunny.

It's barely possible that Eddie had a little recurrence of stage fright in playing the part of Ben's best man, or maybe the fact that the day happened to be Friday the Thirteenth put a jinx on him, but the big occasion didn't pass without a few hitches. Eddie, looking handsome and very natty in an immaculate suit, stood up as Ben's best man. "I guess I was a little nervous," Eddie admitted later. Not that it was a huge audience, because Ben and Pamela had put the wedding together on fairly short notice while Ben's parents were in town. As usual, Eddie had gone through careful preparations earlier, so he didn't expect any surprises. "I did a last-minute check to make sure everything was ready and that I had the ring and so on just before the wedding, but I probably kept fidgeting around and sticking my hands in my pockets before the ceremony began."

The minister appeared, the groom and the best man stood up, the bride walked down the aisle, and the ceremony got underway. Then the big moment came when Eddie was to produce Pamela's wedding ring. With great dignity he reached in his pocket and immediately turned pale. While the minister, the crowd, and worst of all Ben and Pamela waited, Eddie frantically fumbled around and began to search *all* of his pockets.

"How could I lose the ring? I knew I'd just had it moments before!" Eddie began to turn red. Ben's expression showed that at first he thought it was just a joke — until Eddie's search went on a little too long, and then Ben began to scowl.

Eddie made a helpless palms-open gesture, and Ben did a double-take. He nodded, but the flustered Eddie didn't immediately get it and just shook his head until Ben leaned close to whisper, "It's on your finger!"

"I guess it must have slipped on my little finger when I was fidgeting with my hand in my pocket," Eddie said. "I hadn't even noticed it there, because it was so small and light. But thank heavens, there it was. With a silent prayer of relief, I took the ring off my pinkie, finally handed it over, and the wedding went on."

Ben and Pamela Cooper at their wedding reception.

As best man, Eddie's next responsibility was to drive Ben's mom to a bakery to pick up the wedding cake. He then had to deliver cake and mother of the groom safely to the reception. As Ben and Pamela had met on the set of *Wagon Train*, the cake was appropriately decorated with a Western touch: the bride and groom weren't standing figurines, but were seated on a covered wagon atop the tallest tier. Eddie and Ben's mom picked up the cake, which had just been freshly decorated.

"The icing was still in the process of setting," Eddie recalled. "Well, I had a used car, you'll remember — a *well*-used car. It worked all right as transportation, but at that particular time it really needed some brake work. To be honest, what it really needed was a whole new set of brakes." However, as a hopeful actor Eddie had put paying for his portfolio of headshots and costume photos ahead of such everyday expenses as car repairs. Sure, the car needed a little work, but it had held together so far, and he was fairly confident it would get them safely to Malibu.

"Now, the brakes *would* work," Eddie insisted. "It was just that you had to double-pump them just right to get them to take hold." Sort of like a dance step, maybe. Anyway, tapping the brakes became a special skill that he had become accustomed to.

Eddie drove Ben's mother to Malibu with the mother of the groom sitting rigidly upright in the passenger seat and carefully balancing the cake on her lap. Knowing that the cake mattered a great deal to the couple, Eddie drove with caution, keeping within the speed limit and making sure to take the curves gently, and everything was fine until they actually reached their destination. "Now, Bunny's driveway slanted down," Eddie remembered. "And it was pretty steep. I was carefully and slowly edging the car down, gently double-pumping the brakes, and the car jerked a little bit and the wedding cake started to slide. Out of pure reflex, Ben's mom made a grab at the cake to save it, and her hand went right into the side of the thing. She wailed, 'Oh, no!' and I got the car stopped and looked over. I said, 'Don't move your hand. If you pull it out, the whole thing will collapse.'"

So Eddie cautiously got out of the car, not jarring the cake at all, and then went around to the passenger side, opened the door, and took hold of the base holding the cake. "I gave Ben's mom directions on how to swing her legs around and get out of the car and stand up and all the while how to keep her hand in place. Then we did a choreographed walk into the house," Eddie said. "We had to go the whole way with her hand still inside the wedding cake."

They made it into Bunny's kitchen, where they explained to Bunny how the accident had happened and why they had to apply first aid. Bunny surveyed the damage, got a supply of breadcrumbs and then had her mother very, very slowly pull her hand out of the cake.

Eddie said, "The cake wasn't ruined, but there was a fairly big crater in the side. So Bunny stuffed the cavity with breadcrumbs. Well, that at least kept the cake from caving in, but it left this obvious repair, so then it was like dealing with a Christmas tree that has one bad side. We wound up setting the cake on a table that we shoved back into a corner of the room. So there was this apparently beautiful and whole cake sheltered in the corner with the damaged side turned to the wall and out of sight. And you know, we got away with it. No one ever even suspected what had happened."

Not even Ben and Pamela! The happy couple got through the reception and enjoyed it without knowing how close they had come to losing that cake. In fact, Carolyn says, "They never even knew until years later, when we told them over drinks one evening. And they remained our close friends over all those years and afterwards, even with the OOPSes! in Ben's and Eddie's relationship."

Ben and Pamela had a long and happy marriage.

By this time Eddie had finally begun to make some headway in getting cast here and there, and he was feeling more hopeful about his career and also feeling more at home in Hollywood. In those days, Schwab's Drugstore was still the coffee hangout in Hollywood frequented by actors. Two or three times a week Eddie would drop in, and there he met and chatted with people whose names would soon become nationally famous. Just to mention three, they included Don Rickles, a kind and gentle man offstage, not the abrasive insult expert he portrays in his act; Mel Brooks, a writer whose sketches were always not only crazy but hilarious; and the great voice actor Paul Frees, just beginning his work as "Boris Badenov" and other voices in the various versions of the *Rocky and Bullwinkle* cartoon show on TV.

Frees became a kind of inspiration to Eddie. "He did everything," Eddie would say of the deep-voiced actor. "All these cartoon characters, and he acted in movies and he wrote music and he did tons of commercials and other voiceover work. When Disney opened the Haunted Mansion attraction, Paul became the voice of the Ghost Host you hear in the preshow." An odd fact, by the way: Frees also recorded a track for Hartsfield Airport in Atlanta that you heard when you stepped onto a long escalator going down to the subway that took you to your gate. Paul's sepulchral voice would say, "Welcome. You are now entering the transportation mall…." Eventually, though, the airport changed the recording, reportedly because travelers who remembered hearing a voice like that in the Haunted Mansion for some reason started to get very, very nervous about boarding a plane.

Frees was also an actor with a great many screen credits (he is one of the scientists in the original version of the spooky science-fiction classic *The Thing*). In addition to acting in movies, Frees occasionally dubbed in dialogue for other actors, providing foreign accents (he was a master at these) or duplicating the actor's voice to correct a poor line reading. In fact, occasionally he even re-recorded the whole part in a voice that sounded more appropriate for the character seen on the screen than the original actor's own voice. He was a fairly successful songwriter, too, and all in all he made an excellent living at his craft.

Actually, just with his work in national commercials alone — Paul was the voice for the Pillsbury Doughboy and his income from that one series of commercials was solid — he was never unemployed. In an interview someone once asked Frees if he ever regretted becoming mainly a voice talent, and Paul admitted, "Well, sometimes. But it's nothing I can't overcome by looking at my bank balance." That was exactly the kind of versatility and dedication to craft that Eddie shared and hoped he could capitalize on to find the same kind of well-deserved success.

And just about at this same time Eddie also met for the first time a young man who later became his closest friend for the rest of his life. This was another aspiring actor who, like Eddie, had changed his name. He had begun life in Toledo, Ohio, as Jameel Farah (he is Lebanese-American), but after a good many movie and TV appearances, he had decided to change that to the more American-sounding Jamie Farr.

By the time he began billing himself that way, Jamie had already taken roles in some significant movies: As Jameel, he had played the "slow kid" Santini in 1955's *Blackboard Jungle*, an inner-city high-school drama starring Glenn Ford and Anne Francis and based on a book by the prolific writer Evan Hunter. Mystery fans, by the way, know Hunter under his pen name of Ed McBain, writer of the "87th Precinct" series of novels.

In addition to his part in *The Blackboard Jungle,* Jameel had also played an orange peddler in the movie version of the musical *Kismet* (1955) and had a small role as the co-pilot of a bomber in Andy Griffith's Army comedy *No Time for Sergeants* (1958).

When Jamie and Eddie first met, they were in the same boat: Searching for good roles, no matter how large or small, to establish themselves in TV and movies. They had a lot in common, because both of them had served in the U.S. Army (though after serving temporary duty stateside in Astoria, NY and Fort Knox, KY along with a few other places, Jamie had spent much of his hitch abroad in Japan) and both of them had worked for Armed Forces Radio.

Jamie recalls, "At the time I went into the service, my most regular performing job had been with Red Skelton. I'd been in a lot of his TV sketches with him where I literally carried half of the show, and we played against each other in regular roles. He was Cookie and I was Snorkel, and we were two guys in the Navy, and they were pretty popular sketches. So when I went into the service, Red kept in touch with me.

"Now, I was stationed in Japan and working with the Armed Services Radio, and after Red's son Richard died at the age of about twelve from leukemia, to keep himself busy and to work through his grief Red came over to do a USO tour of camps in Korea. He knew I was in Japan, and he requested me from the State Department. I went with him, and we went from camp to camp and entertained the troops all over Korea, right up to the Demarcation Zone.

"At the end of the tour, Red said to me, 'Look, when you get home, it's going to be difficult to re-start your career, so if you need any help, I want you to get in touch with me.' I thought that was awfully nice of him."

Not long after Jamie was released from active duty his father died, and Jamie thought the loss meant he'd have to leave Hollywood to take care of the family. "This was in 1959. We didn't have any money, and I knew I was going to have to go home to support my mother. I stopped by the CBS studio to say goodbye to Red," he remembers, "and he said, 'No, I told you it would be tough to re-start your career, and I won't let you give it up.' Instead Red immediately put me under personal contract right there in his dressing room at CBS. He gave me a couple of one-hundred-dollar bills right out of his pocket for me to send home to Mom, and that kept me in Hollywood."

Skelton asked Jamie to meet him at his home in Bel Air for a strategy session, and as they talked things over there, Red offered Jamie a sweet assignment: "Red said I would travel with him and do an act with him in night clubs and also continue to appear on his TV show, and all that.

One of his first engagements was in Lake Tahoe, at Harrah's, which in November of 1959 had just opened, and he was going to open the South Shore Room.

"So I went along with him. And there was another act playing there at Harrah's, Shaw and Hitchcock, which included these beautiful dancers. I met one of them, this amazing, tall, thin, perky blonde, just as charming as could be, witty and beautiful, and I thought she was just terrific. Her name was Carolyn Springer — and lo and behold, when I came back to California and after I had left Red, I met and became friends with Eddie Carroll. And then later when he introduced me to his girlfriend, it was Carolyn! You know, the Arabs say 'It is written.' Some things happen because they're just fated to happen. You meet someone and somehow you're destined to be part of each other's life."

Carolyn Springer at Harrah's South Shore Showroom in Lake Tahoe, November 1959.

As for that meeting with Eddie, at that time Eddie had become a friend of actor Doug McClure, and McClure in turn was a good friend of Burt Reynolds. McClure, then in the Navy Reserve, had put together a big show with Reynolds and the two of them then recruited other talented young actors, comics, and singers. Jamie had worked up a comedy routine with a buddy of his, Dick Bakalyan and because McClure wanted the act, Jamie became part of the show.

Eddie was also in the show, performing a sketch with Doug McClure. Jamie says he can't remember exactly when or where the show took place, but that's not important. The meeting is. "Anyway, as the show went on, Eddie and I were standing backstage," Jamie says, "and so we just started to chat and kid around and laugh back and forth. And it seems that from then on we were buddies. Eddie was that kind of guy, you know. You met him and five minutes later you wanted to be his friend. And of course I knew immediately that Eddie was very talented — it was a case of 'Gee, I like that person — we think just alike.'"

However, they didn't team up right away. Jamie still had the cushion of his personal contract with Red Skelton, which would continue long enough for him to re-establish his career, and Eddie was beginning to find work in local commercials and especially in stage shows. He could work well and confidently as an actor in a dramatic show, a comedy, or a musical, and in a variety show he could serve as a stand-up comic or a Master of Ceremonies with equal ease. In 1961 he appeared in many such stage shows, some hits and some, well, misses, but they kept him employed and let him sharpen his craft.

He landed a role in one show, *Max*, as one of the two male costars. The other was a young man named Bill Bixby, who had just made his first TV appearance in an episode of the sitcom *The Many Loves of Dobie Gillis*. Bixby, also a magician, would go on to many other TV appearances before becoming famous as the lead in several series, including *My Favorite Martian* (Bill was a long-suffering young reporter who concealed and "adopted" a crashed Martian flying-saucer pilot as his "Uncle Martin," and the title role was taken by stage and screen veteran Ray Walston). Other Bixby series were *The Courtship of Eddie's Father* (the actor playing his little boy was a kid named Brandon Cruz), *The Magician*, and The *Incredible Hulk*, in which Bixby played *half* of the lead role. As long as he was calm, the lead was the handsome and intelligent Dr. David Banner, in the person of Bixby. When he became angry, though — "You wouldn't like me when I'm angry" was his tag line — Banner transformed into the muscular, monstrous, green-skinned Hulk, played by Lou Ferrigno.

These roles, however, still lay in the future. In 1961 *Max* was a modest success for Bill and also for Eddie, and it led to another opportunity for him, one that would re-shape his whole existence. Bill Hitchcock of Shaw-Hitchcock Productions caught a performance of *Max*, liked the young Eddie Carroll's good looks and easy, charming manner, and got in touch with him after the show. Eddie auditioned for and got the chance to star in a touring variety show that would bring Vegas glitter to venues all around the country, *A la Carte from Las Vegas*.

And because he got that show, he would meet a lovely lady who soon changed his life forever.

CHAPTER 7

Carolyn

Carolyn Springer was still in her teens when she first met Eddie, but already she was a show-business veteran. "I began dancing in Chicago hotels when I was four years old, and that was when I had my first professional appearance," she says. The Springers were living then in Indiana, not too far from Chicago. Her father Glenn, bandleader of the Melody Knights, encouraged her talent.

So when Carolyn was six years old, she sang regularly with the Melody Knights both in personal appearances and every Saturday from nine to ten a.m. on the radio — as well as from six-thirty to seven in the mornings Monday through Friday! The family lived in Kentucky at that time. Later, Carolyn took dancing, singing, and piano lessons.

By the time she was thirteen, Carolyn was studying at Baker's Dance Studio in their show class, doing so well that she began teaching for them the next year. She joined the Junior Dance Masters of America. She remembers, "My friend Bobby Barranco, who later was known under his professional name, Rob Barran, taught with me. One Saturday, we went to a mall to eat and we saw Bugs Bunny in person at a store opening — it was someone in a costume, of course, together with the host of a cartoon show on TV, Skipper Frank. Many years, later I discovered that the person inside the costume was a young man named Eddie Carroll!"

Eddie was floored when he learned how close they had come to each other. However, he didn't miss those days of appearing in costume as a famous cartoon character. "Sometimes it was hazardous," he recalled. "Once two kids argued about whether I was the real Bugs Bunny, and to test me, they stabbed a knife into the costume foot. Luckily, it went right between two of my toes!"

When Carolyn was fifteen, she transferred to Hollywood Professional School (HPS), where the children of show-business pros were enrolled. Her classmates included Olympic skaters and gymnasts, some of the original Mouseketeers who performed on TV's *The Mickey Mouse Club*, and other young hopeful performers and actors. Extracurricular activities included classes in dance, acting, singing, musical performance — and performing in TV shows or in films. Instead of fire drills, HPS often had "aud calls," where, Carolyn says, students "would have to get their instruments and music charts, their dance shoes, or whatever the student needed, and immediately change into clothes you could perform in and rush to the auditorium. Kids from kindergarten to grade 12 would entertain us there."

Carolyn's close friend, Bobby Barranco.

Carolyn's class was very small by graduation time, but she treasures the memories and the friendships she made at HPS: "Many of us are still very close: Steve Stevens, Tommy Cole, Allan Brenerman, Tony Butala, and Pat Valentino were all there with me. It was a fun and close group who understood show business and learned what it would take to fulfill our careers."

At the age of fifteen and a half, Carolyn appeared on the weekly *Johnny Otis Show* as a dancer. She also worked as a choreographer, arranging the original "Willie and the Hand Jive" for the show. One of Johnny Otis's guests was Sammy Davis, Jr., who had left the family trio to strike out on his own. They chatted, and Sammy asked Carolyn out for a drink…but she wasn't even sixteen. When her dad came to pick her up, the three of them went out for coffee instead. Years later Carolyn met Sammy again in Las Vegas, and they reminisced about the moment. Sammy explained, "Well, with stage makeup, it's hard to know how old someone is!"

Carolyn had other professional jobs as a teenager, and then, three days after her eighteenth birthday, she went to Las Vegas to open for Milton Berle. "I knew Uncle Miltie from TV," she remembers, "and I didn't realize that in his nightclub act he would do risqué material. Even in rehearsals I didn't hear it, because as soon as I was finished rehearsing my part, I'd run out to the pool. On opening night my family came to see the show, and of course I hadn't warned them about the material. My eighty-year-old grandfather and my twelve-year-old brother were both there. After my dance numbers, I came out into the audience and sat with them…and then Milton Berle came on and turned the air blue! My family looked at me — well, I learned that what you saw on TV wasn't the same as what you would see and hear in a nightclub act!"

Later Carolyn remained in Vegas, working for six months at the Sahara and then another six months in the brand-new Harrah's Resort

Eddie Carroll in costume as Bugs Bunny.

and Casino in Lake Tahoe, where she met Jamie Farr for the first time. She also met a host of stars: Dan Dailey, the agile comedian and dancer Donald O'Connor, the exotic Marlene Dietrich, Buddy Hackett, Victor Borge, George Burns, the Crosby Brothers, Patti Page, Fred Waring, Nat King Cole and…"so many others," she says.

Carolyn was working in South Lake in Tahoe during the winter of

Left: Carolyn in Vegas as opener for Milton Berle. Right: Sisters, Gloria Birnkrant and Carolyn, very early in their career.

1959-1960. New Year's Eve has always been a huge event in Tahoe, the streets jammed with revelers. She remembers, "I had a New Year's Eve dinner with Burt Bacharach at the top of Harvey's. At that time, Burt was Marlene Dietrich's musical director and arranger. We left in what we thought was plenty of time, but the streets and the casino were so crowded that we were late for the midnight show — the only time in my whole life that I was ever late for a performance."

That year, nearby Squaw Valley hosted the Winter Olympics, and Harrah's Casino provided a bus to take the employees to the events each day. It wasn't easy: "We had to be aboard the bus by six a.m., which is a little early when you don't get off the stage until two in the morning. But we slept on the bus to and from the Olympics and had a marvelous, once-in-a-lifetime experience."

At nineteen, Carolyn toured with Marlene Dietrich: the Dallas State Expo, San Francisco's Geary Theater, the Riviera Hotel and Casino in Vegas, the Coconut Grove, and the Ambassador Hotel were among the stops. This time Carolyn's little sister Gloria joined her onstage.

By 1961, despite her tender years Carolyn had become a seasoned professional who had danced in Las Vegas, had toured, and had starred in Hitchcock-Shaw productions for two years. Mature for her age, she had impressed the producers with her professionalism and, just as important, with her willingness to take responsibility. By the time the production company was beginning to mount *A la Carte from Las Vegas*, Carolyn was in fact the person in charge of the entire show when the producers were not around.

Joining her again was her younger sister Gloria, who remembers, "Now, at that time I was really too young to be in the show, but we fudged my birthday a little." Like Carolyn, Gloria — "Glo" is her nickname, and she certainly has a glow about her — was already an experienced dancer.

"I met Eddie the same time my sister did," Gloria recalls. "At that time, remember, I was just a kid, and my sister Carolyn was the person looking out for me on the road."

Carolyn adds, "Now, when Eddie got cast in *A la Carte*, we in the cast had already heard about it before he actually showed up. In fact, one of the singers in the show had seen Eddie in *Max*, had found him attractive, and had set her sights on him. We had eleven women in the show, and this singer, to keep the others away so she would have a chance at Eddie, warned us all, 'I've heard this Carroll guy is a real ladies' man. Watch out for him. He'll try to go through the whole cast alphabetically.' I told her, 'Well, I don't have to worry much, since my last name starts with *S*.'"

Let's face it, it was hard to impress Carolyn, who had performed in Vegas on the same stages as Frank Sinatra, Marlene Dietrich, Sammy Davis, Jr., and other top stars. And she had dated first Burt Bacharach and later Tony Butala, already the lead singer for a hot musical group called The Lettermen. She was unlikely to be impressed by some rank newcomer, and she had the confidence and savvy to put down any womanizer who might make an ill-timed pass at her.

"We were going through a dance routine in the rehearsal hall," Gloria continues, "when this guy in a black turtleneck and western-cut jeans came in and came walking down the stairs, just looking like he owned the place, and he called out, 'Hi, gang!'" She laughs. "My first reaction was that he was trying way too hard to impress us, and I thought 'Well, lah-di-dah!'"

Carolyn agrees: "The way he came breezing in looking so full of himself first struck me as so egotistical! So I didn't even return his greeting, but just turned my back on him and said sarcastically to the dancers, 'Okay, let's take it from the top…five, six, seven, eight!'"

Not exactly an auspicious beginning! However, as rehearsals got underway and Eddie began to participate and reveal his own professional

Rehearsals with Carolyn and singer Paul Fresco.

demeanor, slowly Carolyn's opinion of him began to change. "You're on your guard, you know, in a situation like that. But he was good at what he did, and he didn't mind working hard and he took direction and advice. And contrary to what we had heard, he was very polite and gentlemanly."

That was important to Carolyn, since she really was watching out for her kid sister. Despite what the producers thought at the time, Gloria was really only fifteen, but she had talent as a dancer and she looked gorgeous. Carolyn bought her a tall showgirl headpiece and high heels and when they were home, away from the rehearsal hall, Carolyn taught her how to hold herself and balance the tall hat as she danced — and how to dance in heels, something Gloria had never done before. Gloria was a quick study and aced it. No one out in the audience seeing the show would think that she was as young as she really was. However, Carolyn certainly knew the truth and had the duty of protecting her little sister from men who might take advantage of Gloria's youth, so she was still a little bit wary of Eddie.

However, as the rehearsals went on, more and more Carolyn began to notice Eddie's kind, thoughtful side. He wasn't a spotlight hog onstage, and his attitude was that what was best for the show outweighed any personal vanity. Offstage, Eddie became more relaxed and less focused on impressing others as he settled in and got to know the cast personally, and before long he was his old self, laid-back and easy, kidding around, laughing with the others, and sharing the workload. Eddie was even then a man who was very difficult to dislike.

Gloria and Eddie rehearsing a skit in Ala Carte.

A la Carte from Las Vegas came into shape, the timing was set and the routines were memorized and rehearsed, and the time came for the tour to begin. "The cast and sets were put aboard a train," Carolyn recalls, "and we left Los Angeles Union Station for our first stop on the tour." *A la Carte* was billed as an "off-Broadway show," and their opening was in Fort Wayne, Indiana. Fair enough. That certainly was *way* off Broadway! It was a long, long train trip from Los Angeles, though. When the troupe pulled out of Union Station, Carolyn and Gloria were seated together, trying to make themselves comfortable for the long haul.

After a while they went down to the ladies' room to remove their make-up, brush their teeth, and prepare for the hours ahead. Carolyn finished and went back to their seat, only to find Eddie sitting in it. Eddie looked surprised. "I didn't know where you had gone, so I came over here to sit."

Gloria returned and took the place where Eddie had been sitting, next to their dear friend of many years, Paul DeRolf (actor and choreographer on such films as *The Karate Kid* parts I and II), and so Carolyn sat next to Eddie. They chatted about this and that, time went by, and then as they were passing through Dodge City, Eddie noticed that Carolyn was looking sleepy. He said, "You know, it might be more comfortable if you rested your head on my shoulder. You might be able to get some sleep."

Clever Eddie. Carolyn did just that, and she began to warm up to Mr.

Gloria in dice headdress with Paul DeRolf.

Carroll. The train arrived in Fort Wayne on a Sunday morning, and as the cast got out at the station they found a line of convertibles waiting to parade them through the city. That was well and good, but they were hungry after the long cross-country trip. They asked about breakfast, and they had to settle for the one place that was open to serve food on Sunday mornings.

The Greyhound bus station.

All through his career when such moments came up, Eddie would often joke about "the glamorous world of show-biz." But eggs are eggs, breakfast is breakfast, and the cast laughed their way through it and had a fun time. By the end of the first show engagement, Eddie and Carolyn had begun to date, in a sort of tentative way.

Gloria remembers, "I had the pleasure of going on all their dates with them, including all three of us going to the drive-in movies together. He was a good sport, and I really came to look at him more like a brother than just another performer. You know, one thing about Eddie: If you walked into a room and he came up and said, 'Hi, how are you?' he really wanted to know, and it was never just a social comment. He was always really interested in other people. He was a very easy guy to like."

After Fort Wayne the troupe journeyed to the Elmwood Casino in Windsor, Ontario, just across the Canadian border from Detroit — and *A la Carte* could truly claim to be on an international tour. The showroom in the casino had been closed down for some time, and *A la Carte* reopened it. The evening should have been a gala occasion, but somehow either the management or the media had fumbled the ball on publicity. There had been not a hint in the press or on TV or radio about the show. It was as though the grand re-opening were a Cold War secret. On the first night, there were literally more people on stage than in the audience. "It was a hard room to play!" Carolyn says.

Especially considering all the traveling and irregular hours. After that first show the casino owner came up to Eddie and said, "Hey, kid! You're not getting too many laughs."

Eddie came back with, "Not getting too much sleep, either."

The owner said, "You know what the problem is? Delivery. Talk slower."

Eddie was always open to advice, but he also thought the problem might just be the material. He stayed up all the rest of the night reworking his lines. The next night he opened the show by coming out on stage and just running in circles. It was so ridiculous that the audience started to laugh, and from then on he had them. He did all of his brand-new material, and they ate it up with laughter and applause. When the show ended and Eddie walked offstage, the owner was there beaming at him: "See, kid? Talking slower worked, didn't it?"

Eddie gave him a wide smile and a nod. And then went off to grab a few hours of much-needed sleep.

Today Elmwood Casino has become a rehabilitation center, probably using the same rooms. Carolyn remembers the performers' quarters as separate tiny units, barely large enough to turn around in, but down at the end of each hall were huge bathrooms. Getting through the shows — if it's done well, dancing looks easy, but it's really hard work — and leaning on each other for support, the cast of *A la Carte* pulled together as the tour went on. "Eddie was great," Carolyn says. "He and I and Gloria were a trio. We went everywhere together, and I was so happy that Gloria had double chaperones. Eddie kept the guys away."

After six months of touring, Eddie and Carolyn had fallen in love. They kept Gloria under their wings and they already felt as if they were almost a family. "This is how you know the man really, really feels comfortable with you," Carolyn says. "We were riding on the train again, on that long trip back to Los Angeles. This time I didn't even wait for Eddie to invite me. I put my head on his shoulder and went to sleep. And then he woke me up and said, 'Hey, move your head, please. My arm's gone to sleep.'"

During the tour Eddie and Carolyn had talked a lot about their backgrounds and their professional lives and hopes and dreams. Eddie still played the guitar, and he had continued to write songs. Carolyn really liked one of them, "How Is Julie?" and thought it had potential. Years later, Eddie remembered it as "just one of those teen angst songs" that were popular in the early 1960s, but Carolyn thought it might become something much more.

Before the tour had begun, Carolyn had dated Tony Butala, a classmate of hers at Hollywood Professional School. Butala had formed the singing group The Lettermen first in 1958, with Mike Barnett and Talmadge Russell. They had a lovely close-harmony style that was memorable and distinctive, and in a Vegas revue called *Newcomers of 1928* (yes, 1928 — they shared the stage with veteran bandleader Paul Whiteman, legendary comedian Buster Keaton, and singer Rudy Vallee, among others). Butala took the part of Bing Crosby, who had sung with Whiteman's band, the Rhythm Boys. Audiences went wild.

By 1960, the Lettermen were recording songs (Butala was still the leader, but Jim Pike and Bob Engemann had replaced Barnett and Russell). They released two singles that established them as an up-and-coming recording group, and soon Artist and Repertoire representative Nick Venet signed them up for Capitol Records — an association that went on to last for more than twenty-five years. In fact, even today the Lettermen still tour, filling auditoriums and bringing audiences to their feet with their great hits. Today the Lettermen are Tony Butala, Donovan Tea, and Bobby Poynton.

But in 1961, they were brand-new on the national music scene and hitting it really big with their first album, *A Song for Young Love*. In addition to the title track, it included "I'll Be Seeing You," "Smile," "When I Fall in Love," "The Way You Look Tonight," "Blueberry Hill," "In the Still of the Night" and others — and if those don't raise a smile and send a happy wave of nostalgia washing over you, you weren't around in the

1960s! *A Song for Young Love* was an enormous success, and all during the tour of *A la Carte* Carolyn kept hearing songs from it.

However, Carolyn had not told Tony that she had begun to date Eddie. For one thing, the Lettermen were on tour at the same time the *A la Carte* troupe was, and who knew where they would be on any given day? This was long before cell phones. Touring performers had to rely on pay phones, and it was all but impossible to connect with someone who was out on the road. Then, too, Carolyn did not want to break up with Tony by letter. That was far too impersonal and not her style at all. She procrastinated, telling herself that she would see Tony face to face when they were home again.

When Eddie got back to Los Angeles, encouraged by Carolyn's response to "How Is Julie?" he went to a friend of his, Barry DeVorzon, and sang the song to him. Barry agreed with Carolyn's assessment: the tune had definite possibilities. He had connections at Capitol and called an A&R representative there, Nick Venet — the same man who had signed Tony and the Lettermen up with Capitol not too long before. Nick agreed to listen, Eddie played the guitar and sang the song for him, and it impressed him enough for him to ask for a recorded demo and a lead sheet. As it happened, Nick was on the lookout for just such a song. He had an album under development with a final slot open for a song just exactly the length and mood of "How Is Julie?"

And, he said, it was to be a Lettermen album.

Eddie's heart sank. "Oh, great," he thought. "I'm dating Carolyn. I'll walk in and hand my music to Tony Butala and he'll rip it up and stomp on it."

To lend moral support, Carolyn went along with Eddie to the recording studio two days later. At Capitol Records, they ran into two of Eddie's friends, Billy Strange, guitarist and songwriter for Elvis Presley among many others (and a legend in rockabilly music), and musician, actor, and singer Glenn Campbell. At that time the two were sidemen playing in the musical group backing the new album. While Eddie was catching up with the two of them, two of the Lettermen, Jimmy Pike and Bobby Engemann, saw Carolyn and came over to greet her.

"Hey," one of them said, "does Tony know you're here?"

Carolyn turned bright red. "No," she murmured.

So of course they had to take her to him. Carolyn had steeled herself to the task and gently, kindly, but firmly told Tony that she had fallen in love with Eddie. Tony, who had been a friend of Carolyn's long before they had dated, understood. "I wish you all the happiness in the world," he said kindly. He knew that with the Lettermen hitting it big, in the near future there simply would be little time in his life for both a good relationship and a burgeoning career. Then too, he came to like Eddie once the two young men got to know each other.

Tony says, "I can't even remember exactly when I did meet Eddie first. Nick Venet brought him around, but we were meeting so many songwrit-

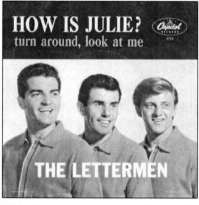

How is Julie *sheet music (left) and record (above). Left to Right: Jim Pike, Bob Engemann and Tony Butala.*

ers at that time that it's hard to recall. There was a whole community of people just bumping into each other, all of them just bubbling under the surface of success. Nick had a good ear for songs that would be right for the Lettermen. I listened to Eddie's demo with him and I agreed with Nick that 'How Is Julie?' would be right for us."

Later, Tony became friends with Eddie, and the Carrolls remained on very good terms with Tony for the rest of Eddie's life. "Eddie was just a great guy," Tony remembers. "He was so talented in so many ways." Tony has special memories of Eddie at the point in his career when his role as Jack Benny emerged — but more about that later. Back in 1962, as Tony says with a chuckle, what mattered most to Eddie and Carolyn was the first royalty check for "How Is Julie?"

The Lettermen did a fine job recording the cut, and it appeared not only on their second album, *Once Upon a Time*, but as the A side of a single (the B side was another track from the album, "Turn Around, Look at Me," which became one of the group's standards). The single came out first and sold so well, securing so much airplay, that when the album hit the racks, Capitol put a sticker on the front of the jacket: "Includes 'How Is Julie?' The Great Hit by *THE LETTERMEN.*"

It was a wonderful break for Eddie, bringing in some welcome income and adding to his sense of security. And as for Tony and Carolyn, their own break was not traumatic at all.

By the way, ironically or maybe just appropriately, the last line that Tony sings in "How Is Julie?" is the plaintive sentence, "She left me last night."

CHAPTER 8

Crushing the Grapes, Sipping the Wine

Carolyn and Eddie grew even closer after the recording of "How Is Julie?" Somehow the next step just seemed inevitable, but Carolyn says, "Eddie never did propose to me. While we were on the road with *A la Carte*, Eddie and I had read Errol Flynn's scandalous, confessional 1959 autobiography *My Wicked, Wicked Ways*, in which Flynn reminisced about his life on screen, off screen, and in some real-life scenes that were about as steamy as the law allowed."

Eddie and Carolyn had enjoyed a funny incident Flynn had written about concerning the movie *Essex and Elizabeth* (1939) in which Bette Davis played a passionate Queen Elizabeth I and Flynn the swashbuckling Robert Devereaux, Earl of Essex.

The film, by the way, is an adaptation of Maxwell Anderson's stage play *Elizabeth the Queen*, but Flynn wanted his character represented in the title. A series of title changes followed: *The Private Lives of Elizabeth and Essex, Elizabeth the Queen, The Private Lives of Essex and Elizabeth*, and simply *Essex and Elizabeth*. It actually circulated, at one time or another, under all of these titles, making it one of the few films that could play a quadruple feature with itself.

As Flynn revealed in his book, he and Bette Davis had a relationship with all of the warmth of a mongoose facing a cobra. The successful and powerful Davis had not wanted Flynn in the film to begin with, campaigning for the role to go to Laurence Olivier. She fumed when the studio gave the role to Flynn, and she never forgave him. Though *Essex and Elizabeth* was popular and could easily have led to more teamings of the two stars, Davis refused ever to work with Flynn again.

So just as one might expect, filming proved tumultuous. On the set, the two stars constantly sniped at each other, maneuvered to distract or upstage each other, and in general got on each other's nerves. This culminated in the passage in Flynn's autobiography that Eddie laughed over: it's a moment when, in the movie script, an angry Elizabeth slaps the face of the Earl of Essex, an act of contempt that breaches all the protocol and decorum of the royal household and that shocks the court.

In real life, acting on days of stored-up resentments, Davis hauled off and really clobbered Flynn, who was in armor. Flynn describes the moment, saying he saw stars and his ears rang from the force of the blow, but because the Technicolor cameras were rolling, he clenched his teeth and got through the scene — which wound up in the finished movie, because he flatly refused to do a retake.

Some months after Eddie and Carolyn had read the story, the two of them were watching TV one evening, sitting on the sofa and holding hands, and the movie of the night was *Essex and Elizabeth.* At the dramatic moment when Good Queen Bess snarls, "You dare to turn your back on your Queen?" and clouts her loyal retainer Essex with a slap hard enough to qualify as a TKO, Eddie guffawed and chortled, and the next instant both he and Carolyn collapsed, holding onto each other and laughing hysterically. They hugged each other, and when they had caught their breath, Eddie turned to her and simply asked, "When we're married, will we still have this much fun?"

It was the first time the subject had come up. Carolyn tilted her head. "Am I supposed to say 'yes' or 'no'?" she asked.

She then kissed Eddie, giving him the answer that really mattered. The question was settled, and from that moment they were engaged.

Yet they had to postpone the wedding, because launching a marriage at that particular time was dicey. After all, royalties from the song stretched just so far, and for his annual income Eddie was still greatly dependent on his success or lack of success with casting directors. Carolyn, ever dynamic and inventive, became a whole new source of inspiration and support for Eddie as his fiancée and later his wife. She had studied psychology and knew something about the power of autosuggestion in maintaining a positive outlook and aiming for success, and Eddie's temperament told him her suggestions were sound ones. Meanwhile, they enjoyed being engaged. As she says, the two had very little money at times, but they were determined to have fun together.

At the same time that Carolyn and Eddie were dating, Jamie Farr had fallen for a wonderful lady, Joy. She and Carolyn became the closest of friends (and remain so today). With both Eddie and Jamie often on shoestring budgets, the couples double-dated. That meant they'd chip in for a six-pack of Coca-Cola and a bag of potato chips and would spend an evening at home playing board games and making each other laugh. "We didn't have enough to invest in even going to the movies," Carolyn says, "but we really didn't need it with Eddie and Jamie there. They were always a floor show in themselves."

At one point Jamie confessed that he envied Eddie: "I'd like to propose to Joy, but I can't even hope to support her with the kind of money I'm making from bit parts." What they needed was a miracle. Jamie says, "At that particular time we were struggling a great deal, but you know what they say in Hollywood: 'One day you're drinking the wine, the next day you're crushing the grapes.' Let's say I'd been crushing the grapes a lot. By then Eddie and I had started to try to write pilots for TV, and we'd get an occasional nibble of interest, but none sold. We even got as far as pitching one to CBS for a live show, but it didn't go anywhere.

"So I was broke and trying to eke out a living. I remember I had this little Renault car I drove everywhere to auditions and so on, just the same way Eddie did — hoping it would hold together, you know. My agent had heard about a big epic religious movie that was about to be cast, *The Greatest Story Ever Told*, to be directed by the great George Stevens. Now, that got me excited, and I told my agent, 'With my face there's gotta be something in that movie for me!' I mean, I'm Lebanese-American, with Semitic features — and this nose is a nose of biblical proportions!"

Jamie's agent was dubious. He pointed out that with his appearances on the Skelton show and elsewhere Jamie had put himself in a kind of rut and was essentially already typecast as a funnyman. If casting directors knew him at all, they knew him as a comic actor, not as someone who could handle drama. He asked Jamie, "Do you have any dramatic role on film that Mr. Stevens could see?"

Jamie thought hard and said, "Well, yeah. I could come up with one thing. I had done an episode of *The Rebel*, the Western series starring Nick Adams, in which I had played a serious role. I said, 'I can get that piece of film if Mr. Stevens would look at it.' My agent told me to go ahead, so I got in touch with Nick Adams and he provided me with a copy of the show, on film. My agent set it up, and so I got in that Renault and drove over to Culver City to hand-deliver it so that George Stevens could take a look at it."

Then it was time to wait and pray. Literally. As it happened, every morning at that time Jamie was dropping Joy off at work. Near her place of employment in downtown Los Angeles was a little Catholic church, and the day after he had taken the film over to the M-G-M Studio in Culver City, Jamie took Joy to work as usual, then stopped at the church.

"I'm Orthodox, not Roman Catholic, but I remembered a story about Danny Thomas, who's a Lebanese compatriot of mine and who came from the same hometown that I did. Danny always said that when he was at a low point in his career he prayed to St. Jude: 'Please help me, and I promise I'll build a shrine to you.' Sure enough, Danny went on to great success and built the St. Jude's Children's Research Hospital in Memphis."

So Jamie decided, "I'm gonna try it. Danny's Lebanese, I'm Lebanese, he's from Toledo, I'm from Toledo, so what the heck, I'll try it. Every morning after I dropped Joy off I would go into the church and light a candle to St. Jude and drop a quarter into the slot, you know. And I'd pray, 'St. Jude, please help me get a part in this movie.'"

Crushingly, about a week later Jamie's agent called with bad news: "Jamie, you can go over to Culver City and pick up your film. There's nothing for you in the movie."

It was almost the last straw. "I was living right on the edge," Jamie says. "My unemployment was running out. Not getting even a bit part was just a disaster for me. So that morning before going to pick up the film I took Joy to work, parked the car, went into the church, and really told St. Jude off. I was mad at him. I didn't light the candle, I didn't give him a quarter, and I told him he had let me down."

However, later that day, Jamie received a second phone call from his agent, who now was both happy and apologetic: "Jamie, I don't know how it got all mixed up, but Stevens likes your look and you have a contract to be in the movie. They'll guarantee you twenty-six weeks at $450.00 a week, and you're going to play one of the Apostles. You'll be Nathaniel Bartholomew. M-G-M wants you to go to the studio tomorrow and have costuming and make-up tests." Jamie, his voice happy after all these years, says, "Well, as you can imagine, that made me feel a lot better toward St. Jude, and I was just elated — that was so much money to me!"

The next day Jamie reported in for the costume fitting and the tests and ran into a couple of big stars, Charlton Heston (who played John the Baptist in the film) and Roddy McDowell (Matthew). Jamie remembers "they were talking about how nice Italy was at that time of year, but I was just thinking, 'I got the part! I got the part!'"

Into every actor's life some rain must fall. Later, Jamie's agent called him again and told him that the studio had looked at the tests and had decided against casting him as Nathaniel Bartholomew. Before Jamie's heart plummeted all the way down into his shoes, the agent added, "Now, don't panic, you will be in the movie and you've still got the same deal, twenty-six weeks at four-fifty a week, but you'll be playing the role of the Apostle Thaddeus."

Jamie rejoiced again — this time because he hadn't lost the job — and called a friend of his with the news. He told him the whole story, including his prayers to St. Jude, and wound up by saying, "And it must have worked because I'll be playing Thaddeus!"

"Who?" his friend asked.

"Thaddeus!" Jamie said.

Long pause. Then his friend said, "Jamie, do you know who Thaddeus is?"

"No."

"He's St. Jude, you jackass!"

Jamie owed St. Jude some candles and a whole pocketful of quarters. On the strength of his contract and the money he made and saved from the film, Jamie proposed, Joy accepted, and the couple got married just seven weeks before Eddie and Carolyn. They are still very happily together today. Don't believe everything you read about Hollywood marriages.

Joy and Jamie on set of The Greatest Story Ever Told.

Just as his friend Jamie had found his own miracle, the year 1962 was an important one for Eddie, too, a time when he reached a higher level in his own career. By then he and Jamie were beginning to write together. They knew that quiz shows were cheap to produce (even with the prizes they offered) and drew in good audiences, and they brainstormed several possibilities for such programs, even filming pilots for a couple of them, sometimes rounding up friends and family, like Carolyn's sister Gloria, to be the contestants.

These got a little traction — at least the networks kept looking at their ideas and considering them — but never quite caught the right wave. When one of their proposals was rejected, the two would immediately begin planning another, determined to get *something* on the air as writers and producers. However, acting came through for Eddie at that point, and just as Jamie caught a break in the movies, so did Eddie.

Another epic M-G-M blockbuster, this one set in the Ukraine of the sixteenth century, was casting. It was called *Taras Bulba*, and it was kind of a Romeo and Juliet love story set against the backdrop of the fierce Cossacks struggling against the Polish overlords who tried to dominate them. Yul Brynner stars as Taras, and Tony Curtis is his son, sent away to Poland to study among the enemy. However, he falls in love with the daughter of a Polish nobleman, and family and national loyalties are strained to the breaking point in the ensuing struggles and heroic battles.

Just as Jamie had a great face for a biblical epic, so Eddie had the right look for a Cossack, and he landed a small role in the film — small, but weighty enough to allow him to join the Screen Actors Guild, a goal that Carolyn had taught him to program himself to approach and achieve. That marked at least a small peak in his upward climb.

From a purely financial standpoint even better news came soon afterward. One day he visited Carolyn, bursting to tell her about an assignment that meant a nice paycheck, though Eddie made an effort to seem very cool and casual. He told Carolyn, "Honey, I just got word that I had a successful interview and got cast in a commercial."

"What's the product?" she asked. Up until then, much of his commercial work had been for strictly local businesses, little fifteen-second bits on the radio for tire stores or mom-and-pop restaurants, the kind of ads that didn't pay the talent very much, and all too often the payment came as a one-shot deal for fifty or a hundred dollars. Not this time, though. This time the product wasn't local.

Eddie calmly said, "It's for Coca-Cola."

Carolyn began to jump up and down. She had done a few big commercials and knew just how hard they were to snag — just as difficult, in their way, as getting a good role in a major movie. Being cast in a Coke commercial was an enormous step up from doing voice work for a radio spot advertising a new coin laundry.

For a national — no, an *international* product like Coca-Cola, the job of filming a TV commercial meant so much more. For one thing, it would be exposure on a grand scale. Having a face that people recognized from commercials would often get an actor a crack at a plum role on TV or in the movies. Then, too, the national commercials paid well, and not just in one check. Commercial actors collect residuals for a contracted period of time after the commercial first airs: so much for the initial payment, and then regular checks for as long as the commercial runs or as long as the contract specifies.

Eddie would say, "When you are an actor who gets these commercials, you strike up a wonderful relationship with your mail carrier. Every day you look forward to the mail delivery and hope there are going to be a few of those wonderful residual checks in there for you."

Despite his calm demeanor, Eddie was really as excited as Carolyn, because the opportunity meant so much for them. It was a sign that they could marry and have a reasonable shot at prospering. It's great to be so much in love that you don't mind sharing a life of poverty, and Eddie and Carolyn had that kind of love going for them, too. On the other hand, anyone who's that much in love wants to provide the very best for his or her loved ones and to guarantee security — as much as it can be guaranteed in the unpredictable world. Now that Eddie felt he had turned a corner in his career, he and Carolyn set the date: April 7, 1963.

By that time, Jamie and Joy had been married for seven long and wonderful…weeks. Jamie was away on location for *The Greatest Story Ever Told*, but he would make time to come to the wedding. And so, about a year after that moment when Eddie had asked one question and Carolyn had answered a different one with a kiss, they were ready.

When Carolyn promised with that kiss that she would marry Eddie, she wasn't just kidding around. Not quite two months after Joy and Jamie said their vows, Eddie and Carolyn were married in Los Angeles in a small ceremony intended for Eddie's friends and Carolyn's family. Two weeks later, on April 20, 1963, they went to Edmonton and had a *second* full wedding service for Eddie's parents and relatives and all his Canadian friends. Finally, more than twenty-five years later, they were married for a third time in China. That is real commitment. A triple knot just will not come untied, and this one never did.

That first wedding ceremony, the one held in California, of course included Eddie's old friend Ben Cooper as best man. He stood up for Eddie and somehow managed not to lose the ring. Eddie always remembered as he was walking toward the minister, Jamie and Joy were sitting at the end of a pew, next to the aisle. "Jamie had come in from Utah, where *The Greatest Story Ever Told* was filming," Eddie said. "He had a full black beard and had let his hair grow long and shaggy, and he was as tan as saddle leather. And just as I passed him, Jamie leaned over and said so softly that only I could hear him, 'Don't do it! You'll regret this later!'"

Jamie's advice was not meant in earnest, and advice that Eddie did not consider taking for one-tenth of an instant. The small, quiet wedding proceeded. Ben didn't have to worry about losing the ring. Five-year-old William Menessee, who was planning on marrying Carolyn himself, carried that in on a pillow. By coincidence, his suit exactly matched that worn by the heckler Jamie Farr. As Eddie and Carolyn, now married, walked back down the aisle, Jamie said quite loudly, "You'll be sorry!"

Eddie said, "Well, Carolyn and I just broke up laughing. I mean, here was my great friend, an old married man of seven weeks, looking like a biblical prophet and giving me that advice at that time!"

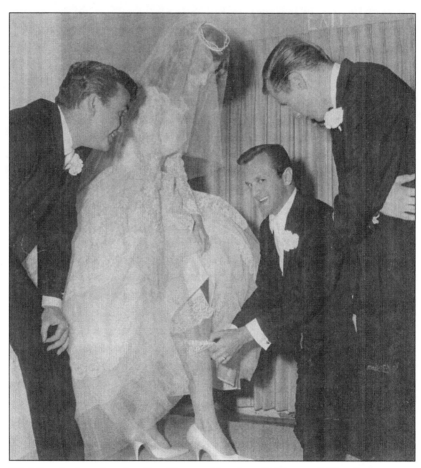

Wedding in Los Angeles: Ben Cooper, Carolyn, Eddie, and Glen Larson.

Mr. and Mrs. Eddie and Carolyn Carroll left the service as newlyweds who felt not only the natural joy that most couples do at such a moment, but also a thrill of hope for the future. Little William jumped into the car with Carolyn and Eddie and rode with them to the reception. For a whole year and a half, ever since he had first met Eddie, William had never spoken a word to him, though Eddie made him

Wedding in Canada.

Carolyn and Eddie laughing at Jamie's "You'll be sorry!"

laugh and would lie on the floor watching cartoons with him. He was terribly jealous of Eddie, but he had confided once that he wanted a special toy rifle.

At the reception Eddie gave him a wrapped package as a gift for being part of the wedding party. When William opened it and discovered the rifle he wanted so badly, he flew from the floor up into Eddie's arms, and they became fast buddies. Things were looking up on all fronts. Eddie deserved it. To use Jamie's metaphor, he had spent a long time now crushing those grapes.

Now a responsible married man, he was eager to sip a little of the wine.

Carolyn's dad Glenn, Eddie, and Ben Cooper as best man.

CHAPTER 9

Ready for his Close-up

After his marriage, Eddie rededicated his efforts to make it in performing. With Carolyn's advice and encouragement, he kept his attitude positive and upbeat, believing in and working for his career and always, always, practicing his craft. Casting directors began to sense how professional he was, always more than punctual and always prepared.

If a casting call went out and hopefuls were advised to show up at ten a.m., Eddie would drive onto the lot at nine. He would find the audition space, sign in, and pick up the sides (the script) of the material to be used in the try-out. He might run into a few other early birds, and he often knew them, because Hollywood is not really that big a town. Eddie would take a little time to greet them and chat a bit, but this was his business, and as soon as he could he would either go outside or find a quiet corner to study and memorize the lines.

He would also analyze them, feeling his way into the role, as far as the material allowed. If he was reading advertising copy, he'd ask himself what there was to *like* about the product. He would sell it the way a friendly neighbor would — "Hey, you ought to try this fantastic grill cleaner that I just learned about." Or if it happened to be a script for a comedy or drama, he'd think about what the scene might mean to the character he would be playing. "In every scene of a script, it works only if the characters have something that matters, something at stake. If the actor can find that, he or she can find what will make the scene work."

Once he had a handle on the situation and character, Eddie would memorize the lines — he was a quick study — and then rehearse, rehearse, rehearse, all to himself. By the time he was called in for the audition, he would nail the scene in front of the casting execs or the video camera. Dreams will come true, he always said — if you believe in them and work for them. He would often tell young people who were coming up in show business, "Remember, this is what you owe to yourself: Every day get up and go to work and do three positive things for your career. You can make it happen." It was a message that Eddie believed in and lived by. He always practiced what he preached.

Breaks did begin to come. In 1963, ABC began its fall season with a one-hour variety program, *The Jerry Lewis Show*, in the line-up, but it didn't last and was cancelled after only three months. The network decided to replace it with a looser show of the same type, an hour of comedy sketches, monologues, specialty acts, and music called *The Hollywood Palace*. Unlike *The Jerry Lewis Show*, the new program wouldn't have a permanent host but would attract viewers with stellar guest hosts: Bing Crosby, Groucho Marx, Joan Crawford, Frank Sinatra, Bette Davis, and scores of other top stars. It debuted on January 4, 1964, and quickly attracted a solid audience, one big enough to sustain the show and make it a long-running success.

The Hollywood Palace was heavy on comedy, and it was a time when the nation needed to laugh: the United States had become involved in Vietnam, President Kennedy had faced down the Russians over missiles in Cuba, and then — on November 22, 1963 — the handsome young President had been assassinated in Dallas. The country's mood was gloomy, and people responded well to the light and entertaining fare offered on *The Hollywood Palace*.

Eddie was cast in one episode, got good, solid laughs and applause, and then went on to perform for a total of six times on the show. "I loved it," Eddie said. "The format of the show meant that it combined acting on stage in front of a theater audience with presenting filmed bits. This was like heaven to me, and I had such a good time doing those shows."

One bit that Eddie remembered very fondly featured Herb Alpert and the Tijuana Brass. Eddie said,

EDDIE CARROLL: They were going to do a medley of all their hits, but they decided it wouldn't be exciting, visually, just to have the camera on the band as they played. So they had Carolyn and me come into the studio and we were going to be audience members listening to the medley.

Now, as the music begins, the camera pans over the audience and focuses on Carolyn and me, and I look sleepy. I nod off and then there's a dream dissolve and you see what I'm dreaming about. As the Tijuana Brass play "The Lonely Bull," suddenly there I am in costume as a bullfighter in the middle of this field, very, very stylish but not all that intimidating to the bull, who gives me a look that says, "You've gotta be kidding me." Then they go into "Tijuana Taxi," and then there I am with this huge mustache, as the wild-eyed taxi driver. And then "Zorba the Greek," and there I am dressed like Anthony Quinn in that movie, and so on.

It was four or five days of filming to get all those sequences done, just long and exhausting days, but it was so much fun! And of course there I was with my beautiful wife in the live audience, looking as if I was asleep. So because my eyes were closed, Carolyn, without giving any indication

Hollywood Palace starring Herb Alpert advertised in Variety.

of what she was doing, had to watch for the cues and squeeze my thigh to let me know when to react. But it was so much fun doing that, and it led to a lot of other things for me, too.

Eddie was also finding employment doing small roles in TV sitcoms. He had roles on *The Andy Griffith Show* (if you catch a rerun of the episode in which Aunt Bee wins a trip to Mexico, watch for the clerk at the airline counter. It's a young Eddie), and then made four or five segments of *Gomer Pyle, U.S.M.C.*, a service comedy that had spun off from *The Andy Griffith Show*. Eddie remembered, "It was terrific working with Frank Sutton, who played Gunnery Sergeant Vince Carter, and Jim Nabors. It was a one-camera show, so it meant a long shooting day."

Eddie also enjoyed meeting and working with Don Knotts, then famous as the high-strung Deputy Barney Fife, on *Andy Griffith*. He said, "I had great admiration for Don, who had developed this fantastically comic characterization and who could do a perfect take to point up a funny line reading." Later on, Eddie would have more experiences working with Don, including doing sketches with him when Knotts hosted *Hollywood Palace,* and that led to an even more exciting opportunity.

Above: Eddie on The Andy Griffith Show, *"Aunt Bee Goes to Mexico." Below:* Gomer Pyle, U.S.M.C. *with Eddie and Frank Sutton.* COURTESY TV LAND

In late 1968, Eddie also had a chance to be on TV with one of his personal idols, Jack Benny. Jack had semiretired — his weekly show had ended, but he was still appearing in two specials a year. One that would be aired on Valentine's Day (by coincidence, also Jack's birthday), 1969, was *Jack Benny's Birthday Special*. Early in his radio career, Jack had integrated commercials with the show, and that tradition continued. Texaco sponsored the special, and toward the end the last commercial featured Eddie.

Jack Benny Birthday Special, 1969. Eddie with Jack Benny. COURTESY JACK BENNY FAN CLUB

As Jack stands on stage thanking the audience, Eddie, headphones covering his ears, carries out a stool and a clipboard and says, "Mr. Benny, it's time for the commercial." He puts the stool down, Jack sits on the stool, and Eddie gives him the script. As Jack reads the copy aloud as though he's seeing it for the first time, Eddie as the stage manager waves in the set pieces. Two islands of gas pumps glide in, a gas-station backdrop flies down, and finally Eddie motions on a flat representing Jack's old Maxwell. It stops so that from the camera's position, it looks as if Jack is behind the wheel of the car. As Jack reads, "So tell your Texaco man to fill her up!" an actor playing the attendant shows up and says, "Fill her up, Mr. Benny?" Cheapskate Jack gives him a pained look and says, "Uh — one gallon, please."

It's a funny bit. As they began to rehearse, Jack told Eddie how to pace everything, when to wave down the station backdrop, signal for the gas pumps, and so on. Eddie remembered,

EDDIE CARROLL: So it was "Now, when I get to this line, the station should be coming down, y'see, kid? And then I want the pumps to come on at this line, all right, kid?" Jack broke off and said, "Oh, for heaven's sakes, I can't just call you 'kid.' You need a name. Lookit, kid, what's your name?"

I told him my name was Eddie Carroll.

Jack thought for a second. "Eddie. Eddie. Okay, from now on your name is gonna be Eddie." He raised his voice and called to the director, Fred de Cordova, up in the booth, "Hey, Freddie, from now on this kid is gonna be named Eddie." Then he turned to me and asked, "Is that okay with you?"

I couldn't resist. I did an impromptu Jack Benny impression and said, "Gosh, I certainly *hope* so. It's the name my mother *gave* me." Then for several beats, Jack just stared at me silently in that everything-happens-to-me expression of his.

Finally he turned and yelled up to the booth: "Forget it, Freddie. The kid's a schmuck, and he doesn't *get* a name!"

But Benny couldn't keep pretending to be angry, and he immediately began to laugh, as did Eddie. It was a moment that one of Eddie's dreams had come true, because he had always admired Jack Benny's comic technique.

At the same time Eddie and Jamie had formalized their partnership as Carroll-Farr Productions. "We wrote pilots for three different game shows during this period," he recalled. "I remember that we pitched all three of them to ABC, where they had just hired this young producer named Michael Eisner. He was encouraging, but didn't pick up any of the shows. There was also another show, a sitcom called *Our House* that we had high hopes for at CBS, but again it didn't spark a purchase."

They kept plugging, though. Eddie now had even more reasons to work hard: in 1967 he and Carolyn were expecting their first child. The date that the obstetrician had predicted as the target came, but Eddie had to keep working, and he was shooting a Gain commercial and worried sick about what might be going on back home. "There I was," Eddie said, "all dressed up as the heroic railway engineer in this immaculate white uniform."

These, remember, were the days before cell phones or even pagers. The cast and crew of the commercial sympathized with Eddie, though — so the helpful male cast kept ducking out to find pay phones to call Carolyn to see how she was doing. She had to report that it looked like there would be no arrival that day.

And in fact more days passed...three, four...six, seven...nine, ten! The commercial shoot had ended, and when it came time at 1:00 in the morning on April 29, 1967, for Carolyn to go to the hospital, like many men facing imminent fatherhood, Eddie temporarily lost his mind: "Carolyn was ready, and she was understandably eager to get to the hospital. So I was flustered, and there I was running around, getting dressed, putting down my keys and losing them, finding them again, tearing the closet doors open, looking in every nook and cranny."

Carolyn, who had the feeling she couldn't wait all that long, called out, "What are you looking for?"

Frantically, Eddie said, "The diaper bag! I know we packed the diaper bag! I can't find the diaper bag!"

Tina at 2 years old.

They had packed it much earlier, anticipating the big day. Fortunately, Carolyn had the presence of mind to recall the bag and said, "Don't you remember? You said you didn't want to lose it in all the excitement. You locked it in the car trunk three weeks ago!"

At least Eddie had enough of a grip on his nerves to drive Carolyn to the hospital, both of them laughing about Eddie's sitcom-like dithering. It was a long labor, but at last she gave birth to a beautiful little girl, Tina. To Eddie she was immediately and forever his Treasure. He was a doting dad, and from that point on the Carroll family was richer and happier.

Luckily, Eddie continued to find success with commercials and with the occasional role on TV. He remembered being in a special reuniting the stars of the Road movies: Bob Hope, Bing Crosby, and Dorothy Lamour. "I worked with three of the greatest names in show business, and I loved doing it — but I never once thought of asking for a copy of the show! It was incredible to see them act together and to see them in private moments. We did a Western sketch in which Crosby was the marshal, I was his deputy, and Hope was the outlaw Black Bart. Whenever we had a break, Bing would saunter off, get a cup of coffee, and sit down, light his pipe, and leaf through a newspaper. Bob would be surrounded by a dozen assistants, and he'd be talking a mile a minute: 'Okay, we need a line for this, and when we go to Cleveland we gotta put together a monologue, and tell Bing we gotta go to Malibu tomorrow —' He never stopped for a moment, and maybe that's why he lived so long."

Eddie's turns on *Hollywood Palace* led to an even bigger break in 1970: Don Knotts became the host of his own variety program, *The Don Knotts Show*, and the producers hired Eddie as a regular co-star. It was an engaging program, with not only the usual rotation of comedy sketches and musical numbers, but two spots that always appeared. One was a segment about the effort of putting on the show itself — something

The Don Knotts Variety Show *episode: Eddie, Don Knotts and Dennis Weaver, 1973.*

like the strategy of the *Jack Benny Program*, in which Benny would often say, "You know, while we were putting together this show…" and that would segue into a "behind the scenes" skit lampooning the show itself. (It would also be reflected much later in *The Gary Shandling Show* on HBO.) The second was "The Front Porch," in which Knotts and the guest star of the week would sit in rocking chairs on a porch set and simply… chat about life.

Eddie had a ball as a major player in the NBC series. At the same time, his writing and producing partnership with Jamie Farr finally was paying off. Jamie Farr remembers that when they formed Carroll-Farr Productions, "we set up an office and put in long hours working on ideas for shows. At the same time we were always ready to dash off if the phone rang and there was an audition possibility for either one of us. Both Eddie and I smoked pipes at that time, and the office was so small that before long it smelled like an ashtray. We thought we were big-time producers in that office on Sunset Boulevard. Eddie bought a used Cadillac and I bought a used Lincoln, and we were ready to burn up the town."

They were still laboring to create a game show and attracted interest by using accomplished people to host their run-throughs: Chick Hearn, the sportscaster known as the voice of the Lakers, and the handsome Johnny Gilbert, later the announcer for *Jeopardy*, were hosts for some of the run-throughs. Jamie says, "We had some of the best try-outs, but nothing went on the air. We developed a great reputation and got wonderful comments, but no success."

But then Carroll-Farr Productions finally created and sold to M-G-M a syndicated series that did go into production. It was a unique premise: titled *Man to Man*, the series was a sports-talk show featuring both professional athletes and celebrities who played or enjoyed the same sport. NFL stars Roman Gabriel and Merlin Olsen hosted. Eddie and Jamie wrote and produced all the episodes, which were taped at the Merv Griffin Theater on Hollywood Boulevard — and years later, when Jamie received his star on the Hollywood Walk of Fame, the star went right in front of the Merv Griffin Theater. Jamie laughs and says, "About two years later the building burned down, and now it's a Bed, Bath, and Beyond, so that's where my star is today."

In all, twenty-six episodes of *Man to Man* aired, often pairing up really first-rate celebrities with star athletes. Jamie Farr remembers Peter Lawford, Clint Eastwood, and Rock Hudson as among the celebrities who accepted the five-hundred-dollar payment to sit down with a sports celebrity and talk about sports. It worked not because of the money — pocket change for that caliber of star — but because the guests truly were excited about the sports they got to discuss. "We wrote scripts," Jamie recalls, "but the stars loved it because they were free to ask their own questions and just chat with the sports stars, too."

One of the biggest stars they approached, just out of the blue, was Bob Hope. Eddie tells what happened:

EDDIE CARROLL: We were planning a golf show, and we got Sam Snead and Jack Nicklaus as guests — we always got the best in the business. Now, as our celebrity guest we wanted a big name who also loved golf. I was working regularly on a show at that time, and across the hall from our studio Bob Hope was taping his monthly special. I called Jamie and said, "I'm going to go ask Bob Hope if he'd do our show."

So I just walked next door and explained to Bob that we were producing *Man to Man* and mentioned that we had a golf show coming up featuring Snead and Nicklaus.

Bob immediately broke in with "Oh, yeah, you got the best!"

I explained that we paired the sports figures with a star, and he didn't even let me finish: "Yeah, that sounds great! When are you doing it?"

"Next week," I said.

Hope said, "Sure, I'd love to do it! Just talk to my manager Jimmy."

So I told the manager, who just gave me a pitying look. "This is Bob Hope," he told me. "He's booked solid for two years. I'm sorry, but there's no way he can do it."

Well, that's the way it goes. So I got together with Jamie and said, "Forget it, Bob Hope's too busy." We looked around for someone else and got Forrest Tucker, who had starred in the TV comedy-Western *F Troop*, to be the other guest. He was a big star and he loved golf, so he'd be perfect.

Now, we taped the shows back-to-back, and on the day we were doing the Snead and Nicklaus episode, it was to be the second one we taped. So we were prepping for the golf show while another show was taping in the studio. Tucker came in and we went over the script, and backstage we got him into makeup and got him a drink, and then all of a sudden there was this horrible noise, and a moment later a page came running in and said, "Mr. Carroll, a helicopter just landed on the studio roof!"

I thought it was the police!

And then the back door opened and I heard, "Hey, how ya doin', pally?" It was Bob Hope. He said, "There was nothing good on television, so I came in to do the show."

Oh, my gosh, what are you going to do? I'm not going to tell Forrest Tucker, "Okay, you can go home now." But how could we turn down the biggest comedy star in the country?

And Hope came breezing into the dressing room: "Hey, Tuck, how ya doin'? What are you here for?"

"I'm here to do the show."

Hope said, "What? I'm gonna do the show."

I tried to explain, "Forrest, you're not going to believe this, but we asked Bob originally, and he was too busy to show up — "

Forrest said, "If it was anybody but Bob Hope, I'd be upset, but Bob really helped me out at a low point in my career by taking me on his USO tours, so I'll tell you what: Send me a case of Jack Daniels, Bob can go on, and I'll just watch the taping."

Bob said, "No, no, you're not. We're both gonna do it!"

Jamie and I had fifteen minutes to rewrite a half-hour script to accommodate Bob. Somehow or other we did it.

And that turned out to be the best episode we ever shot!

Eddie was working long hours, and it never stopped. Once, dazed from lack of sleep, he got up one morning, stood in front of his closet in the bedroom stark naked, jumping up and down and waving his arms, thought and thought and thought, and finally wailed to Carolyn, "What am I supposed to wear today? What day is it? What day is it?" He couldn't remember if he was due to be a producer at *Man to Man*, a performer on "*The Don Knotts Show*, or a writer at Carroll-Farr Productions.

Busy as he was, Eddie adored the life he and Carolyn were living. And no wonder. They had a beautiful daughter, and Carolyn was pregnant for a second time. This time it was tough on her, not nearly as easy as her first one with the now three-year-old Tina. A concerned obstetrician had ordered her to spend the second trimester of her pregnancy off her feet. Thanks to the Carroll's friends, Carolyn's parents, and Tina, who young as she was proved to be a great helper, Carolyn was able to obey doctor's orders.

The obstetrician was worried because though the due date had arrived, the baby Carolyn was carrying had lost weight, and the doctor planned to induce labor on October 28, 1970. When the time came, Eddie drove Carolyn to the hospital. He was thinking about staying with her, but Carolyn firmly insisted that he leave her in the doctors' hands and go to the rehearsal for *The Don Knotts Show*, and in addition to that he had a wardrobe fitting at noon for a commercial. Nervous and jittery, Eddie went on his way. Carolyn's first labor with Tina had lasted nineteen hours. The second one lasted nineteen minutes! Good thing she was there at the hospital.

While Eddie was off the set of *The Don Knotts Show* being fitted for his wardrobe, the baby arrived. The obstetrician was a family friend, and he considerately called from the delivery room with the good news, but because he wasn't able to reach Eddie directly he left word with the NBC operator: "Tell Mr. Carroll that he has a son who weighs five pounds and ten ounces."

Eddie returned from his costume fitting to see a huge banner hanging over the rehearsal hall stage: "Congratulations, Eddie. It's a boy!" Don Knotts and his guest star of the week, Andy Griffith, broke out cigars and champagne for the cast to celebrate, and the receptionist gave Eddie a note of what she *thought* the doctor had said: "It's a baby boy that weighs five pounds and is ten inches long."

Leland at 18 months.

Ten inches? *Ten inches?*

Eddie panicked and phoned the hospital. He got through to Carolyn in her room and asked tentatively, "How is the baby? How does he, uh, look?"

Carolyn told him that the baby was beautiful and weighed five pounds and ten ounces.

A relieved Eddie said, "Thank God!"

Though on the small side, the little boy was healthy. Today Eddie's son, Dr. Leland Carroll, is six feet two inches tall and is in splendid health. All in all, Eddie could look back on 1970 as a fine year, one that saw the realization of so many of his hopes and dreams.

CHAPTER 10

Mr. Cricket Enters

In *Pinocchio,* a couple of characters joyfully sing, "An Actor's Life for Me!" In real life, Eddie sometimes wondered if the actor's life would really be for him. Sadly, *The Don Knotts Show*, which Eddie loved so much, ended after only a year on the air. *Man to Man* was popular in its markets, but as a syndicated show it just never picked up a mass audience that would carry it past twenty-six episodes.

On the other hand, Eddie and Jamie had come to the attention of Hanna-Barbera, the animation studios that produced cartoons especially for TV, beginning with *Ruff and Reddy* and going on through *Huckleberry Hound*, *Yogi Bear*, and many others. Eddie and Jamie became a writing team producing scripts for Hannah-Barbera shows, including *The Amazing Chan and the Chan Clan*, a take on Charlie Chan in which the numerous children of the Chan family performed rock songs in every episode — songs that Eddie and Jamie wrote.

In addition to writing, Eddie deeply loved performing, and he kept finding little bits and pieces of success, but then periods would go by when nothing clicked for him. Never a proud man, Eddie now and then took sales jobs to keep his family going — but he sold only products he believed in. However, even in tough times Eddie had self-assurance, and together he and Carolyn were an impressive, formidable couple who could weather just about any storm. In 1970, they took stock and made some fateful decisions.

Eddie always said these turned out to be the crucial years of his career. But let's let him talk about some changes in attitude and philosophy and direction that made all the difference:

EDDIE CARROLL: The decade of the 1970s brought many changes and new things in our lives. Actors have times of feast and also of famine, and after a difficult stretch Jamie and I even thought at one time about giving up acting completely and going into writing full time. However, we both still loved that experience of performing for an audience, so we tried something a little different. Carolyn had learned hypnotism and positive programming while performing in Lake Tahoe. Now, an actor needs confidence, and at that time I thought I needed to program myself to get out of the writing mode and into an acting mind-set whenever a call might come for an audition.

Man from Glad commercial: Smells bad, need to wrap it!

So we took classes and learned psychological techniques that changed our thoughts. You know, thoughts are things, and once those changed, so did our outlook on life. I remember we wrote out goal contracts of the things we wished for in our future. That was a wonderful feeling, because a peace and calm came into our home with a sense of finally being in control of where we were going with our lives. Now we felt like we were driving the car instead of going for a ride with someone else behind the wheel. We now had destinations to head for and could see we had to stop going around in circles.

This new attitude and approach immediately worked like a charm. My acting and voiceover career picked up immensely, and so did the writing. My peers and friends started to call me "The King of Commercials." I did commercials for toilet tissue, deodorants, cars, tires, cake mixes, soda drinks, beer, chairs, gas companies, TV stations, dog food, cat food, insurance, appliances, food products, and you name it! My professional income steadied nicely, and residual checks started showing up in thick envelopes, the checks rubber-banded together.

Then one day our mailman, Ray Baker, rang the doorbell and said, "Mr. Carroll, could I ask you a favor? Would you please move your mailbox away from the curb and get one that attaches to the front of the house?"

That was unusual because the rule in Encino was to have the mailboxes on the curb for the convenience of the mail carriers to drive their trucks and just reach into the box to dispense the mail to the residence. "Well, sure," I said. "But I thought that was against the rules. Why do you want us to do that?"

"It's for your protection," Ray said, and he went on to explain what had happened. A boy living behind our home had opened the mailbox, removed the envelopes, and took some checks out. With our permission, Ray told the boy's family where we lived, and right away his mom dragged her son to our front door, twisting his ear and ordering him to apologize and return the checks to us. I got Ray's point, and we placed our new mailbox on the wall right next to the garage!

Lots of laughter and humor has always filled our home and even that grew. Our family loved parties, weddings, and holidays. We have always tried to find the joy in our everyday living. That is what makes getting out of bed worthwhile and insures you're going to have a good day.

In those times, there were no cell phones or pagers and if Jamie or I were out playing tennis when an agent called with news of a role one or the other of us could try to land, Joy and Carolyn would have to pile the kids into a car and come and find us and give us the audition information. Just as when I first started with my old clunky car, the trunk of the family car was a mobile wardrobe closet containing clothing from a mechanic's jumpsuit to a conservative three-piece business suit and everything in between.

Finally feeling that we were financially secure, in 1973, Carolyn decided to move into a larger home because with the family growing, we needed another bedroom. We sat down and each of us drew a layout of the home we would love and sketched in a description of what we wished for in our dream home.

Now, this shows you how close Carolyn and I were as a couple: We drew the same house, but with me being left handed, I drew a mirror image of Carolyn's drawing, although aside from that the two were identical in a floor plan. We also agreed that we liked yellow with white trim. Well, we were out looking at properties with our realtor and were driving through a neighborhood when we saw an agent just pounding a For Sale sign into the front yard of a house that, frankly, I didn't like the look of.

Carolyn wanted to stop and I didn't want to even go inside the house. The driveway was a cracked and broken mess, and the house was not the yellow and white trim we had programmed. The place had been painted in ugly and clashing shades of green.

However, when Carolyn entered the place, she loved the step-down living room with the corner white stone fireplace and the step-up formal dining room, just the way we both had sketched. I didn't even get out of the car because the driveway was so pot-holed and I kept thinking how unattractive the paint was. Carolyn loved the entry way and the living and dining room, and after she had walked around admiring them, she came to the door and called out to me, "Oh, come on and at least take a look at it!"

Well, I felt a little besieged, so just to make Carolyn happy I got out of the car and went in and my jaw just dropped. The layout was an exact mirror image of my sketch. And when I thought about it…paint's not permanent! We later found out there had been a difficult divorce and the ugly paint job was the husband's expression of anger. Well, of course we wound up buying the place and immediately set about making it a little more like the dream house we had programmed ourselves to expect for our lives.

A couple of months later, as we were having the house repainted, our next-door neighbor came over to welcome us and told us how nice the house would look after we finished the new yellow-and-white color scheme. He mentioned the house had always been an attractive yellow and white until the previous owners started getting a divorce!

The redecorating must have exorcised all the bad feelings left over from the previous owners, because Eddie and Carolyn went on to spend nearly forty years in the white-and-yellow Encino house, filling it with family, friends, and many, many happy memories. Eddie's Eleniak relatives regularly visited for a Ukrainian Easter meal and for the Christmas holidays. Eddie and Carolyn's children, Tina and Leland, grew up there, learning when they were very young never to disturb Dad or Uncle Jamie when the two of them were working hard on a new writing project or a new show to pitch (though they both say that the laughter coming out of that room sometimes made them suspicious that it was mostly play and little work).

Then in 1972, an audition brought Jamie Farr a totally unexpected shot at the big time. Jamie says, "My agent called to tell me that Gene

Reynolds wanted me for a small role in the TV show M*A*S*H. It would be the fourth show of their first year, "Chief Surgeon Who?" I hadn't even seen the movie M*A*S*H, but it was $250.00, so I said 'Okay!'

I owed the chance to Gene Reynolds, who had directed me in an episode of F Troop in which I had played Standup Bull, a Native American stand-up comic who had lines like 'Is this an audience or a war council?' Gene remembered me and wanted me for this small part in M*A*S*H. Now, Larry Gelbart had created this character Maxwell Q. Klinger, but I didn't know anything about him."

Jamie drove to the Twentieth Century-Fox lot and "they showed me to this trailer dressing room, and there was a Women's Army Corps uniform hanging there. I asked if I was sharing the dressing room with a woman, and they said, 'No, this is your costume.'"

Not too sure about all this, Jamie donned the uniform and went onto the set, and everyone cracked up at the way he looked. Jamie learned that Klinger wanted so desperately to leave the Army that he was cross-dressing in hopes of getting a Section-8 discharge. He picked up his script and saw that he had only a few lines: Klinger, in WAC regalia, is standing sentry duty and has an exchange with Sorrel Brooke, playing an apoplectic regular-Army officer, General Barker. The episode director, E.W. Swackhammer, had Jamie play the role in a very fey style. "I was talking with sibilant s's and making broad, gay gestures and so on." The next day Jamie's agent called with a request that he return because Gene Reynolds wanted a re-shoot.

Jamie felt terrible: "I felt like I had done something wrong. They asked me, 'How can we make this character work?'

I said, 'Why don't we just play him straight and let everyone else comment on him? Let me have a cigar and just play it straight and masculine, and let's see if it works.' Well — it worked for eleven years!"

At first, Jamie wondered if there would be anything more to Klinger than just that one joke, but with Eddie's encouragement and the guidance of Gene Reynolds and Larry Gelbart, Jamie began to supply Klinger with depth and background. Klinger eventually shared Jamie's hometown of Toledo, his devotion to the minor-league Toledo Mud Hens, his extended family, and his intimate knowledge of Toledo's restaurants, pool halls, and dives.

Though Jamie's starring role in the great ensemble cast that made up M*A*S*H led to his appearing on quiz shows as a guest — a very popular one — and diminished the time he had available to work with Eddie in Carroll-Farr Productions, the Farrs and the Carrolls remained good friends through great success as they had during the lean times. Eddie's and Carolyn's friends from show business would drop in at the new Encino house for a meal or coffee or drinks or just for a chat.

Jamie and Joy Farr came often, of course, but many others: Ben and Pamela Cooper, Bill and Jen Farmer (Bill voices Goofy and Pluto for Disney), Tommy and Ida Banks, Tony Butala and Janie, director/choreographer Rob Barran, comic and master impressionist Fred Travalena and his wife Lois, Tom and Betty Kennedy, International Jack Benny Fan Club president Laura Leff, Wink and Sandy Martindale, and a host of others, from actors, singers, and musicians to writers, agents and directors.

Bill Farmer, voice of Goofy and Pluto.

The charming and busy new house was not the only change for the better. Eddie's more positive attitude and outlook just seemed to open up all sorts of new avenues for him, and he became more active than ever as opportunities opened up. One, of course, came along with an important and quite unexpected phone call, literally as though a bolt had come out of the blue: "It was my agent, Herb Tannen, telling me that Disney was auditioning for a new Jiminy Cricket and they wanted an exact sound-alike of Cliff Edwards, who had performed for years as Ukulele Ike. He had passed away two years earlier, and of course Cliff was the first voice of Jiminy Cricket. Could I do it? Being an actor I said, 'Sure!'"

Eddie has already told the story of that fateful call. He added some details from time to time, such as the way he first attempted to "get" the vocal quality of Jiminy just right:

EDDIE CARROLL: We'd always been sure to have music and books in the house for our children. At that time Tina was six and Leland was three, and they had some children's albums and I thought I remembered one of the records had some songs from Pinocchio and a good little clip of Jiminy on it, so I went into Leland's room and found the Disney album with excerpts from all the famous movies up to that time. Fortunately for me, the album did contain the clip of Jiminy saying, "I'll bet a lot of you folks don't believe, about a wish comin' true, do you? Well I didn't either. Of course I'm just a cricket singin' my way from hearth to hearth, but let me tell ya what made me change my mind." And there was the bit in which Jiminy warns Pinoke to tell the truth and keep his nose from growing. That gave me something to work with.

It's a mark of Eddie's wonderful recollection that nearly forty years after he practiced that bit for an audition he could still recite it perfectly word for word, and he still sounded exactly like the original Jiminy. His vocal training and his actor's ability saw him through, and after practicing the little speech over and over and programming himself to duplicate Cliff Edwards's distinctive Midwestern vocal quality, Eddie thought he was prepared for the audition.

Then when he was getting ready to record, much to his surprise he heard a far different-sounding Jiminy voice. It was the demo that Disney was asking actors to duplicate, but Eddie's instincts told him it wasn't really what the studio wanted:

EDDIE CARROLL: Herb had a little recording booth where I'd record audition tapes, and when I went in he gave me three little pieces to read, and he told me that Disney had a tape I needed to listen to first. So I listened to a tape that Disney had sent over for me to hear the voice, and it was completely different from what I had practiced. As we age our voice has a lower register. The Disney tape was Cliff's speaking voice from the very last session he had done for the character, and it was not the youthful, energetic sound everyone remembered from the movie.

I pointed that out to Herb, and he agreed we should listen to the movie instead, so I called Les Perkins at Disney and asked if the studio would screen the first five minutes of the movie for me. They did, and this gave me the right pitch and intonation for Jiminy. What they really wanted, you see, was that bright, youthful sound that Jiminy has in the movie. That was the voice that I had practiced and could do well, and it was all thanks to my son Leland's record that I realized this!

When Herb got the acceptance from Disney, he was just bouncing up and down as he shared his enthusiasm over the accomplishment of getting the role. Well, fair enough, it would be a financially rewarding session, I figured. You see, I thought it was for a one shot, but then Herb explained it was so much more than that. "Eddie, you don't understand. You'll have a job for the rest of your life. This is *a career!*"

Herb was exactly right about that. And then came the day that I was actually going to record the voice of Jiminy for the first time ever.

You have to remember that by 1973 I had been working professionally in entertainment for thirteen years, and from the outset I had decided I was going to explore every facet of show business. If you're lucky enough to look like Brad Pitt or George Clooney, you've got an image that works for you. I looked like Joe Everybody, so I had established all these avenues of not only acting on the screen but writing and so forth, and I had done a ton of voice work for commercials and considered myself pretty professional. And then came my first recording session with Disney.

Once I got the role of Jiminy Cricket, my first official job was to go to Studio B on the Disney lot to record a new stereo version of "When You Wish upon a Star," Jiminy's signature song. Now, I had done musical comedy, I was fine with singing, and in fact a day or two before the session I met the musical director and he sat down at the piano and we went through the song to make sure I had the right pitch and phrasing, and it had been fine. I was confident that I could record the song with no trouble, and I was really looking forward to it. It was going to be a lot of fun.

And I have to say this: At that point I had completely forgotten about the first time I had seen the movie *Pinocchio* and how fascinated I had been with Jiminy. It wasn't even on my mind. I came into the studio and the full orchestra and the choral group were there and everyone was ready. We chatted for a few minutes and then the conductor asked, "Are you ready to start?" and we said, "Sure, let's take one."

So the music started, and I sang the first three or four bars, and suddenly a tear rolled down my cheek! At first I thought something had dripped on my face from the ceiling, and I looked to see if there was a leak up there, wondering, "What the heck is that?'"

The conductor stopped the musicians and asked, "Are you all right?"

I said, "Yeah.'"

He said, "You want to go again?'"

And I said, "Yeah, let's take another one." And at the same point in the song, tears from both my eyes rolled down my face. Now, I don't feel sad, I'm not emotionally upset or anything — just tears! I can't figure out what's going on. The musical conductor said, "Eddie, do you want to take a moment and collect yourself?"

I said yes, and I went and got a cup of coffee and I stood outside the studio in the sunlight to drink it. I said to myself, "Look, you're a grown man. You're a mature human being. You're a professional in this business. You're singing a song that you know. So what is your problem?"

And all of a sudden that little kid inside of me, the six-year-old I had once been came to the surface, and I remembered it all, how I had loved Jiminy when I was so little and how I had told my mom that I was going to meet him one day and he would be my friend. I had not only met Jiminy Cricket and had made him my friend, but I had become that very character.

Eddie recording voice of Jiminy.

Those tears weren't from sorrow, but from the joy and affirmation and validation of that little kid. I'm a living example that the lyrics of that song are so true — if you wish for your dream and never lose sight of it, you can make that dream come true.

Now at peace with his younger self, Eddie finished his cup of coffee, went back into Studio B, and on the third take nailed the song. In fact, he probably did it better for having paused to think about what it and Jiminy meant to him.

It was important to the studio because of the significance of the tune: "When You Wish upon a Star" had won the Academy Award as Best Original Song, it is near the top of the American Film Institute's list of the hundred best film songs of all time, and of course it is practically the anthem of the Disney Studios. Eddie learned a lesson from the experience, and he spoke about it often. Aspiring young actors who heard him tell of this moment have themselves broken into sobs because they know exactly what Eddie meant when he spoke of affirmation, of validation, and of joy.

From that moment to the very end, Eddie was in truth Jiminy's best friend. Performing the role never once became "just a job" for Eddie, and he never lost the wonderful sense of joy that he had recaptured in that first recording session. In turn, with Eddie as his champion, Jiminy was never just a cartoon character — and definitely not just a bug! The little fellow's personality had its own richness and its own integrity, and Eddie sensed that, loved that dimension of the role, and protected it over the years. Late in his career, Eddie would observe, "I know how Jiminy thinks. Sometimes I'll stop and say 'We need to do something with this line because Jiminy would never say it that way,' and we'll adjust because Jiminy is always both homespun and philosophical. Many times we'll find the right way to put the line, and then it works."

Eddie had achieved a milestone in his career. Wishing on a star is a wonderful, hopeful experience, and when you have the kind of determination and love for what you are doing that Eddie always possessed, the wishes do indeed come true. Beginning with that recording session, Eddie and Jiminy merged. The next thirty-seven years brought more and more recording assignments for Eddie to perform as Jiminy, sometimes coming in almost daily, and each and every time Eddie took up the persona of Jiminy Cricket, he brought to the role a tenderness, a joyousness, and an integrity that all shine through with true warmth and sincerity.

And with Eddie's help, Jiminy Cricket no longer had to sing his way from hearth to hearth. Instead of a hearth, he had had found a heart to live in. From that home he would reach out to touch the hearts of millions of Americans, of millions of people young and old, all around the whole world.

CHAPTER 11

"Happy and Fulfilling Years"

Eddie had attained a measure of financial security with the role of Jiminy Cricket, just as Herb Tannen had predicted. Eddie said, "The first really big assignment was to re-dub much of *Pinocchio* for a new release." Later the same process was repeated for the film's release on VHS and DVD. However, the assignments didn't end there. Because Jiminy had a pleasing and easily understandable voice (unlike, say, Donald Duck), he increasingly became the "voice" of the Disney studios in TV spots and in the theme parks. Soon Eddie became the most widely-heard and most easily-recognized star that no one ever saw!

The years from 1973 to 1980 Eddie remembered as practically a blur — "the next years just flew by for all of us." The new house in Encino became a welcome refuge after long days of work in commercials, at Disney, and in TV roles. Eddie remembered "the house just full of so many great memories. I keep pictures of them all in my mind, and the soundtrack is laughter." Eddie's younger brothers Dale and Bob eventually followed him to California, where each became successful. Soon every holiday was an Eleniak festival, with the house full of relatives, good Ukrainian food, and — yes, laughter.

Eddie's appearances on TV continued during the 1970s: He acted in such shows as *Sanford and Son*, in which he played a bartender, had a short role as an emcee on *The Mary Tyler Moore Show*, and performed in a run of episodes from *Maude*, where he became something of a fixture, playing different characters in several different shows. He also had a comic bit as a puzzled Las Vegas casino card dealer in an episode of the Sally Field sitcom *The Girl with Something Extra*. Umm…in case you don't remember the short-lived series, Sally Field played a newlywed bride with extra-sensory perception — not someone a card dealer wants on the other side of the table!

In 1977, Eddie became an emcee in another way, as Jiminy Cricket, in a new version of the episode "From All of Us to All of You" from

Walt Disney's Wonderful World of Color. Many middle-aged people fondly remember this Yuletide special. Broadcast on Christmas Day, the episode featured Jiminy as the host and the wrap-around narrator who sang the catchy title song and offered viewers a holiday present of Disney animation. The show combined old and new animation and for years was a holiday staple in reruns, with no two broadcasts being exactly the same

Eddie in The Mary Tyler Moore Show.

because the last segment would present advance clips from movies under production in the current year. Both as part of the original TV series and then as stand-alone rebroadcasts on The Disney Channel, "From All of Us to All of You" recycled every year for over twenty years — and we understand that in Sweden it's still a favorite, broadcast each Christmas day at exactly 3:00 p.m.

And of course in addition to his acting roles on TV and small parts in movies, Eddie's commercial work continued, guaranteeing more of those nice residual checks. Though commercials didn't get him name recognition — very few stars are identified in TV ads — they did give him wide exposure and more experience in his field. It was work that Eddie enjoyed, even though at times the deadlines and shooting schedules were short. He had no trouble in memorizing lines at short notice or in taking direction so that most of the time retakes of scenes were not really necessary, unless another actor made a blooper or something went wrong with a prop or with the equipment.

By this time, Carroll-Farr Productions had tapered off. Jamie's popularity as Max Klinger had soared, and he had no time left over for writing or producing: "It was a grinding schedule," he remembers. "Especially if we were shooting exteriors out on the ranch, I'd have to report before sunup for make-up and costuming. And suddenly I was in demand as a game-show guest, so I was working seven days a week, like Eddie."

Eddie in Sanford and Son.

Over his years with *M*A*S*H,* Jamie textured the initially one-dimensional Klinger beautifully, giving him unexpected emotional depths and unsuspected dimensions. He successfully carried many memorable episodes of the show, and eventually at the end of the decade, when Max Klinger replaced Radar O'Reilly (Gary Burghoff) as company clerk, Jamie was even able to trade in the cocktail dresses for regulation Army fatigues. But even though both Eddie and Jamie were too busy to write together during these years, their friendship never wavered, and whenever they could, Jamie and Joy got together with Eddie and Carolyn.

Eddie was keenly aware that his increasing involvement in performing, exhilarating though it was, made heavy demands on his time. To compensate for the long hours and frequent trips his profession required, work that threatened to keep him away from his family for long stretches, Eddie talked things over with Carolyn and they came up a plan. Together, he said,

"We made a firm commitment to have family vacations twice a year. Every winter we would go to Lake Tahoe, and every summer we promised each other that we would vacation together either in Mexico or Hawaii. And finally, very early in our marriage Carolyn and I made a promise to each other that we would have some time together on every anniversary and that we would go on a date once a week — to make up for all those times when we were actually dating and had to stay home and watch TV because we didn't have any money."

On their very first anniversary, when Eddie was still scrambling for acting jobs, "We scraped together enough cash for us to spend the night in a small hotel in Palm Springs. Literally all we could afford to do was just take a long walk together, but it was so much fun." Their second anniversary was spent in a friend's home in Las Vegas. Carolyn had worked with her, and they had roomed together in Lake Tahoe for six months, and the friend was glad to lend the house for their getaway. On that occasion Eddie and Carolyn took food to cook so they wouldn't have to spend money to eat out, and they had a grand total of fifty dollars to spend on fun. That had been in 1965, and as they were driving out of town, Eddie took in the bright lights all around, then turned and said to Carolyn, "Honey, one day we're going to come back here, and I'll work on the strip."

Jamie as a Southern Belle.

"What will you do?" Carolyn asked him.

Eddie shrugged. "I don't know," he said, "but I will."

It took a while. Eventually those anniversary trips became easier as Eddie began to find success in performing. By the 1970s, though he had achieved considerable success as a voice-over artist, an occasional actor, and the King of Commercials, Eddie still didn't know exactly what he might do to work on the Strip, but as we will see, that would be another wish that would eventually come true.

The Disney Studios had realized how versatile Jiminy could be, and in these years Eddie had frequent recording calls, sometimes to do just a quick spot, sometimes to record longer bits for the TV shows or the theme parks. As Eddie became more and more occupied with his role as Jiminy Cricket, Carolyn kept busy, too. First Tina and then Leland started to attend Hesby Street School in Encino (a few years later it was renamed Hesby Oaks School, as it remains today).

In the next years, Carolyn devoted herself to school activities, serving

Carolyn and Joy Farr.

as PTA president for Hesby Street for five years and also as a Brownie and Girl Scout leader — as well as producing and directing school performances in the annual talent show. Tina and Leland remember this period as a great time, though as young children neither of them was particularly aware of show-business glamour.

"My dad was just my dad to me," Tina says. Although she and Leland both knew that Eddie was the voice of Jiminy Cricket, that didn't make him a celebrity in their eyes. Like all kids, they had a close-up view of their father, and the man they saw was quite human, with a good sense of humor and a devotion to them that they appreciated. Even so, they both saw his little eccentricities. Tina remembers, "We always used to tease him about being a Virgo because he was always so obsessively neat and clean. I remember once I got out of bed in the middle of the night and went out to use the bathroom, and when I came back to my bedroom, Dad had made up my bed!"

Regardless of how busy Eddie was, he was always supportive of both his children, she says. "He encouraged us to find things we loved to do, and he was there for us to help us along." She also recalls that her father "was so tender-hearted. When my brother Leland was little, we went on vacation to Puerto Vallarta in Mexico. We had a very nice place, but these little geckos would get in and creep over the walls. I liked them, but they sort of freaked Leland out, so Dad tried to calm him down by moving the geckos outside. Dad tried to carefully scoop them up with a big plastic cup, then take them out and release them, but he accidentally cut off one of their tails with the cup, and he felt so bad about that!"

When Tina was very young, she and Carolyn once went to the airport to see Eddie off on a flight to Arizona, where he had a commercial shoot with actor Michael Conrad, later very famous on *Hill Street Blues* as Phil Esterhaus ("Let's be careful out there"). The commercial involved their being handcuffed together, but no one quite remembers the product.

As soon as Carolyn and her daughter met him in the boarding area, Conrad fell in love with little Tina and carried her all around on his shoulder. Because the airport was fogged in, the planes were all grounded and everyone faced a long wait for the weather to clear. When Tina became fidgety and bored, as children will do when forced to wait and wait and wait, Conrad cheerfully said, "It's okay. Tina and I are going to share a peanut butter and jelly sandwich!" Soon he had her laughing again.

Eventually the fog cleared, planes could take off, and Eddie and Michael Conrad flew to Arizona. That same evening, in the Carrolls' home, Tina was watching an episode of *The Virginian* in which Michael Conrad guest-starred as a rancher confined to a wheelchair. When his ranch house caught fire and burned to the ground, Tina sobbed uncontrollably because her friend who had shared his sandwich with her had suffered so much.

Carolyn explained to her that it was all make-believe, but Tina was inconsolable until Carolyn called Eddie long-distance. Eddie couldn't ease Tina's fears either, so he went down the hall and brought Michael Conrad to his hotel room to explain personally that when Tina saw him on TV, he was only acting, and that acting was just pretending.

A little later, on an episode of *The Don Knotts Show* when Dan Blocker (Hoss Cartwright on *Bonanza*) was the guest star, the show included a flower-child Western sketch in which instead of six-shooters the characters were armed with flowers — but used them in a shoot-out. On the TV screen, Eddie took a fatal daisy to the chest, and again Tina got upset until Carolyn reminded her that it was all pretend, then told her to look on the sofa behind her and there sat Eddie. And as soon as she had, the phone rang: Tina's cousin Cami, Bob Elen's daughter (Bob had changed his name from Eleniak a few years earlier), called, bawling, "They shot my Uncle Eddie!" It was Tina's turn to explain that acting was all make-believe.

As for Jiminy, Tina says, "Dad didn't make a big deal out of it, but it was neat. Once I got a little embarrassed when we were all at Disneyland and all the people fussed over him so much! But normally when he got home from doing a Jiminy Cricket session, he didn't talk about it all that much. He just wasn't the type to brag. A lot of my friends didn't even know he was Jiminy, though occasionally he would do the voice for them at a birthday party or something, and then they would be impressed." She smiles. "He was more likely to do Jiminy's voice with complete strangers, just to prove that he really was someone they had heard, even if they didn't know him."

The school that the children attended was an excellent one. Eddie admired the way that "Hesby truly had moms and dads involved with their children's lives. No white gloves or teatime here!" He treasured the way that Carolyn devoted so much time to lead the PTA and to put on an annual talent show featuring the Hesby School students. With her experience and assurance, Carolyn nurtured the children's talents and encouraged them to do their very best — no tears in the cloakroom at Hesby Street!

And busy as he was, Eddie made sure to have time for his son as well. Leland says, "Dad was always interested in what I was doing and what I wanted. It's hard to think of many specific times, because I just remember him as an overall constant presence, always there for me. One thing that impresses me is his temperament. Dad always had a very even keel — oh, he'd get upset every once in a while, but overall he was very consistent. One of the biggest things I remember about him when I was growing up was his sense of humor. He loved to tell jokes, he loved to laugh and make other people laugh, and that was my dad."

Tina would grow up to pursue an acting career herself, but Leland says, "Dad knew that I was never stage-struck. If I was involved in anything like that, I was always more interested in being behind the scenes. Once he asked me if I'd want to be an actor someday, and young as I was, I said very seriously, 'I think I'd rather be the producer.'"

Remembering a family vacation, Leland says, "Once when I was pretty young, we were in Lake Tahoe, and I started this little ritual. I'd be walking along and I'd make a snowball and throw it at Dad. But he never did throw one back. Instead, whether I hit him or not, he started to pick up the snowballs I'd thrown, and he'd tell me with a smile, 'I'm saving these up!' He actually kept count over the years, and from time to time he'd remind me how many snowballs he hadn't thrown at me…yet. He kept me in suspense, but he never actually saved them up and hit me with a thousand snowballs at once!"

Leland was occasionally a little more adventurous than Eddie when it came to things like skiing: "Dad was never the daredevil in the family. He knew his limits and his capabilities. I'd go on roller-coasters, but he didn't like to do that because they made him dizzy. He didn't mind physical activity, but he always said he'd rather exercise his brain than his body."

As the children grew, Carolyn also became busy outside the house as she completed her doctorate in psychology. She also became a master of Tai Chi Chuan and began to teach Tai Chi. Carolyn created and offered a series of motivational seminars designed to extend to others the same kind of approach to success that she and Eddie practiced in their own professional lives, often traveling to deliver these programs all over the country.

And yet with all of this, both Eddie and Carolyn constantly found time to be closely involved in their children's lives. Eddie remembered, "Tina had started taking roller-skating lessons, and they eventually led to eleven years of her going into skating competitions all over California and later all around the United States. And then a little later Leland wanted to get into karate."

Leland recalls, "Dad would talk things over with me, and once he noticed that karate classes were beginning nearby. He said, 'Do you think you'd like to study this?'"

Leland agreed at once: "It looked really cool, and I got interested and said yes. The karate classes were at the YMCA, and I think I was the youngest kid in the class. It was a mixed group, with adults, teens, and children all in one class. At the beginning of each lesson, whoever was the highest-ranking belt would lead the class in a moment of meditation before the instruction began."

After taking Leland in every Saturday for six months or so, Eddie said, "I decided that instead of just taking him and dropping him off at classes and then waiting for him to finish, I'd take lessons too. Before long, Tina and Carolyn joined us. When the four of us got in the car, each one dressed in a white *karategi*, we looked as if we were on our way to a slumber party."

At the time, Leland had gained a couple of belts on Eddie, so "I led the meditation, and Dad was behind me in the class, but he accepted that. And you know, he took it very seriously. We sparred together and practiced, and mostly he was partnered with another adult, but Dad was never one of those fathers who had to outperform his kids. He never tried to overtake me just so he could start the class with the meditation!"

Just as Eddie involved himself with Leland's karate, he also helped Tina with her skating. Tina smiles as she remembers her busy dad "always showing up at the regionals or nationals to cheer me on. He seemed so proud of me." Along with his role of Jiminy, Eddie took his role as dad to heart.

It was a time of change for America. Lawsuits challenging unequal integration of schools in Southern California led to a mandate for the Los Angeles area schools to bus students to achieve a more even distribution of ethnicities. Carolyn worked with Hesby Street to find ways of pairing with good schools to which they could bus children and finding students who could be bussed into Encino to attend Hesby Street.

The spirit of cooperation worked wonders, and Eddie always thought "the semester that Tina was bussed turned into the best one of her elementary-school career." The Carrolls had found that a positive outlook and dedication could lead to good times for everyone, even when things threatened to get chaotic. So the 1970s passed with the family remaining close-knit and loving even as Eddie's professional life became increasingly demanding.

As for Eddie, he summed up the era like this: "Those were happy and fulfilling years for all of us."

CHAPTER 12

"Hello again, this is Jack Benny talking…"

As the 1980s began, the Carrolls had found a point of balance that brought their family close and that allowed both Carolyn and Eddie to pursue careers while being full-time parents. Big changes were looming on the horizon, a few of them apparent setbacks but almost all of them positive, and some of them were destined to change Eddie's life forever.

Eddie recalls a difficult time right at the beginning of the decade:

EDDIE CARROLL: I was doing well in commercials and TV, but then in July of 1980, a Screen Actors Guild strike began…and it would last for 154 days, nearly half a year. The strike had been called to establish contract terms for new sources of income for the studios and cable stations involved in production: pay-TV and videocassettes were beginning to add to the studios' profits, and there was as yet no clear way of sharing those profits with the artists. Soon the American Federation of Television and Radio Artists and the Federation of Musicians joined with SAG in the strike.

As a result, the entertainment industry came to a virtual standstill. The Los Angeles area was especially hard hit, with no work for actors, extras, musicians, wardrobe staff, catering companies, stage crews…plus all of the allied businesses involved in making a shoot. The strike even affected the police department, because production companies always hired off-duty policemen to protect the location and to take care of traffic control during taping and filming.

It felt strange to be idle after so many years of constant auditioning and performing, but most of our neighbors, who were also involved in some way with show business, were in the same boat. As the weeks went by, the entire city was hurting financially.

And yet the issues were huge for the future of the business on both management and production sides. The strike led to a long, contentious, and hard-fought struggle, and when at last after five months it ended with compromises between the two factions, I could almost feel a huge sigh of relief coming from the whole city.

As the industry resumed production following the strike, Eddie's career began to rev up again, too, and the Carrolls decided to improve their home

Eddie and Gloria doing Karaoke.

by adding a swimming pool. Eddie explained, "Originally Carolyn didn't want to buy a home with an existing pool because our children were so young. Now that they were old enough, though, it was time to add one. I remember we all had fun designing the pool. After drawing out ideas on paper, we figured out a fun way of seeing just where it should go. We used a bag of flour with a hole cut in one corner to let the flour stream out and leave a trail. We marked out the perimeter just by walking around the yard and letting the flour trickle out. If we made a mistake, or if we got too close to the shrubs, we just got out the hose, watered it down, and started again."

The pool construction company admired the Carrolls' ingenuity in laying out their work for them: "It was simple for them to see exactly where the pool and Jacuzzi should be built," Eddie said. And thinking green ahead of the rest of America (Jiminy Cricket, after all, is a big environmentalist), the Carrolls put in a solar-heating unit for both the pool and the Jacuzzi, giving the family two extra months of extended use every year.

Leland, who had inherited his mother's scientific bent, used to rise early every day while construction was going on. Eddie said, "He watched daily until time came for him to walk to school. He took photos of every stage and even put together a project for a school presentation."

Rob doing Karaoke.

The new pool made the Carroll home even more of a social center. From then on, Eddie and Carolyn constantly hosted barbecues, parties, and casual get-togethers. He discovered Karaoke and bought a Karaoke machine for the family, which they installed in a special party room that opened into the backyard pool area.

Every summer the backyard and pool filled up with visiting kids, friends of Tina and Leland, and Eddie remembered the Jacuzzi fondly, too: "The four of us would sit in the Jacuzzi and have great philosophical discussions, and as we looked up at the stars we would solve all the problems of the world — or at least we thought we had solved them!"

One of Leland's closest friends, Chuck Magnus, became such a fixture at the house that eventually he became known as "TOS," which is an acronym for "The Other Son." Leland remembers one occasion when he and Chuck, just by being typical kids, frustrated Eddie: "We had the Karaoke machine, and Dad really took it seriously. He was a singer, and he would rehearse his performances. Chuck and I saw it as more of an opportunity to goof around. I can't remember what song we were doing together, but when we were supposed to be practicing it, Chuck started doing this silly high falsetto voice, and I joined in. We butchered the song on purpose! And we turn around, and Dad is standing there in the doorway just staring at us. He didn't say a word, but he gave us a grim look and shook his head as if we had just disappointed him badly. Chuck and I couldn't take him seriously, so we broke up laughing, and Dad just turned and walked out on us."

During one summer afternoon swim-in, Leland brought three friends to swim and on their way to the pool they walked through the game room. Eddie recalled, "Jamie and I had some idea, and we were sitting there working on a project. So these four kids, one of them my son, were standing there looking at us, just staring at us. One of them said to Leland, 'Nah, he's not!' Leland insisted, 'He is, too!' Later I asked Leland what all that was about. Well, he told me that the three other kids agreed that Jamie was an actor, because they all knew *M*A*S*H* and he looked just like Klinger. I, on the other hand, didn't resemble Jiminy Cricket at all." Eddie would always sigh. "I suppose one out of two isn't bad!"

Carolyn recalls these years as the time when Tina really concentrated on roller dance. "She had got into it in a big way, skating with a partner and pairs and so on. It wasn't always easy. She was dropped many times and went to a chiropractor many times!" As it turned out, the trips to take Tina to her chiropractor were to be a major influence on Leland, who would sit there mesmerized as Curt Buddingh, D.C. put his sister's spine back in place again. Leland was also fascinated looking at the x-rays, and Curt would take time to explain them to him. Then as he later neared adulthood, Leland became interested in the field himself, first as something to study and then as a career.

Tina and her skating partner, David Nordlund.

Supportive mom Carolyn made all of Tina's skating costumes and boot covers. In turn, Tina devoted herself to developing her skill, taking lessons and practicing six days a week and competing almost every Sunday. She truly loved the sport, and at the competitions, her brother and parents were always there to cheer her on. On other Sundays, Eddie drove her to the rink to practice, and he enjoyed these afternoons out with his daughter, while at the same time Carolyn often took Leland to play tennis or football.

The next year, 1981, brought yet another Writers Guild Strike, this one lasting three months. Once more the entertainment business came to screeching halt. Eddie's income from performing dried up — any actor with a Guild card could not cross a picket line. The Carrolls tightened their belts once more and wished on their lucky star. At least this strike was shorter than the first one.

A little later, once production had resumed again, Eddie had a role in a film, just a supporting bit, like many others he had acted over the years. This time, however, something happened seemingly at random that again opened doors for him. Eddie described the ad-lib and the result:

EDDIE CARROLL: They say that life is what happens to you while you're making other plans, and I think this experience proves it. We were shooting one scene and had trouble with it, so we did re-take after re-take trying to get it right. Thirty, forty, fifty tries, and for every single time something would go wrong — an actor would flub a line or miss a mark, a light would blow, a camera would malfunction, just anything that could foul up the take did.

Tensions were getting pretty high — everyone on a set can get frustrated at times like these. We were doing the latest of a whole day's worth of takes, the scene was finally going well, and then suddenly, off-screen, a grip dropped something that crashed and clattered and ruined the scene again!

On the spur of the moment, I did an impromptu impression of Jack Benny, yelling, "Oh Rochester! If that's my Stradivarius, you're fired!" Everyone laughed, so I added one of Benny's catch phrases: "Now, cut that out!" That got an even bigger reaction, and it at least broke the tension.

We finally got the scene in the can on the next take, and then afterward the director came to me and told me, "You do a good Benny impression, and you know, you actually started to look like him too. There's a Broadway producer, a friend of mine, who's putting together a one-man show about Jack Benny. You ought to audition."

Jack Benny, a legend in show business, had died nine years before, the day after Christmas, 1974. Born Benjamin Kubelsky in Chicago on Valentine's Day, 1894, he grew up in middle-class surroundings in Waukegan, IL. Much later in life, when he contemplated writing an autobiography, he said the first difficulty was that he had no rags-to-riches story to tell, because his family was always fairly comfortable. He claimed that he thought of calling the book *I Always Had Shoes*. An early school dropout (one of his keenest regrets), he became a performer — not a comedian initially, but a violinist.

Later Benny used the violin as a source of many gags, but he was good enough at it as a young man to go on the Vaudeville stage, first locally, in an act with young singer Ned Miller. In 1911, he once had to follow the one act no one in Vaudeville wanted to follow: the Marx Brothers. Their unpredictable, largely ad-libbed and madcap act made the next act's life a misery. Benny did well enough, though, and as a result Minnie Marx, the boys' mother and manager, actually offered him a spot as a musician, meaning he would tour the country with the Marx Brothers. His parents thought Benny was too young and refused, and not until he teamed with the motherly Cora Salisbury a year later did he actually begin to tour.

Over the years Benjamin Kubelsky changed his name several times. When professional violinist Jan Kubelik thought their names were too similar, he became Ben K. Benny for a while. Then later when bandleader Ben Bernie objected to *that*, he became Jack Benny. He was successful as a novelty and popular violinist, and when Cora's mom's ill health forced Cora to leave the act, he teamed with pianist Lyman Woods. They billed themselves as "Benny and Woods, from Grand Opera to Ragtime."

When the United States entered World War I, Benny enlisted in the Navy and was stationed at the training station at the Great Lakes Naval Station. "I joined the Navy to see the world," he later would complain, "and they put me on a base from which I could see my father's house." While on duty at Great Lakes, though, he took part in a show the sailors had put together and for the first time did a real comedy bit. He enjoyed getting the laughs. After the end of the war, Benny again took to the Vaudeville stage, this time as a comedian who more and more used the violin just as a prop — and who began playing it badly just for laughs.

During his Vaudeville years, Jack met and married Sadie Marks (who changed her name to Mary Livingstone when she became part of Jack's act). After a few not-very-notable turns on various radio shows, Jack made a one-shot appearance on an Ed Sullivan broadcast, opening with, "Ladies and gentlemen, this is Jack Benny talking. There will now be a short pause so everybody can say 'Who cares?'" That led to his landing his own radio program — and then from 1932 up until just before his death, Jack was always on the air on radio, on his TV series, or on TV specials.

In real life a generous and cheerful man, Benny built up a persona that was everything he was not: stingy, vain, unwilling to admit his true age (he perpetually claimed to be 39), a woman-chaser (he was married to Mary for nearly fifty years), egocentric, grouchy, sarcastic, and a braggart.

And yet audiences loved him, probably because Benny always gave his supporting cast the best gags and was happy to be on the receiving end of their put-downs. He accumulated a stellar cast: ditzy "boy" tenors (first Kenny Baker, later Dennis Day); rotund announcer Don Wilson;

jive-talking bandleader Phil Harris; Mary Livingstone (in the show Jack's assistant, in real life, of course, his wife); gravel-voiced Eddie Anderson as Jack's valet Rochester; and occasional characters such as Sam Hearn's "Schlepperman" and Artie Auerbach's "Mr. Kitzel."

Another semi-regular was Frank Nelson, who was a utility character, showing up one week as a doctor, the next as a doorman, the next as a cop, and so on. When Jack approached him with an "Oh, mister!" Nelson would answer with a glissando "Yessssss?" And for no reason at all, each of Nelson's characters despised Jack Benny on sight, treating him with fiendishly withering scorn and scoring big laughs. And finally, lending the radio show a variety of character voices and a host of sound effects, celebrated cartoon and radio voice actor Mel Blanc was a valuable member of the cast.

Benny was thoroughly professional as the force behind the show. His writers praised him as unquestionably the finest comedy editor ever to work in radio, because he had such an unerring understanding of a joke's tempo and impact that he could nudge a line from being merely funny to being a moment of comic genius. Oddly, though he had a strong sense of humor, when he was editing the scripts the writers could anticipate only a "Now, that's funny" from Jack, never a laugh.

The flat statement, coming from him, translated as high praise. Yet in real life, and sometimes onstage, Jack would crack up often and completely. His good friend George Burns could reduce him to helplessness just by glancing at him.

If you catch a TV version of the *Si-Sy* routine, in which Jack runs across Mel Blanc as a morose, monosyllabic Mexican, you'll see Jack fighting back giggles. Until late in its run, the radio show was broadcast live, and when inevitable line fluffs happened, usually Jack topped them with a joke. In one broadcast Mel, playing the role of a sound-effects man, tells Jack that everyone in America thinks they heard a door slamming, but "my family in Canooga — Can — Canoga Park know it was me."

Jack shoots back, "Not with *that* reading they don't!"

Though Fred Allen claimed that Jack "couldn't ad-lib a belch after a Hungarian dinner," actually he could be quick with a quip. Once on a TV show when Mel Blanc was playing an old friend from Jack's childhood, Jack had him come from the audience up onto the stage and, chatting, asked him what he did for a living, and Mel said, "Oh, I'm still in insurance…what do *you* do?" That was the laugh line, but Jack ad-libbed, "I'm the voice of Bugs Bunny," which broke Mel up, perhaps in revenge for all the times it was the other way around.

Jack most frequently ad-libbed when something went wrong, and he maintained his composure in the face of verbal foul-ups from his cast. Well, usually. The most famous example of Jack's *not* coming up with a great covering line occurred in the show broadcast on January 8, 1950. First, Don Wilson flubbed a line, which was supposed to be "I read about it in Drew Pearson's column." The spoonerism was spectacular when instead Don said, "I read about it in Drear Pooson's — uh — "

Jack did a quick ad-libbed cover for that boo-boo, but he was unprepared for what happened at the end of the same show. In an interview with the newsletter of the International Jack Benny Fan Club, Frank Nelson told about the occasion: "I had a joke where Jack said, 'Are you the doorman?' And I said, 'Well, who do you think I am in this uniform? Nelson Eddy?'"

Jack didn't particularly like the joke, and he asked his writers to try to come up with a funnier line, but they couldn't think of anything. Nelson told Laura Leff that Don's blooper got a big laugh, "and the next thing I see is the writers are motioning for me to come into the booth. And so I went in and said, 'What do you want?' They said, 'Hey, when you get to the line, say, *Who do you think I am in this uniform, Drear Pooson?*'" Nelson at first refused — "You don't ad lib with Jack." However, the writers promised to take the heat, and when the time came, Jack said, "Oh, Mister, Mister."

Nelson did his familiar *"Yesssss?"* and then when Jack asked if he was the doorman, Nelson came back with the Drear Pooson line, really hitting the silly name hard.

According to Nelson, Jack's "eyes got like two saucers, he began to laugh. He grabbed hold of the microphone, he slid down the microphone all the way to the floor, and he pounded on the floor. He got up and staggered all the way across the studio to the far wall, hammered on the wall, turned into the drapes, grabbed the drapes, slid down the drapes, pounded on the floor some more, and the audience is in hysterics this whole time." It was one of the top three longest laughs on the *Jack Benny Program.*

Jack's radio audiences had fun, and they loved him for bringing it to them. When TV came along, Jack and his ensemble sailed right into it, continuing their weekly series for a long run, and then when he semi-retired, Jack continued to perform in TV specials and appear in concerts for the benefits of orchestras around the country. America had a long love affair with Jack Benny.

When Benny died, two networks mounted commemorative specials celebrating his life. Quite touchingly, one reported, "Jack Benny was born in Waukegan on Valentine's Day, February 14, 1894, and he died at his home in Hollywood on December 26, 1974. At the time of his passing, his age was…thirty-nine." Everyone loved Jack Benny. And now he was about to be the inspiration for a one-man show. Eddie had a special reason to want to be involved:

EDDIE CARROLL: Remembering the one time I had appeared on *Jack Benny's Birthday Special*, I thought hard about the opportunity. Now, over the years I've worked with all sorts of big names. On *The Don Knotts Show*, every week there were top stars, singers and actors and comedians, and I had worked with them all. But sharing the stage with Jack Benny was delightful. I was in awe of the man, but in fact of all the stars I'd ever had the privilege of working with, he was the most approachable and least assuming star that I'd ever met.

I'm sure he had a healthy ego, but talking to him you had the feeling he was still Benny Kubelsky of Waukegan, and he could put anyone at ease. Anyone could come up and talk to him and he would be the nicest guy you could hope to meet. Who wouldn't want to portray him?

So I was just so thrilled at the notion that someone was going to do a tribute to Jack Benny, but at the time I was so busy in Hollywood that I just didn't see any way that I could take time to go to New York to audition. I told the director so, and then I figured that was it.

But what I didn't know was that the producer, Ted Snowdon, was having terrific casting problems. He could find people who could sound like Jack Benny and some who looked like Jack Benny, but no one who had both the voice and the physicality that was just right for the role. The word got to Snowdon, and by then he had just about exhausted the talent pool in New York, so he decided to come to Hollywood to audition people there. I got a call from the film director's assistant to ask me to see Mr. Snowdon, and I was definitely interested.

So I looked in the mirror and thought that I had a similar cheek structure to Benny's. We both came from Slavic backgrounds, so there was a kind of facial resemblance. He always wore black horn-rimmed glasses, so I found a pair and took the lenses out to emphasize the eyes. Ever since we had got married, I had been complaining to Carolyn that my hairline was receding, but now I realized that if I brushed my hair straight back, I could come very close to Jack Benny's hairline. And I could sort of purse my lips and get his expression.

Together Carolyn and I went through my closet and found one of my jackets that could pass as a 1950s-era coat. Now I needed to study Jack

Benny's physical appearance and mannerisms, but I had no reference material on Jack, and nobody had any tapes or films of him. And then, as if it were a gift to me, that very week CBS began re-running *The Jack Benny Show*, followed by *Burns and Allen* and *Love That Bob!*

I watched every night and worked on Benny's attitudes and gestures and walk and everything for the rest of the week. So we set up the audition

Ted Snowdon, showing Eddie how to play the violin.

with Ted Snowdon. By then I had learned that his approach was that he had to find the right actor for the job. His attitude was "Either I'm going to find someone who'll do this properly, or I won't do it at all."

When I arrived, there were about five or six other actors scheduled. I took my time and put my name in the last slot on the sign-up sheet, and then I went around the corner to a dark little area and took a seat and waited. One by one all the other actors went in and auditioned, and by the time the last one walked out, it was late. Ted knew there was one other actor waiting, so he opened the door and looked out into the dark atrium and asked, "Is there anyone else here?"

So I got up and did Jack Benny's walk from the darkness into the light, saying in my best Jack Benny voice, "Oh, Ted, listen, I heard you were gonna make a show of my life. So I got special permission to come back, because if *anyone* is gonna play me on stage, it's gonna be *me*."

Ted's mouth dropped open and he said, "Oh, my God!" I went into the rehearsal hall, and there was a table with the script on it. I picked up the script, assuming I would read from it, but he took it out of my hands and said, "You've just auditioned. Come in Monday, because we'll take the PR photos and start rehearsals then."

And so I was cast as Jack Benny in Ted's show. That one was called *A Small Eternity with Jack Benny,* and I thought it would be a good stage vehicle for me.

Little did I know what it would lead to.

CHAPTER 13

Eddie and a Small Eternity

Eddie approached the one-man show with his usual professionalism and with growing excitement. Since moving to Hollywood, he had done a great deal of acting for TV and the movies and in voiceover work, and he had appeared often on stage: in *Ben Blue's Review*, *A la Carte*, *Of Mice and Men*, *Twelve Angry Men*, as one of the poker players in *The Odd Couple*, *When Last I Saw the Lemmings*, and in *End of a Man*. However, this would be his first time carrying a one-person show. Just as Eddie had worked hard to find and then protect the personality of Jiminy Cricket, he explored Jack Benny's character.

Still, the methods of presentation were very different. "When I do Jiminy," Eddie said, "I'm all alone in a recording studio with headphones on. The director will talk me through the script and tell me what he's looking for, and then I'll try to give that, with variations, so that they'll have several different line readings to choose from. A lot of the time I'll be talking to another character, but of course ninety per cent of the time the actor who is voicing that character isn't there, and I don't hear the voice of whomever I'm supposed to be talking and responding to, so I'm flying solo and playing to the mike.

"It's completely different when I walk out on a stage in a play or in the one-man show. Then I have to be conscious not only of voice and inflection, but of my stance, my eye contact with the audience, my gestures, my expressions, everything, and I'm not alone. The whole audience is there to interact with." Though Eddie jumped at the chance to be in it, and though it's almost impossible to imagine any other actor succeeding as he did in the title role, *A Small Eternity with Jack Benny* would offer its own kind of challenges. On the other hand, Eddie couldn't have asked for a more savvy producer than Snowdon, whose Broadway shows now include the hit *Spring Awakening*, for which he won a Tony. Eddie determined to work his hardest to bring the one-person show to vibrant life.

Eddie remembered the lead-in to the show's California run:

EDDIE CARROLL: Once rehearsals started, I had so much to do to successfully act the role of Jack Benny. From the outset, I wanted to make it clear to the audience that what I was doing was not an impersonation. An impersonation is quick, it's over with in thirty seconds or a minute, and it's like a caricature of someone, exaggerating all the features. Instead of that, I wanted to create an oil painting, a lifelike rendering, an embodiment of the real person who was Jack Benny.

Now of course as we began to rehearse I had a lot of studying to do to get the famous Jack Benny walk, and add to that the voice and all the mannerisms, and I continued to watch the reruns of the show at nine o'clock every weekday night to get all that down.

But the most difficult thing of all was learning to play the violin. I simply had to learn it well enough to play Jack's famous theme song, "Love in Bloom." When I was only eight or nine, my father, Peter Eleniak, who played the violin himself, made one for me and my folks got me lessons, but I was more interested in the guitar. Before long I started to use the money they gave me for my violin lessons to go see a movie instead and was skipping the sessions with my violin teacher. I would hide my violin under the front porch because I couldn't take it with me, and then get it back before I came back into the house.

My mother, Marie Eleniak, finally got suspicious when she realized I'd been practicing the exact same little piece for about three weeks. One afternoon as I came into the house I heard my mother talking to someone in the kitchen. It was my violin teacher. When I came in, she looked at me and said, "All right, if you don't want to play it we're not going to force you."

Coming back to the violin as an adult was one of the hardest efforts of my life. I had a good ear and could play a range of musical instruments, but the violin is incredibly challenging. There is no middle C on a violin; you have to create it, not just put your finger on the strings to produce the note. And just to make it a little worse, I'm left-handed and Jack of course was right-handed. I couldn't play the violin left-handed because people knew what Jack Benny looked like when he was playing and it would spoil the illusion. So I knew going in it would be a hard instrument to master, but I'd had no idea how really tough it was really going to be.

So I went to Carolyn, who used hypnosis as a tool in her practice, and told her she had a new customer. And the price was right! She worked with me, hypnotizing me several times each day for a couple of weeks. Each time she put the suggestion in my mind that my right arm and hand were just as dexterous as my left and that I could play the violin right-handed. Hypnosis can really help someone who sincerely wants to bring about a change in life, and at that point I really wanted it. It began to work, and I improved in my playing to the point where I could perform a squeaky rendition of "Love in Bloom" just about as well — which really means just about as badly — as Jack Benny!

Eddie can play "Love in Bloom."

Then, because that was a success, I also asked Carolyn to help me memorize the script, all 110 pages of it. After a few weeks, it was all coming together. Just to be sure about the violin, I asked a family friend, Noni Fagott, who was a violinist, to give me lessons. She taught me staccato first, then glissando, short notes while sliding my finger along the strings. Then harmonics, holding the note while sliding my finger and doing a controlled bounce of the bow. Noni kept telling me, "Press on the string, but don't hold it down."

Even with my motivation and with the help of suggestion, learning the violin was a struggle, and I felt like someone rubbing his stomach with one hand while patting his head with the other. It was worth it, though. Playing the violin always gave me a good laugh, and the audience enjoyed it, too, though I'll admit I'm always relieved when that part of the show is over.

As Eddie developed his musical skills and the show opening approached, he had one deep regret. His father Peter had passed away the year before Eddie was cast in the show. Peter Eleniak would have been delighted to see his son on stage playing the violin, even if he were playing it for laughs.

In memory of his father, for a long time whenever Eddie acted the role of Jack, he played Peter Eleniak's violin on stage until the TSA cracked down and made carrying anything other than an overnight bag onto an airliner problematic. Even rosin for the violin strings became a problem, as it becomes a white powder after it is applied. That looks suspicious to the TSA, and the violin and case always had to be checked with white fabric squares and the violin wiped with cotton swabs to insure that the powder wasn't anthrax. A few times during tours all this extra attention came close to making Eddie and Carolyn miss connecting flights.

Eddie remembered that "Dad always used to tell us the violin was a Stradivarius, and my brothers and I would laugh at the joke." Later, however, as Eddie was using the instrument the bridge started to lift, so he and Carolyn took it to be repaired. The expert took loving care of it and then said in a reproving tone of voice that Eddie really should get a better carrying case for the violin. The craftsman explained that if you look through the f-shaped sound hole on the instrument you can see the maker's name and the year of manufacture printed inside.

It turned out that this violin had actually been made by a member of the Stradivarius family. "From that time on I gained a new respect for that fiddle," Eddie said. "Carolyn and I bought a grand new hard carrying case as its new home, and from then on I took my music lessons more seriously."

At the same time he was learning to bow right-handed, Eddie was researching the life of Jack Benny, reading all the interviews and biographical material he could find on the beloved star. His goal was to find his way inside Jack's personality, so that not only the outward appearance, the voice, and the mannerisms came through, but a bit of Jack's spirit as well. He proved successful. The show opened at the Mayfair Theatre in Santa Monica in the fall of 1983, and Eddie's performance completely won over the audience.

Eddie's mother Marie had flown in from Edmonton for the show. She was so proud of Eddie — and so moved that he had used Peter's violin in the show, as a special gift for his parents. Other audience members came up to Eddie after the show and told him how accurate his portrayal had been.

As the show's run went on, a few very special audience members added their words of praise. One was Dennis Day, the Irish tenor who had worked with Jack since 1939. For years Day had appeared with Jack every single week, acting with him in sketches in which Dennis played the role of a none-too-bright "kid." Once when Dennis complained to Jack that he didn't want to go swimming because the year before when he'd gone out onto the diving board everyone in the pool had laughed at him, Jack said, "Well, kid, that's nothing. Maybe you had a funny expression on your face. Maybe your swim trunks might have been a little torn —"

And in his high-pitched, breathy voice, Dennis interrupted him with dawning realization: "Ohhhhh! *Swim trunks!*" As if by magic, however, when Jack said, "Sing, Dennis," the clear tenor tones he produced were a bewitching work of musical art.

The night Dennis Day came up after the show to congratulate Eddie was a memorable one. A little hesitantly, Eddie asked, "How did I do?" He expected a stock response: "Fine" or "I liked it." Instead, very seriously and with emotion in his voice, Day replied softly, "I closed my eyes and I heard Jack. I opened my eyes and I saw him."

Eddie received many glowing reviews, but that was one that he always treasured. A little later, veteran comedian Jack Carter saw the show and was similarly impressed. Jack's daughter Joan Benny remembers, "Jack Carter came to me and told me I had to see this show. I said that I really didn't want to, because I had seen all these impressions of my father and none of them seemed very good. But Jack insisted. Now, Jack Carter didn't like *anything*, so I thought his recommendation was pretty special. I did go to see the show and it moved me to tears."

Carolyn says, "Joan's visit was such a great honor for us. A theater employee came to me and said someone was waiting in the lobby who would like to meet Eddie. When I saw who it was, I choked up. I hugged her and thanked her for coming and took her back to Eddie's dressing room. I knocked on the door and told Eddie that Joan Benny was there to meet him."

Eddie was overwhelmed and deeply honored that Joan had come to the show. She was gracious and was moved again to see that Eddie had hung photos of her dad and mom on the dressing-room walls. Carolyn says, "I was in awe of her, and to this day she always has given such good support to the show. She has a marvelous book about Jack that she wrote, *Sunday Nights at Seven*. It uses Jack's manuscript for the autobiography he planned, and in it one chapter is by Jack, the next by Joan. I love it! Joan is just like her dad in many ways — she has a great sense of humor and a great laugh. Later Eddie and I met the four grandchildren as well, all such special individuals."

Others in the Hollywood community also showered accolades on Eddie's performance. Comedy writer and actor Morey Amsterdam was very impressed, and dozens of people who had known Jack in real life commented on the amazing acting job Eddie had done and on the respect and affection that Eddie obviously had for Mr. Benny.

A young man who was just beginning his own theatrical career was likewise impressed. Frank Ferrante recalls, "In 1983, I was a drama student at the University of Southern California and it had entered my mind to perform a one-man show on my comedy hero Groucho Marx. I set out to see as many one-person shows in the Los Angeles area as possible: Jack Klugman as LBJ, Lewis Stadlen as Groucho, and William Windom as James Thurber. I saw shows based on Dorothy Parker and Albert Einstein. And of course the granddaddy of them all — Hal Holbrook as Mark Twain.

"But it was Eddie Carroll's portrayal of Jack Benny at the Mayfair in Santa Monica that may have moved me most. The Mayfair itself was a stunningly ornate theater perfectly suited for a show about the legendary vaudevillian. The house was packed the night I attended and there was a wonderful buzz from the audience. And then there was this actor Eddie Carroll who completely nailed Jack Benny. I remember my exhilaration following his performance and found myself imitating Eddie Carroll embodying Jack Benny on my drive back to my USC dorm. 'Well!' I inflected over and over." Frank's admiration endured, and he and Eddie were to cross paths later and become firm friends.

Best of all, Eddie's family was justifiably proud of his accomplishment. It's quite a feat for any performer to walk out on a stage alone and hold an audience for an hour and forty-five minutes. Eddie always said it felt a bit like a gladiator going into the Coliseum to face a lion: "The trick is to get the audience to root for the gladiator!"

The printed reviews were uniformly very kind to Eddie. There was a problem, though, and it was one that Eddie couldn't personally overcome: the script wasn't quite right. The writer began with the idea that Jack Benny has just been allowed a little time off from Heaven and that he's come back to Earth to prove he really wasn't a cheapskate! Eddie thought that got the show off on the wrong foot: "We all know that Jack Benny's dead, so why hit the audience with that right off the bat? I'd much rather have acted it as if Jack were simply strolling onstage in 1983 to entertain an audience, as he had always done."

The reviewers, after praising Eddie, usually went on to say that unfortunately the material was not as strong as it could have been. However, the original writer was insistent on keeping the opening in, in which before anything else Jack announces that he has returned from Heaven for a one-night engagement.

Even so, struggling to improve the script's pace and humor, eventually the production brought in George Balzer, a veteran comedy writer and a longtime member of Jack Benny's own writing staff. In fact, Balzer was one of the group that Benny himself always enthusiastically credited with his show's longevity (Jack was as generous with gratitude offstage as he was tight with a penny onstage). George and Eddie went through the script and did what they could: "We moved some things from Act I to Act II and vice-versa. We spent many nights cutting and pasting, moving material around until two or three o'clock in the morning. There was also some new material. Between performances I had to relearn the entire script. Then the producer asked the original writer to create some additional dialogue to help us out. He came back three days later to report his progress: he was working on *a* line."

So after its try-out run, and despite Eddie's virtuoso performance as Jack, the show closed. Eddie said, "Everyone involved in a show like this is part of the family, and then it's over and you go your separate ways. It's like losing someone dear to you. I remember we had the staff come to our house that year for Thanksgiving dinner, and then everyone went back to the theater for the evening performance. And then our run ended and the show closed. I regretted that. We loved the theater, the tech crew, and the production staff. It was a sad farewell, but it did open up new directions for us. Ted Snowdon always hoped to work on the script, get it in shape, and then open the show in New York, and I looked forward to the time when it would happen."

The hoped-for New York run of *A Small Eternity with Jack Benny* never quite materialized, though Eddie had a feeling he wasn't finished with Jack Benny, and he was right. He recalled something that happened a few months later:

EDDIE CARROLL: In 1984, through my agent I received a letter from a fifteen-year-old young lady from the Midwest. She told me she was a big fan of Jack Benny and had even started a fan club in Jack's honor. Her name was Laura Leff, and because that first letter she has become a very close friend of ours.

Laura does a marvelous job as the President of the International Jack Benny Fan Club, which moved online and now has a tremendous following, a wonderful community of Jack Benny fans. All the members of the club are knowledgeable about Jack's life and career, but Laura is beyond a doubt the world's top authority on Jack Benny. She has published books about him and edits a regular newsletter for members of the club.

Eddie eventually contributed several articles to the newsletter, and even though his show had had such a limited run, before long he became

Mark and Clark and their dueling pianos.

well-known to Benny fans all across the country. Eventually Laura Leff would be instrumental in Eddie's portraying Jack at a variety of venues, just one sign that *A Small Eternity* was not the final word. There were others, too. Encouraged by the reception he had received in the one-man show, Eddie told of the next installment:

EDDIE CARROLL: The year after *A Small Eternity with Jack Benny* closed, I went to Las Vegas to join the cast of *Legends in Concert* at the Imperial Palace. This was a variety show in which performers re-created true legends of stage and screen: Hank Williams, Marilyn Monroe, Buddy Holly, and, of course, Elvis Presley. As Jack Benny I was the emcee and did bits with the other performers.

This engagement led to other runs of *Legends* at Caesars Atlantic City and then a three-month-long run at C.M. Schulz's Goodtime Theater at Knotts Berry Farm, where in addition to performing I became the show's co-producer. It was a grind — five shows every day, seven days a week. And every single day something would go awry and Carolyn and the kids would wait to hear what had happened and how we managed to work around it. Once a week we still would manage to go to the park and enjoy some family time together.

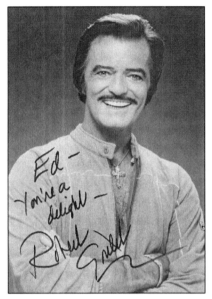

Robert Goulet in Atlantic City spending Mother's Day with Eddie.

Carolyn says, "This was the beginning of many of our most spectacular memories. I took Tina and Leland to Vegas for the first time, and the lights and glamour fascinated them. They had been to Tahoe, but that's a much smaller and more subdued place than Vegas. At thirteen, Lee loved the buffet, and Tina and Lee both had a terrific time seeing the show (many times) and got to know the cast well.

"When we were in the audience, the cast would know it and play to us. One night Jim Owens, portraying Hank Williams, took off his hat as he bowed and threw it down to our table. Like a bowling ball, it made a strike, knocking over every single drink. It was funny, so we actually didn't mind being splashed, but Jim was embarrassed. The audience loved it."

And of course that star of Eddie's was still shining for him. On their second anniversary as they left Las Vegas to drive back home to California, he had assured Carolyn that one day he would return to Vegas and play the strip. He had now done just that, and he would repeat his achievement many times.

The other venues for *Legends* were great, too. Working Atlantic City's flashy Caesars Palace, Eddie often found himself reminded of films he had seen, so many of them showing the famous Boardwalk. "Clothes had changed," he said, "and casinos had been built on it, yet for me it was still filled with magic. I met the twins Mark and Clark [Seymour], who in their act 'Dueling Pianos' played matching pianos and sang and did comedy bits. Their show in the Tropicana Lounge was just wonderful, and some of us would always go there after work."

Carolyn and Eddie had great fun in Atlantic City. She remembers an odd detail: "Outside the showroom entrance stood two nude statues, one male, the other female. Back in the 1980s, slot machines took only coins, and after hours of play the gamblers would have blackened fingers from handling so many quarters, dimes, and nickels. Once after the midnight show we noticed a man with a small brush cleaning the genitalia of the two statues. It turned out he did that every night — as they passed by, the slot players seemed to be enjoying the statues!"

On their anniversary, the casino hosted a fantastic dinner for the Carrolls and then presented them with an amazing wedding cake. Hard though it can be, show business does offer perks, and Eddie and Carolyn thought this was a great one. That year on Mother's Day, Bob Goulet and Eddie spent the whole day together, and then went to see Wayne Newton's show. Eddie called Carolyn to wish her a happy Mother's Day, and in the background Robert Goulet was carrying on — "They sounded like they were back in high school," Carolyn says. "It was a great Mother's Day gift to me just to hear them being so silly and laughing so hard."

Eddie was portraying a legend onstage, and his costars were acting the roles of others, but more was to come. Before long, Eddie would find himself before the cameras with a lady who was not only the greatest comedienne that television had ever produced, but a true living legend and the real-life next-door neighbor of Jack Benny.

Her name was Lucille Ball.

CHAPTER 14

Lucy and Later

By the 1980s, Lucille Ball had spent more than fifty years in show business. She began her career as a stage actress in New York in the very early 1930s, working briefly in a revue put together by impresario Earl Carroll (no relation to Eddie, of course) and stuck with a career that for the first twenty years largely landed her in small parts or supporting roles, though in the 1940s she became known as "Queen of the B's" for appearing in a wide range of B-movies.

Oddly, film directors had little idea of her real gifts and she was often cast more as decoration than for her comedic talents. She wasn't bad in the films, but she just didn't have much chance to shine in vehicles like *Five Came Back*, or *Dance, Girl, Dance* or *The Dark Corner*. On radio, she had a little more luck, often playing smart-mouthed "dame" roles in comedies. Working on one of them, *The Wonder Show*, which starred future Tin Man of Oz Jack Haley, Lucille met Gale Gordon, the blustery comic foil with whom she would work on and off for the rest of her career.

Gregg Oppenheimer, the son of the man who produced *I Love Lucy*, Jess Oppenheimer, remembers his father's stories about how Lucy herself learned just how to use the medium of radio. In a radio script, he wrote for an old-time-radio group to perform, Gregg recreates a pivotal moment in the redhead's career as Jess Oppenheimer counsels his client:

> JESS: You're forgetting the studio full of people right here who *can* see you. *They're* your audience. The folks at home take their cue from *them*. Believe me, the moment you look up from your script and start acting things out, the listening audience will know the difference. And they'll love you for it.
> LUCY: I just find that hard to believe.
> JESS: Did I ever tell you about my first job in Hollywood?
> LUCY: I don't think so. Why?

JESS: I wrote for Fred Astaire's radio show. And every week the highlight of the show was Fred's big *dance* number. Dance. On the radio. And the only people who saw it were the studio audience.
LUCY: Well...
JESS: My next job was on Jack Benny's program. You know, Jack always gets bigger laughs *between* the lines than he does for the jokes themselves. Know how he does it?
LUCY: No — how?
JESS: He lays his hand against his cheek, opens his eyes wide, and slowly looks out at the audience, slowly turning his head, like a comic lighthouse. And the longer he looks the more they laugh.
LUCY: But what if they don't laugh when *I* look at them?
JESS: Don't worry, they will.
LUCY: Listen, Jess, we're finally got a sponsor, our audience is growing, and CBS is happy. All I'm saying is, why risk changing anything when we're doing just fine?
JESS: Because *just fine* just isn't good enough. Not for me. And it sure as hell shouldn't be good enough for you. You could be the best comedian in the business. But not if you keep performing with one arm tied behind your back.
LUCY: It sounds more like you want me to perform with my *script* tied behind my back.
JESS: Well. It couldn't hurt. (Pause) Here, I've got something for you.
LUCY: Jack Benny tickets? What are *these* for?
JESS: I want you to go to school.

The schooling worked because Lucy was a great student and Jack a great teacher. In the late 1940s, Lucille Ball was cast as the star in her own radio comedy, *My Favorite Husband*. It gained a strong audience following, and when television came along and she was asked to develop the show for the small screen, she insisted that the only man who would play her husband on TV was her husband in real life: Cuban bandleader Desi Arnaz. Her stubbornness on this point overcame network resistance. *I Love Lucy* was born, and before long Lucy was the female equivalent of Milton Berle: the unquestioned top star of TV comedy.

She held that position for most of the rest of her life, through the run of several sitcoms, and she remained popular even after she and Desi split and she married comedian Gary Morton. In addition to her success onscreen, Lucy was the force behind Desilu, a production company that brought out a string of solid, successful shows: *I Love Lucy* and later sitcoms featuring Lucille Ball, of course, but also *The Andy Griffith Show, Mission: Impossible, The Dick Van Dyke Show,* and even the original *Star Trek* (and many, many more) were either produced by or shot at Desilu.

In private life, Lucille Ball and Gary Morton lived on Roxbury Drive in Beverly Hills, next-door neighbors to Jack Benny. In the mid-1980s, after he had appeared as Jack Benny in the stage show and in the revue, Eddie was cast in an episode of Lucy's last TV series. He was playing "Herb," a dorky neighbor with no sense of style at all.

Eddie loved the idea of working with Lucille Ball, who had been a great friend of Jack Benny — the two of them frequently traded guest-shot appearances with each other, and in fact Lucy had guested on the same *Jack Benny's Birthday Special* on which Eddie had worked, though she and Eddie had no scenes together. He loved telling the story of the first cast meeting to read through the script for that episode:

Gregg and Debby Oppenheimer. Father of Gregg and co-author with him is Jess Oppenheimer, creator and producer of I Love Lucy.

EDDIE CARROLL: I was honored to be cast in an episode of *Life with Lucy*. Now, the first thing you do when you begin to rehearse a TV script is to meet the whole cast to sit around a table for an initial read-through. This one was scheduled for early in the morning on a soundstage, and when I got there it was freezing cold. Lucy showed up with her coat collar turned way up and her hair in curlers. As we all sat at the table, she kept her eyes on the script and didn't look up at all. I noticed how deep her voice was. She always had a low voice, but first thing in the morning, it was way down there — *basso profundo*.

Now, I played the next-door neighbor Herb, and she and Gale Gordon lived in this great big three-story Victorian home with their grandchildren. They had a yard sale, but it started to rain, so they brought everything inside. I played the neighbor who came over for the sale and started to haggle with Lucy.

When we started to read through our scene and got to my lines, Lucy interrupted me almost right away: "Now, when you get to that line as we do the show, it's gonna get a big laugh. Up until then we'll be in a two-shot, but be sure to pause just at that point because we'll have to clear and set up a close-up so you'll be able to react on the laugh line...." She went on to give me this incredibly detailed set of instructions. I glanced at the director, and he just shrugged at me in a "what the hell am *I* doing here?" kind of way.

Lucy went on and on with her directions, and when she finished, she said, "You got that?"

I couldn't resist. I got up from the table and in my best Jack Benny voice, I said, "Well! If you wanted *that* kind of actor, you should have hired Al Pacino!" And I sashayed off in Jack's walk.

Lucy burst out with her great booming laugh, and from then on, the rehearsal was scrubbed. Lucy, Gary, and I just sat around for two hours trading stories about Jack Benny.

And I loved this one that Lucy told: When the Mortons lived next door to Jack Benny there on Roxbury Drive, they were always dropping in on one another. Now, Jack's wife Mary Livingstone always had something going on — she was out shopping, or off playing Mah-Jongg or what have you.

Jack liked to have just one cocktail around five or six before dinner, but he hated to drink alone, so several times a week he'd phone Lucy and say, "I'd like to come over and have a drink if it would be okay," and it almost always was. He'd go over, they'd have one drink, visit for half an hour, and then Jack would go home.

So once Jack called around five-thirty and Gary answered the phone. Jack said, "Hi, Gary, is it all right if I come over for a drink?"

And Gary said, "Jack, ordinarily we'd love to have you, but Lucy has relatives in from out of town. We're about to have an early dinner, and then we're going out because we have tickets to a show at the Ahmanson Theater."

Jack said, "Well, go ahead, and I'll come over another time — no, wait a minute! Wait a minute! I've got a great idea. You go ahead and have dinner, and I'll come over in a few minutes and serenade you with the violin while you're eating, but don't tell Lucy, ya see."

They hung up and Lucy asked Gary "Who was that?"

"I don't know, wrong number," he said.

Well, Lucy and Gary and their guests sat down and started their dinner, and of course her relatives were already in awe because there they were in Hollywood at Lucy's table. And then the back door opens, and in comes Jack Benny dressed as a Gypsy! He's taken Mary's eyebrow pencil and drawn a mustache on his face, and sideburns. He's put a little cap on and has his shirt open to his waist with gold chains hanging over his chest and a sash around his waist. He doesn't say a word but just bows and then starts playing a Gypsy melody, and he strolls all around the table.

And Lucy's guests are freaking out. They whispered to her, "Is that Jack Benny?"

And just like it happened every day, she said, "Oh, yeah, please pass the salt." Like she could care less, you know.

Jack plays the whole table, winds up beside Gary Morton and finishes with a flourish, tucks his bow and violin under his arm, and just stands there like he's waiting for something. Gary just ignores him for minutes, then looks up and says, "Oh, that's right. Here you are." And he hands Jack a dollar.

Jack says, "Thank you. Same time tomorrow?"

Gary says, "Yes," and Jack bows and leaves.

Now the real punch line comes later. Jack goes back home and discovers that Mary must have come in and left again, because all the doors are locked and he didn't take his key and so he can't get in! He's pounding on the front door, but there's nobody home.

And just at that moment, the tour bus that takes people around Hollywood to see the homes of the stars comes rolling down the street. Warm summer afternoon, all the bus windows are open. And the driver is saying on his microphone, "Ladies and gentlemen, we have just passed the home of Miss Lucille Ball, and coming up is the home of Mr. Jack Benny — wait a minute, I think I see Mr. Benny now!"

The driver parks the bus! And dressed like a Gypsy and with nowhere to go, Jack takes his violin over to the bus, plays a little ditty, and then walks along under the windows holding out his hat. He collects sixteen dollars, the bus rolls off. And Jack told Lucy, "Then I went into my backyard and screamed for an hour."

Unfortunately, Lucy's last sitcom wasn't a hit, though Eddie had fun making his one guest appearance with her and Gale Gordon. As the show was actually being taped before the studio audience, there came a pause when the cameras were being re-set and loaded with fresh videotape. Lucy came out to the front of the stage to talk to the people in the studio auditorium. Eddie had stepped off into the wings, dressed in his mismatched wardrobe of long black socks, dingy white sneakers, checkered shorts, a striped shirt, and a floppy-brimmed khaki hat. As Lucy talked to the audience she saw Eddie out of the corner of her eye and said, "Hey, I want you to meet someone who does the best Jack Benny you've ever seen!"

Carolyn was out in that audience and Eddie shot her a look of despair. He was meticulous when it came to playing Benny in *A Small Eternity* or *Legends,* and he was definitely not an impressionist. But he did his best, smoothing his hair back and coming out in Benny's walk. Lucy started to pepper him with questions and he responded in Jack's voice and with Jack's gestures.

Here was the queen of television comedy becoming the straight-man for Eddie Carroll. From offstage Lucy's husband Gary yelled, "Lucy! Just give Eddie the mike!" She did, and Eddie did a little bit of Benny for the delighted audience. The business with the cameras and lights finally was done, the cast was called back to finish the last scene, and a marvelous moment ended. For the rest of his life, Eddie carried that memory in his heart.

At the same time, his other career was revving up and keeping him, well, hopping. Eddie said, "Jiminy, my beautiful conscience, always seemed to be around to put me in the correct place when the time was right. Like Pinoke, I had Jiminy as my guide. At this time the Disney Studios had me doing some great projects: a Valentine's Day TV special, then another Christmas Special, and *The Constitution,* a U.S. history special with Richard Dreyfuss. For a humble cricket, Jiminy brought so many bright memories and wonderful people into my life!"

Meanwhile, Ted Snowdon had become so busy with other Broadway projects that he had no time to pull together all the elements to open *A Small Eternity with Jack Benny* in New York. First, the script still needed work, then the theaters were all booked, and all in all, prospects of Eddie's taking to the stage again in the one-man show did not look bright.

That was too bad, because the show was shaping up and the rough spots were being smoothed out, but Eddie still had opportunities to play Jack Benny. In 1985, *Legends in Concert* opened for four months in Miami Beach in a hotel that, literally, was right on the beach. For the first time that year the Carrolls broke a family tradition and did not spend Christmas at home.

Instead, Eddie said, "we spent Christmas Eve riding in an airboat through the Everglades. Then a dear friend, the great film and television editor Michael Economou, and his daughter spent the evening with us. We put up and decorated a tree, and Carolyn made some home-baked goodies that we munched on as we laughed with Michael." On Christmas day itself, Eddie and Carolyn with Tina and Lee lounged in beach chairs before Christmas dinner.

Unfortunately, because the family had never eaten out for Christmas, they neglected to make reservations. "We had no idea they were needed,"

Carolyn says. "We were naïve about that! We visited every restaurant in reach and finally settled for a Denny's, where we *still* had a long wait. Well, live and learn. Then when the meal finally came and Eddie saw the tiny portion of stuffing he was given to go with his turkey, he immediately asked for seconds. The waitress said there would be an additional charge, and Eddie said, 'I'll pay it, I'll pay it!' He wanted his dressing, and it was no time to play it as cheaply as Jack Benny might have."

And a classic moment occurred at one matinee, one that always made Eddie laugh as he told about it:

EDDIE CARROLL: At the Marco Polo in Miami, we had a 2:00 p.m. show — a real early-bird special. A great many elderly people would be in the audience for these. One afternoon I walked on for my entrance, and in character I opened with, "Good afternoon, ladies and gentlemen, and welcome, welcome to our show."

At the very front table sat a little old couple. The wife said in a loud voice to her husband, "Who is that?"

I paused and gave the audience one of those Jack Benny everything-happens-to-me looks. The little old lady must have had a serious hearing impairment because the husband roared, "It's Jack Benny!"

I couldn't even open my mouth for my next line before the woman said, "Who? Who is it?"

And the husband shouted, "Jack! Benny!"

By now people were laughing. I did the hand to the cheek and sighed, just waiting. I knew it wasn't over yet.

And sure enough, the lady said, "I thought Jack Benny was dead!"

The husband shouted back, "Jack Benny *is* dead! This is a guy who *thinks* he's Jack Benny!"

And after the following roar of laughter had died down, still in character, I said to them, "Well, I'm glad we got *that* settled. Now do you folks mind if I go on with my act?"

And the gentleman said, "Go on, go on, young man. Don't worry. You look like him, you sound like him, you'll be good."

The rest of the audience laughed and applauded, and all I could say was "Well!" And one other time, with a similar elderly audience, I was in the middle of a monologue when an old fellow got up from his table and said to me, "Listen, I gotta go to the restroom, but don't worry, I'll be back. You're doing good, just ignore me and go on."

I had to laugh out loud — but that's what Jack would have done, too. And once again, the audience loved it.

So even without a full production of *A Small Eternity,* Eddie kept busy. He was in *Legends in Concert* in the Wang Theatre in Boston for the month of July 1988. While there, he and Carolyn decided to take advantage of the opportunity. Eddie said, "Carolyn and I were always interested in history. She was always studying AAA books to find places we'd love to visit or experience. We walked the Freedom Trail together not once

A show in Miami had members of audience talking to Eddie on stage. Eddie perplexed as Jack Benny.

but many times, even on one day with the thermometer at 99 degrees and the humidity at 99% — not to mention the occasional sudden downpours.

We visited the Mayflower II, an exact replica of the original Pilgrim ship, and we were amazed to think about how people could have stood the cramped quarters for the sixty-six days they spent crossing the Atlantic. We saw Plimouth Village, a meticulous re-creation of the original Pilgrim settlement, with replicas of the fort, wigwams, and the Pilgrims' cabins. It was very realistic, including actors who do the daily chores and take the parts of the founding settlers, down to the accents."

Mischievously, Eddie tried to get just one of them to break character, casually asking the "Pilgrims" what they thought of contemporary politics or space travel. Not one of them cracked. They had the kind of professional concentration that Eddie shared and admired. He even started to feel a little out of place, because "they were in authentic costume, and there I was wearing shorts. That kept me from fitting in."

One drawback for that particular production of *Legends in Concert* was the sheer size of the theater. Sitting in the back row of the sharply-raked auditorium, Carolyn thought that Eddie looked about the size of a year-old toddler. She took the producer up for a look — "the seats were so steep that we had to take an elevator to get up there — " to show him why selling out that theater might actually be a *bad* idea for a show that depended on creating the illusion of stars from the past coming back to the stage.

The tour continued. Eddie recalled, "The show then went to a theater-in-the-round, actually a huge circus tent on Cape Cod. Carolyn and I kept humming that Rothrock-Yakus-Jeffrey song from 1957, 'Old Cape Cod.' We had a chance to visit the Kennedy compound — just amazing.

"From there we were off to the Queen Elizabeth Theatre for the Toronto Expo. Our schedule was for five shortened shows a day, seven days a week, for three weeks." For the Carrolls, a nice perk was that the theater in Toronto stood just across from the big concert hall, and the management gave them complimentary tickets for the concerts after the last shows of the evening. The Carrolls enjoyed wonderful performances by Huey Lewis and the News, George Michaels, and the Tower of Power. It was a good way to round off the evening.

And yet all through the Toronto engagement Eddie began to feel unusually tired. The schedule was a crowded one, but he had become used to that. The dressing rooms in the Queen Elizabeth had brick walls, and Carolyn remembers Eddie nearly collapsing in a chair in the dressing room between shows: "He would pick up a newspaper and after just a few minutes it would sag out of his hands, and he'd have his head back against the bricks, sound asleep." And even awake, Eddie felt draggy and tired all the time.

Carolyn thought he might have a touch of flu, though it was the wrong season for that, but Eddie insisted he'd be okay. Two days before the *Legends* run in Toronto ended, Carolyn flew back home to Encino. When she and Tina drove to the airport to pick Eddie up on his return, she was shocked at how sick he seemed: "This was an Eddie I had never seen. He just wanted to sleep, and he complained that his shoulder and elbow joints were achy."

She had done a little medical reading and had started to suspect the problem: a Lyme disease epidemic had occurred in Massachusetts that summer. The malady was only beginning to be understood, and not until 1982 would researcher Willy Burgdorfer publish findings that the disease organism responsible for the illness was tick-borne, and the specific species of tick that hosted the spirochetes would not be positively identified until 1987. Carolyn had read about Lyme disease research then going on at Boston Memorial Hospital and about the unprecedented outbreak that had occurred just at the time the Carrolls were in Boston.

Carolyn got Eddie to their family doctor immediately, but Lyme disease was at that time almost unknown in California. She says, "Our primary physician was a great detective, yet it took him almost a month to reach the diagnosis. Once again we were blessed: our doctor was an authority to whom the Centers for Disease Control in Atlanta referred patients suffering from tick-borne diseases. He showed us a picture of the deer-tick bite associated with Lyme disease."

Immediately Carolyn recognized the distinctive bull's-eye shaped lesion. She had seen it on Eddie's thigh the night after he returned from Toronto. He had thought maybe the Jacuzzi would offer him some relief for his achy joints, and Carolyn had noticed him scratching the place. At the time, neither of them knew what it could be — just some kind of insect bite or sting that Eddie had suffered when they were visiting the wigwams at Plimouth Village the day he was wearing walking shorts. In fact, Lyme disease is terrifically dangerous, and Eddie faced a much more serious health challenge than he would have thought possible.

The therapy was long and stressful. The doctor prescribed three different antibiotics, and he warned Eddie that he would have to take them for months, not just for a couple of weeks. He explained that tick bites can subject a human victim to 32 different parasites as well as Lyme disease. And the antibiotics would take time to work. Carolyn remembers that soon after Eddie's return the two of them made a trip to Pismo Beach, and again Eddie had none of his usual zing or humor. He was listless, exhausted, and obviously worried about how ill he felt — so ill that he couldn't think of performing yet. Carolyn says, "He felt so terrible, and he was just beginning to realize how long this fight might last. That was the first time I had ever seen him depressed."

In the end, Eddie had to remain on medication for more than five years — Lyme disease is not only debilitating, but stubborn, and at that time physicians were still struggling to find the best, fastest way to treat the illness. For the first six months, Eddie had to battle abnormal fatigue and depression, but gradually he began to improve and to regain his optimism.

Then, too, just as he had been inspired to overcome his paralysis by seeing an old man fight to swallow his food, Eddie realized that, sick though he was, he was blessed: "We would walk into our doctor's office and see other victims of this same disease in such bad shape, confined to wheelchairs and hooked to IV drips. Who was I to feel sorry for myself?" He not only began to improve, but to others who had Lyme disease he offered cheer and encouragement, becoming for them a hopeful example and a shining star.

And of course, being a trouper, Eddie soon began looking forward to performing again. In 1989, he got a wonderful opportunity. Again he would play the role of Jack Benny, this time at the Academy Theater in New York, in a variant of *Legends in Concert* that would be called *Legends on Broadway*.

He and Carolyn went to the Big Apple, where Eddie said "We had a great time and we were always tourists! On my days off we ventured to every landmark in the area and we loved it. We had an apartment, but the wiring was so old that we could run only one appliance at a time. If we tried two, we burnt out a fuse. The apartment was a fourth-floor walkup — no elevator — and the fuse box was in the basement, so whenever we blew one I had to walk all the way down to replace it. It was just what I needed to regain my strength: regular exercise!"

Carolyn recalls more details: "Food shopping for our little love nest was always a funny ordeal without an elevator. Every time we bought too much to carry. Eddie loved his Coca-Cola, but those big cartons get heavy once you pass the second-story landing. On a shopping day, we'd go to the greengrocer, the butcher, and the corner mart. Then slogging up the stairs to the fourth-floor apartment we would feel our arms stretching and getting longer like a gorilla's. Every time we'd be huffing and puffing but giggling, and on the third floor we always promised ourselves that we'd remember the next time. We never did."

To the Carrolls, the neighborhood was picturesque — but, as Eddie said, they were tourists. What did they know? Carolyn tells how they learned better: "One day Art Metrano, the actor who became famous as Mauser in the *Police Academy* movies, called and was talking to Eddie, who invited him over. The actor asked for our address, and Eddie told it to him. Even I could hear his voice, and I wasn't on the extension — we didn't have an extension! The man yelled, '*You are in f— in' Hell's Kitchen!*'"

"We thought it was a joke, and Eddie and I laughed at the very idea. Then two days later the TV broke and we carried it to have it fixed. On our way back we took a little walk and found a cute little park, but as we went into it, we saw a sign: *Hell's Kitchen Park*. 'Oh, my God!' Eddie said. 'Art Metrano was right!'" And he and Carolyn cracked up again.

Soon Carolyn went back home to the kids, but Eddie stayed in New York for the run of the show. However, *Legends on Broadway* had to close early when the FDNY checked and discovered the theater was under code — it had too few sprinklers to handle an emergency. Eddie called home and told Carolyn about the development and asked her to find him a cheap way to get back to California.

At that time Braniff Airlines was about to go under and had offered a special fare to attract passengers: $69.00 to Ontario, California. That was about an hour's drive from Encino, but because Carolyn was seeking a bargain fare on only two days' notice, it worked out. Once more the Carrolls enjoyed a small blessing that had taken care of a problem.

Back home again, Eddie kept thinking that he should do a one-man show again, but with a new script. He spoke with Ted Snowdon, who told him that he might as well try it — he couldn't see any way of remounting *A Small Eternity* for the immediate future, and he gave Eddie his blessing. Eddie takes up the story:

EDDIE CARROLL: Some years back I had done a *Mary Tyler Moore Show*, and as I thought about what I really wanted to do with Jack Benny, I called friends and writers and talked it over with them. I called Allan Burns, a co-creator and writer for *Mary Tyler Moore*, and asked if he would want to write a Jack Benny show with me.

He said right away, "Eddie, you ought to write that yourself. You know Jack Benny better than anyone."

I thought about that. I settled down and re-read all my books and other materials about Jack Benny's life, refreshing my memory. If I wrote a script, I wanted it to be as accurate as I could make it. I started sketching out the shape of the show, though now and then I decided to stretch the facts, mostly for humor and entertainment. Later, that kept getting me taken to task by members of the International Jack Benny Fan Club. They're true fans, and they know all the details of Jack's life. However, I often explained to them that I was only taking a little artistic license, and they understood.

But neither they nor anyone else would see the show for some time, because writing a one-person show is a tricky business, and Eddie was a perfectionist. In the end, when the new project did debut, everyone was delighted with it, occasional inaccuracies included, and even Laura Leff, the ultimate Jack Benny expert, loved the show and gave it her blessing.

In the meantime, another marvelous opportunity opened up to bridge the gap until Eddie could go on solo as Jack once again. The Music Box Theatre in San Francisco mounted a production called *Benny, Monroe, and Cagney*. It was another re-creation of celebrities, with Eddie (of course) as Jack and Christopher Weeks brilliantly playing James Cagney. The show settled in for a successful eight-week run, and the Carrolls had fun again as tourists, loving the city.

Carolyn, though, became a victim of her own enthusiasm: "Being a dancer and singer since the age of four, I always have to move. In addition to Tai Chi Chuan and yoga, I had taken up power walking for cardio exercise. In San Francisco, I decided my walk would be to Fisherman's Wharf and back. You know what? San Francisco is built on hills! I started out climbing up the hills and back down and up again and down again as I headed toward the wharf. After about an hour, my shins began to feel sore. I couldn't hop on a trolley because I was close to my goal and they were all full. So I walked the whole way, had a nice hot Irish coffee, and took the trolley back."

Then the next morning, she got out of bed well before sunup to use the bathroom, but "I barely got to the foot of the bed when my shins cramped so hard I couldn't walk. I screamed so loud with the pain that I woke Eddie, scaring him and probably the rest of the hotel guests. I had given myself excruciating shin splints. That walk wasn't the most brilliant idea I'd ever had, and it took a long time for my legs to feel normal again."

From San Francisco the show moved to John Ascuagas's Nugget Casino in Sparks, Nevada, a suburb of Reno. Ascuagas had a meteoric career, starting as a bus boy in a small casino, saving his money, and eventually buying the place thanks to a loan. By the time he paid it off, he was well on the way to expanding the property and bringing in stellar entertainment for the Celebrity Showroom.

Eddie said, "John is a true model of the American success story. His life should be made into a movie." A part of the show was an act that duplicated the "Blues Brothers" (John Belushi and Dan Aykroyd) from *Saturday Night Live.* Carolyn, recovered from her shin splints, helped choreograph their act so it was closer to the original that people remembered from late-night TV.

Carolyn remembers marvelous times at the Nugget: "On my birthday I arrived while Eddie was performing and in our room I found a table brought in especially to hold bouquets of roses, a bottle of champagne, a diamond-heart necklace, and a beautifully hand-lettered birthday note about the rest of my day. We had a wonderful dinner and Eddie gave me forty dollars to spend on the slot machines. While he was onstage for the second show, I played a three progressive clown machine. A stagehand walked by and asked, 'Losing Eddie's money?'"

Carolyn, who had been staring at the machine, had a great comeback: "No, I just won us $1,199." By the time she came backstage, the whole cast knew about her good luck. Eddie asked her to join the crew in the wings just before the curtain calls. When the cast was all onstage, they wheeled in a gorgeous, full-sheet birthday cake with sparklers twinkling away and with "Carolyn" written on the frosting. The entire cast and crew sang "Happy Birthday" to Carolyn as the finale. Carolyn adores the memory: "It was a perfect, loving, romantic day for me. Bless our friends. They are still there for us. At moments like that, I truly felt love from all around us."

CHAPTER 15

Private Moments

Busy though he was with Jiminy and Jack all through the 1980s, Eddie remembered the pledge he and Carolyn had made when they began their married life. Traditions were very important to Ukrainians, and that went for their family, too. So regularly every year the Carrolls took two family vacations, a beach resort in the summer and Lake Tahoe in the winter, when they could all be together, have fun, and enjoy each other's company.

These vacations were always times of great fun and relaxation, giving Eddie a welcome chance to unwind after the stress and strain of performing every night in *A Small Eternity with Jack Benny* and touring with the *Legends* shows. However, even a fun vacation was not always without its moments of excitement.

Eddie remembered their trips to Hawaii and one scary moment in particular:

EDDIE CARROLL: All of us have stories about our trips, memories we wouldn't trade for anything. The first time we took Tina and Leland to Hawaii was when Tina was ten and Lee almost seven. That first Hawaiian vacation started in Maui, and the kids loved the beach and the food and just everything about it.

Later for history and to see the landmarks we flew from Maui to Waikiki. The kids were naturally excited, but I remember they were extremely well-behaved because before we had even left the house, Carolyn had explained to them very seriously that they had to act maturely to go on an adult vacation, and if they didn't, we'd send them back to Los Angeles to stay with Grandma and Pops.

That worked *almost* all the time. They loved these trips and they really always tried to stay on their best behavior. But the day when we flew to Honolulu from Maui and landed at the airport there, a limo was waiting to pick us up. That was the first time that Tina and Lee had ever been in one, and as it drove us to our hotel, they sat together in the back seat and leaned together and kept whispering something to each other that sounded pretty serious and intense. It was the kind of conversation that rouses a mom's suspicions. "What's this all about?" Carolyn asked them.

They clammed up and would only answer "Nothing." Carolyn looked at me and shrugged, then said gently, "It's okay to tell us about it. We promise we won't get mad."

Lee burst out with, "We want to go back to Maui!"

"Why?" Carolyn asked, surprised.

And they said, "Because this looks just like Santa Monica!"

That was a relief. I told them, "You're not seeing the whole place yet. Don't worry, it's not *that* much like Santa Monica."

Sure enough, they soon were enjoying the beach. One afternoon, Lee took out his boogie board. He had done that many times in Kaanapali on Maui, and he always practiced safety, the way he had been taught, so we had no great fears. He was already a great swimmer and that day the water at Waikiki was very calm, blue and crystal-clear.

Well, Lee had been paddling around for a while before I suddenly noticed with a shock how far out he was. He didn't appear to be kicking, and when we yelled, he was so distant that he didn't seem to hear us. We panicked. I went running out along the breakwater — not my most brilliant idea, because I was slipping and sliding all over the place. Carolyn grabbed the other boogie board, but as she raced down to the water a young man jumped up and called to her that he was a champion swimmer. He said he would swim out and bring Leland back.

And that's what he did. When that wonderful young swimmer brought our son safely back to shore, Lee told us what had happened. The water was so perfectly clear that he saw the coral down below and thought it was closer to the surface than it actually was. He wasn't paddling or kicking because he didn't want to get all cut up on the coral. Well, that wasn't our last trip to Hawaii, but it was the last time we let Lee take his boogie board out into the ship lanes!

And even that frightening moment wasn't the end of Leland's problems. As the Carrolls were waiting at the airport to board their flight home, Carolyn noticed that Leland was lugging his little flight bag as if it were much heavier than it should be. "What did you put in that?" she asked him suspiciously.

"Just stuff," Leland said, looking totally innocent.

He had packed a lot of stuff indeed. When they were back home in Encino and unpacking, Carolyn solved the mystery. Leland had filled the flight bag with a collection of coral — the very thing that had scared him in the water — and had brought it back home.

"You know you're not supposed to bring back chunks of lava because that makes Pele, the volcano goddess, angry," she says. "And I understood the same thing applied to coral. I told Leland we didn't want any bad luck, so I packed it up and sent it to the Chamber of Commerce in Honolulu explaining what had happened. They sent the nicest 'thank-you' note back to us."

Leland says with a grin, "I don't know if the rest of it's true for everybody, but coral brought *me* bad luck."

Their winter trips to Tahoe always began the second day after Christmas, and the Carrolls would stay there until January 2. Times have changed since then, but in those days Carolyn remembers she would freeze the left-over ham from Christmas Eve and the turkey breast from Christmas Day and take them on the plane to Tahoe — there was no TSA back then to keep dangerous and potentially explosive items like ham and turkey off the flights. "Eddie and I had been through enough lean times not to waste food," she says. "And taking the frozen left-overs meant we had delicious breakfasts and tasty sandwiches while we were there."

The Carrolls always stayed in a condo or in a cabin when they were visiting Tahoe, and the kids enjoyed visiting the buffets. While Eddie and Leland kept up their game of snowball tossing and counting, Carolyn and Tina never got into that kind of winter sport. Instead, the two of them would build snowmen, and the whole family enjoyed tobogganing. New Year's Eve was always spectacular, because Tahoe closes down the boulevard and everyone spills out into the traffic-free street to celebrate.

However, the snowy slopes of Tahoe offered both enjoyment and danger. Just as Leland gave his parents a scare in Hawaii, so did Tina one winter in Tahoe. Eddie remembered the occasion like this:

EDDIE CARROLL: By this time Tina was in competition skating, in great physical shape, and she had blossomed into a real daredevil. One winter, she decided she was going to make the toboggan run not with Carolyn as her partner, but all by herself. I remember she was wearing a bright-red snow cap. She climbed aboard the toboggan at the top of the run and shoved off, zooming downhill.

We were up the hill, and as we watched, Tina got almost to the bottom of the run, where there was a slight turn — and she took the curve too fast, missed making the turn, and because only one person was aboard it, the toboggan was light and couldn't hold the track. It leapt right over the snow bank that was supposed to be a protective barrier.

Up at the top of the run we watched in horror as the toboggan shot over the embankment, and all we could see was that red snow cap vanishing into space. We rushed down to help her and discovered that, just as with Lee in Hawaii, our lucky star was still shining.

Tina had rocketed off the run and down the mountainside, but before she had gone very far, she hit a small tree and came to a stop. We were so lucky — the tree that caught her must have been the identical twin to the one Charlie Brown decorated for Christmas. It was all of two feet tall and had a total of four little flexible branches that caught and held the toboggan before anything really terrible happened. Tina was scared but safe, and as we picked her up and brushed her off, I said, "God bless that tree!" At that moment, I thought it was the most beautiful tree I had ever seen.

As the years went by and as Tina grew up, she took to skiing, a sport she always enjoyed. Her brother Leland never was a skiing enthusiast, but being physically fit from her skating and having a great natural sense of balance, Tina loved zooming down the slopes. Besides, even Eddie had to admit that in her teen years his daughter looked terrific in ski pants. "The young men who were the ski instructors," he said wryly, "were always *very* anxious to help her learn her way around the slopes."

There were other young ladies in the Carrolls' life in those years, some of them daughters of family friends, some schoolmates of Tina and Leland, and a few relatives. Two in particular were their nieces. Cami Elen is the daughter of Eddie's brother Bob, a partner in the Davis-Elen Advertising Agency, representing an impressive list of clients from Toyota to McDonalds. Cami is a terrific singer who often came to Eddie for guidance and advice about her career. Eddie always had suggestions for songs she might perform and led her to listen to tracks from many great singers whose work has unfairly faded over time.

Cami is a fast learner, and she always valued Eddie's help and insights into building a career. She has a wonderful voice and can sing anything from 40s ballads and jazz to rap music — she is just as versatile as she is talented.

Another niece is Erika, oldest daughter of Eddie's attorney brother Dale. When she was just a little girl, she became interested in modeling and acting, and she made a memorable debut in a little movie called *E.T.: The Extraterrestrial*.

You'll remember the scene: while the cute alien E.T. is back at the home of the boy who rescued him, Elliott, the little space creature vegging out while watching a romantic movie on TV, young Elliott is in science class at his elementary school, where the students are about to dissect live frogs. Picking up on E.T.'s environment-friendly vibes, Elliott suddenly yells, "Free the frogs!" and heroically rescues and releases the amphibians, thrilling a pretty young classmate, whom he embraces with all the flair of an Errol Flynn and whom he romantically kisses.

Talented nieces Cami Ellen, singer (left) and Erika Eleniak, actress (right).

The classmate was Erika, whom Stephen Spielberg appropriately billed as "Pretty Girl." It was a very special debut, in one of the highest-grossing films of all times, and everyone smiles when they remember Erika's first screen kiss.

When she was an aspiring young actress, Erika remembers that "whenever I had a question about acting or contracts or anything about show business, I would come to Uncle Eddie with it. He always helped me out with advice." Even more, she said, he helped her by being a role model. "I knew how hard he worked and how dedicated he was to his profession. He was an inspiration."

A good one, it seems: Erika went on to stardom as the lead in *Baywatch* for several seasons, and later she made another memorable entrance — though a decidedly more adult one than in *E.T.* — in the Steven Seagal movie *Under Siege* when she emerged from a gigantic cake. The cake was covered with frosting, but Erika was covered only in Erika. In the slam-bang action film she grows from an initially rather ditsy dancer to a tough gal who helps Seagal's Navy Seal-turned-cook defeat a whole shipload of bad guys, led by a menacing Tommy Lee Jones and Gary Busey.

However, like Leland and Tina, Erika's strongest and fondest memories of Eddie are not of acting or even of his advice and counsel, but rather of his personality. She says, "He had such a great sense of humor, and he made everyone feel so relaxed and at home when we came over to visit." She admits to being nostalgic over the wonderful Ukrainian holiday meals and the parties that Eddie and Carolyn frequently hosted. Though her career took her away from home often and for long periods, she always looked forward to coming back to California, going over to the Carroll home, and relaxing with her favorite uncle and aunt.

And they always made sure that she was welcome to the warmth and hospitality of their home. Eddie valued his "extended family," but he adored all his Eleniak kin, and they felt the same about him.

CHAPTER 16

Jiminy, Jack, and the Curse of Goofy

As the 1990s neared, Eddie often reflected on one of his favorite sayings: "Being in show business is like piloting your own plane. You experience two emotions: pure ecstasy and stark terror."

On the one hand, his career as Jiminy Cricket was really taking off. Jiminy had landed a plum role in *Mickey's Christmas Carol*, a featurette in the style of the Disney Studio's *Mickey and the Beanstalk* segment from the 1947 film *Fun and Fancy Free*. The new animated *Christmas Carol* was, of course, a Disney take on the Charles Dickens classic, with tight-fisted Scrooge McDuck playing Ebeneezer Scrooge, Mickey and Minnie as Bob and Mrs. Cratchit, Donald as an improbably cheery and mild-mannered Nephew Fred, and Goofy as a bumbling Marley's Ghost.

Jiminy was cast — very well! — as the Ghost of Christmas Past, a kind of conscience reminding Ebeneezer that once his cold, stingy heart had been warm and generous. When Jiminy first introduces himself to Scrooge by revealing his gold badge, which for the occasion has been changed from "Official Conscience" to "Ghost of Christmas Past," Scrooge mockingly objects that the Ghost should be taller. A stern Jiminy retorts, "If men were measured by kindness, you'd be no bigger than a-a-!" Even after Scrooge has insulted his own height, plan-thinking, honest Jiminy can't be too sarcastic, though, so he ends up with an indignant, " — a speck of dust!"

Joining Eddie in the cast of *Mickey's Christmas Carol* were voice actors, some veterans, some fairly new. Clarence "Ducky" Nash voiced Donald, as he had from the Duck's first squawk. Wayne Allwine was the third voice of Mickey (following Walt Disney himself and then James MacDonald); Hal Smith was Goofy. And Scrooge was played by Alan Young, well-known as Wilbur from *Mr. Ed*. Young was to become one of Eddie's buddies. In the cartoon he had a number of wonderful "cheap" gags:

When Jacob Marley had died, Scrooge observes that he had left Scrooge enough money to buy him a tombstone — so Scrooge had him buried at sea.

When that project proved to be a popular success, Disney found other uses for its smallest (but biggest-hearted) star. Jiminy also was the host and provided the links for *Jiminy Cricket's Christmas,* a video

Alan Young with Eddie.

release that joined together many classic shorts and tuneful bits of Disney animation. For stretches of the video Jiminy is off-camera, just a voice on the soundtrack, but of course he also made visual appearances in the piece.

Here Eddie ran into another wrinkle of voice-overs, because in addition to new footage, the studio recycled some classic animation of Jiminy from *Pinocchio* and other sources. Except, of course, they had to replace the original lines. Eddie said, "Ordinarily when you record the voice for a cartoon, you lay down the vocal tracks before the animators start to work on the drawings. That way they animate for the speeches and there's no problem and you don't have to worry about lip movements, because the artists take care of that.

"But when you're re-dubbing established animation, you have to say the lines so that it still looks as if the character's mouth is synced to the new words. It can be tricky to squeeze in the words, and sometimes it calls for rewriting a line here and there."

In 1983, Disney had launched The Disney Channel, a family-friendly cable network. The studio had a huge backlog of material to draw on, of course, but they also began to create new shows for this outlet. One was called *D-TV*, a takeoff on MTV, which excerpted musical moments from Disney shorts and features and repackaged them as music videos. And who better to host these than Jiminy?

So Eddie voiced the character in a number of *D-TV* productions (many of them later made available for home video as well): two Valentine's specials, in one of which he worked with legendary Paul Frees, whom he had known for years and who was the Viennese-accented voice of Donald's kooky but brilliant uncle Ludwig von Drake. In the other Valentine's show, a new voice for Goofy joined Eddie: Bill Farmer, who was soon to become one of Eddie's close friends.

The *D-TV* shows led in turn to a series of *Disney Sing-Along* videos. Although it was only in archival footage, in one of them Eddie as Jiminy appeared together with Phil Harris, who had played Jack Benny's boozy, hipster bandleaders on radio for many years and who had gone on to voice Baloo the Bear in Disney's *Jungle Book*, where his jivey rendition of "The Bare Necessities" stole the show.

In addition to these roles for Jiminy, Eddie frequently recorded little bits for the Disney Channel or for the theme parks. At first it had looked as if his road trips with the various versions of *Legends* might interrupt his Jiminy voiceover sessions, but he and Carolyn worked out an arrangement with Disney that made it possible. Wherever Eddie might be, the Disney people had only to fax the script to him and find a studio where he could drop in and record the lines. By this time Eddie knew Jiminy so well that he really didn't need close direction, and the road-show method of laying down the little cricket's voice tracks worked like a charm.

Meanwhile, still just missing the chance to go onstage in another full-scale evening with Jack Benny, Eddie continued to work on his dream of bringing a one-man show, this time his own, back to the stage. There was no question that he had nailed Jack's personality. While in San Francisco, he was cast to play "Jack" in a TV spot, opposite Frank Nelson, the mustachioed nemesis on so many of Benny's radio and TV shows. The script was set up like a typical Benny bit: Jack, looking for help, sees a man with his back turned and says politely, "Oh, Mister? Mister?"

And Nelson whirls on him with a manic, nearly satanic grin and says "Yessssss?"

Eddie said, "Well, you can imagine how intimidating it was doing the Benny role with the wonderful Frank Nelson. It was just the same as with Dennis Day — I was dying to know what he thought of my performance. We shot part of it, where I'm all agitated — 'Oh, for heaven's sake! Why must you always aggravate me?' — and then cut for a different set-up, and I asked Frank, 'Am I doing okay?'"

Frank gave him a strange look and unbuttoned his sleeve and rolled it up. Eddie said, "He just pointed to his arm. It was covered with goose pimples. In a sort of quavering voice, Frank said, 'That's how good you are.' It was an honor that choked me up."

No wonder that Eddie wanted so badly to put together another one-man show about Benny. He plugged away at developing his new script, but that was demanding work. As he said, it was to prove a long and difficult process:

EDDIE CARROLL: I had finished writing and rewriting and editing the Jack Benny theatrical show and had titled it *Jack Benny: Laughter in Bloom*. Well, I say "finished." I mean it was in shape to be tried out, at least. As an actor, I knew that once I hit the stage with the show, I would find places that needed further revision and rewriting.

When you see how the material plays before real audiences, you begin to learn about points where the timing or the blocking needs to be different, or maybe the audience laughs its head off over a throw-away bit but doesn't react to the jokes you've really struggled to write, showing you where the script has to be re-thought. Inevitably, over time there would be many changes in the structure and the material of the play, and the running time would shrink or grow as I edited and revised the script. But once I had a version of the script that I could at least begin with, I began to look for casinos and booking agents that might be interested in producing it.

One production team asked me to fly to New York to audition the piece and to check out theaters in the city and in Atlantic City as possible venues. Finding a place to play in either area is unbelievably tough. Most theaters in both cities have a waiting period of a year, minimum, before they can commit to a show opening.

In the meantime, I began doing bits of the show in seminars about the acting business in California and I tried out slightly different versions of it in one-night appearances all over the country. The show always ended well as I picked up the violin that had been in plain sight all evening long and massacred "Love in Bloom" the way Jack always did. The audiences would applaud, laugh, and even stamp and cheer when I finished with a flourish and a triumphant "Ha!"

Those audiences helped me gauge the success of the material, but it got awfully lonely for me out on the road, away from Carolyn and the kids. I found the one-night stands worked better for me in letting me pace the material. I coaxed Carolyn to come along with me and direct the show on those occasions, and it made a tremendous difference.

She would set up the sound and light cues in tech rehearsals and would be the stage, lighting, and sound manager during the performance. Her presence cured my loneliness and made the show run so much smoother that I knew she would have to be part of any big production.

Now that Eddie had mostly recovered from the debilitating effects of Lyme disease but still lacked a permanent home for the full show, in 1990 he and Carolyn took a special trip, one they had dreamed about for a long time. They had visited Europe more than once, but both of them found Asian culture and history fascinating, and they had been on the lookout for an opportunity to travel to that part of the globe. Eddie checked into tour prices and the Carrolls decided they had two choices: for about the same money they could either visit Japan or else take a tour that included Singapore, Thailand, China, and Hong Kong. After some discussion, they decided to put Japan on hold.

Eddie often told stories of the journey:

EDDIE CARROLL: In Singapore we noticed an impressive mosque. From the street, it appeared to be very close to our hotel, but somehow we could never find our way to it. We wandered for literally hours without being able to locate it.

Then on our last day in the city we were walking up the hill toward the hotel when we heard bells and chimes ringing out from somewhere just below the hotel driveway. We ventured over to look down and started to laugh. The elusive mosque we had been searching for was just down the hill below the driveway.

That beautiful structure was right on the hotel doorstep. I thought we were just destined to see that mosque before we left Singapore, and if it hadn't called out to us so musically, we would have completely missed it. What good timing!

After Singapore the Carrolls ventured to a village in the north of China, where they saw a wedding taking place in an open temple. Carolyn thought it was interesting that the bride and groom wore red, not white, but in speaking with the Chinese, they learned that in China people wear white to funerals, not weddings.

As they were talking with the keepers of the temple, one of them told Eddie and Carolyn that for a small fee they could have a Chinese wedding ceremony. "Well, why not?" asks Carolyn. "We'd been married already in

Eddie. the voice, with "Jason the Underwater Robot" in Epcot.

Los Angeles, California and then again in Edmonton, Alberta. The third time is the charm, so we did it!"

Eddie had told Carolyn before their first marriage ceremony, "I can't promise you security, but our lives will never be dull or boring." They never had been dull or boring up to the Chinese wedding service — and they never would be afterward. Eddie and Carolyn had their photo taken as they sat on their thrones in red silk wedding clothes.

"By then," Carolyn says, "we were so married that it had to last forever — and it did." Not very many Hollywood marriages last that long or make the couple as happy together as Eddie and Carolyn always were.

After China came Thailand, where they admired the people, who had a great sense of humor and were always smiling. Thailand has an ancient and rich culture, and Carolyn, especially, enjoyed seeing the temples and wats. She took Eddie to so many of them that at last he pled, "Please, not another one. I'm watted out!"

Still, the Carrolls visited eight of them and stood in awe before the giant reclining Buddha in Bangkok's Wat Pho. The enormous statue is over 140 feet in length and is covered in brilliantly shining gold leaf, making Eddie and Carolyn feel as dwarfed as Jiminy would be by a reclining NBA star. Then it was on to Hong Kong, which Carolyn thought was "one massive ongoing shopping mall." However, she adds, "I was not born to shop." Still, they found so many wonderful places to explore and sights to take in that they made their trip a grand adventure. They loved taking a ride on a real Chinese junk, and they agreed that they had experienced a glorious three-week vacation.

The Castle all dressed up for the 25th Anniversary.

Soon it was back to California and back to work. Eddie did a few personal appearances as Jack Benny and then lots more because of his role as Jiminy Cricket. In 1990, Eddie, who had been with his family to Disneyland scores of times, was invited to the other coast to record some tracks and do some promotions for the upcoming twentieth anniversary of Walt Disney World in Orlando, Florida.

The sheer size of Disney's dream park thrilled the Carrolls: "In Disneyland, the Magic Kingdom is only one small park, but Disney World has the Magic Kingdom, the World Showcase, Epcot, the Studio, the water parks — it would take a family at least a full week to visit all the different themed areas of Disney World. It's truly magnificent, and I thought of the whole expanse as the Country of Disney. It has as much acreage as some small nations."

And speaking of Epcot, it takes a good ear to recognize Eddie's voice in the staccato tones of Jason, the Underwater Robot, at the Living Seas attraction, but that really is Eddie in yet another voiceover role. During this trip not only did Eddie record tons of Jiminy material, but learned that the Disney folks wanted him back soon.

Accordingly, the next year, when the family returned to Disney World for the actual Twentieth Anniversary celebration, "as we drove into the parking lot with our radio tuned to an in-park station that gave helpful hints, suddenly Jiminy popped up, advising us on how to get to the parking areas and then how to find the right tram to the theme parks." There was Eddie talking to himself in the material he had recorded months before. The Carrolls came down with a serious set of giggles that made the folks on the tram wonder what these folks knew that made them enjoy even a tram ride to the Magic Kingdom.

Glenn and Dorothy Springer (Carolyn's parents) in front; Russie Taylor (voice of Minnie Mouse), Eddie, and Wayne Allwine (voice of Mickey Mouse) behind them.

EDDIE CARROLL: And when we got into the parks, seeing the parades and the fireworks show was awesome. Whenever Jiminy was coming over the speaker system, I loved watching the faces of the fans in the parks — it gave me a sense of extraordinary excitement. No one knows that I'm the voice they hear as Jiminy, but even so, the people we meet are all truly nice, just like the Disney employees and all the dedicated Disneyana Fan Club members. It was such a joy to visit the parks and just let our inner children come out to play and enjoy all the shows and rides!

Carolyn remembers that in California's Disneyland the family always went on the Pinocchio ride (the attraction was not duplicated in Orlando). Eddie was the voice of Jiminy in it, naturally, but he had also voiced a couple of other characters for the ride's brief encapsulation of the film, and the Carrolls always enjoyed the experience of being "in" *Pinocchio.*

By the time of the 1991 Disney World trip, Glenn and Dorothy Springer, Carolyn's mother and dad, were living in Florida and joined Eddie and Carolyn on the occasion of Dorothy's seventieth birthday. The Carrolls arranged for a special birthday luncheon at the Liberty Bell Tavern in the Orlando Magic Kingdom's Revolutionary-War themed Liberty Square, and the next night they treated Glenn and Dot to dinner at the upscale Victoria and Albert's Restaurant in the magnificent Grand Floridian Hotel, which is on the monorail line to the Magic Kingdom and has a wonderful view across the lagoon of the theme park.

Bill Farmer, voice of Goofy.

The menus came with Dorothy's and Glenn's names embossed in gold on the cover, and Eddie thought of this as another gift from Jiminy: "Even though they had lived only ninety miles away for about four years, that occasion was my in-laws' first trip to Disney World. Their excitement thrilled me. What an experience we shared."

The working side of the trip gave Eddie a rare chance to do voice acting alongside other actors, because part of the celebrations involved a number of radio interviews with Disney characters. Eddie and Carolyn got to know Bill and Jen Farmer better as Eddie's Jiminy shared the microphones with Bill's Goofy.

The Farmers, like the Carrolls, are unassuming and cheerful, and they hit it off very well indeed. Bill speaks very warmly of those years: "I met Eddie a few months after I began voicing Goofy. I started doing Goofy in early 1987, and they introduced us not long after that time. I knew that Eddie had been doing Jiminy, but had never met him before that. He was one of the first real actors that I really met in Hollywood — you know, my mother always warned me, 'Don't go to Hollywood, the people are awful and the Mafia owns the whole town' [Bill's mom in his interpretation sounds unnervingly like Jonathan Winters's Maudie Frickert]. But Eddie was very down to earth, just a great guy, always genuinely interested in what you were doing and he always put you at ease."

Though Eddie had worked with Disney for so much longer than Bill had, he never offered unsolicited advice — though Bill occasionally would ask him for a tip about this or that. "At first we didn't get to see each other all that often," Bill says, "because like all the other voices, I usually was stuck into a recording studio alone, just as Eddie was. But we'd get together a couple or three times a year, sometimes at one of our homes for holidays or barbecues, other times at Disney celebrations, and it was always like seeing an old college buddy."

When asked if he saw much of Jiminy in Eddie, Bill laughs and says, "Of course! When you do a character like Jiminy or like Jack Benny long enough, they sort of influence your personality, or vice-versa, maybe. Like me and the Curse of Goofy."

The curse of Goofy? Surely people will want to know about that, and Bill obliges:

BILL FARMER: There is a curse that comes along with Goofy. I blame everything on Goofy, anyway — if I ever get stopped for speeding, I'm gonna try to use Goofy to get out of it: 'Gawrsh, Officer! I didn't know I was goin' too fast!' The curse says that once you begin to play Goofy, goofy things begin to happen to you.

Anyway, a few years ago I was out in our yard wearing sweat pants, putting Christmas lights around the gutters of the house, and I had a stepladder out and all. I was climbing down to the ground when a riser from our sprinkler system caught my heel and tripped me up. Now ordinarily, you'd just either catch yourself or fall to the ground, and that would be it. But the curse of Goofy means there are more levels to it. It's layered. It's complex.

All right, there was a rose bush behind me. Normally you'd expect I'd fall into the rose bush and that might be funny. However, this is the curse of Goofy. So I stumbled into the *first* rose bush sort of spinning and trying to get my balance, and the thorns caught my sweat pants and ripped them right off. And then, with no pants, I fell into the *second* rose bush. Backward. And as I fell, involuntarily I gave the Goofy yell: Yah-hah-hah-hoowie!

Bill's lovely wife Jen, a film director and producer, is laughing by this point in the story. She says, "I'm upstairs at the computer and I literally heard his Goofy yell and I thought maybe I should go downstairs and see if I was a widow. But, hey, it's Bill. Anyway, I was working on an e-mail and thought I'd finish that first. So I did, and by the time I got to the top of the steps, here came Bill limping inside, clutching his pants all wadded up in his hand. You remember that cartoon series 'Love Is' with all the little naked cherubs? I don't remember a single one of them that said 'Love Is…pulling thorns from your beloved's butt!"

Bill grins sheepishly. "The next day I had a recording session as Goofy. So I went in to the studio and they said, 'Okay, Bill, we'll get you a stool to sit on and we'll get started.' I said in a small voice, 'I think I'll stand today.'" With a shrug, Bill adds, "See, Eddie was lucky. He got the nice guy, Jiminy, to influence his life. I got Goofy!"

Tina was a beautiful bride.

Not long after that second trip to Disney World and Dot Springer's birthday celebration in 1991, Eddie had yet another role to play in real life: Father of the Bride. After a five-year-long courtship, Tina was getting married, and she was a radiant, sensational bride. All of the Carrolls' friends and family attended the festive occasion. Carolyn admits she had a rough moment when the doors opened and Leland escorted his mother down the aisle while the soloist sang "Ave Maria." Carolyn had to light a candle, which she did with shaking hands.

And then Eddie had a tough entrance himself:

EDDIE CARROLL: I walked in with my lovely daughter Tina on my arm as the organist played "Here Comes the Bride." My adorable little girl was having me walk her down to give her away to the man who was becoming her husband.

You think of the little things at such times — the occasion when as a teenager Tina had scratched the car or some such thing and I was bawling her out and my voice just slipped into that wonderful Jack Benny frustration mode. Tina stopped me and said, "Dad, I could take you more seriously if you'd scold me as yourself and not as Jack Benny," and of course I had to laugh, and there went my anger out the window.

So many beautiful memories came flooding in, and my heart was just so full. When we arrived at the altar, I lifted Tina's veil and kissed her. I saw her groom Rick Monti mouth to her, "You look beautiful!"

Then I walked over and stood next to Carolyn. Through the rest of the service we held hands, remembering our own weddings — all three of them. The reception was a sensational party filled with fun and laughter, and then the most thoughtful thing happened. Tina and I were to dance together for the Father of the Bride dance, and Carolyn had the DJ surprise me by playing Linda Ronstadt's version of "When You Wish Upon a Star." Lovely, just lovely.

CHAPTER 17

Jiminy Does Japan, Benny Does Cucamonga

As the months after Tina's wedding passed, Eddie found both of his major roles gaining steam. By now he was comfortable both in Jiminy's tiny shoes and Jack's size sevens:

EDDIE CARROLL: Jiminy voice-overs and Jack's one-person show began to pick up enormously in my career. I no longer complained about my high hairline because all I had to do to get into character for Jack was to comb my hair back and change my glasses, and there he appeared. After much consideration, Carolyn and I had decided to take a bold step to open each performance of *Laughter in Bloom:* with the permission of Jack Benny's estate, we would play three minutes of bits from the real Jack Benny TV show, funny moments that always got big laughs.

One was a TV version of the holdup sketch, in which a bandit stops penny-pinching Jack (in a pouring rain) with a gun and the snarled threat, "Your money or your life!" Jack has a sustained, pained silent pause in which laughter builds like a rising tide. When the impatient gunman repeats his demand, Jack waspishly snaps, "I'm thinking it over!"

Another was a sketch in which Jack, having lost a bet with his valet Rochester, has to do the shopping. In the grocery he passes a table offering free samples of cake. However, because the sign at the table is not specific — it just says "Free," not "Free: One Slice" — Jack takes the whole cake, sets it in his shopping cart, and then licks some stray icing off his fingers. Then he remembers to collect the silverware. Then the tablecloth. Then the sign itself, to whoops of audience laughter.

While the audience in the theater is enjoying these, I'm backstage speaking along with Jack's lines to get into his cadence and speech rhythm. After the multimedia pre-show there was a blackout. I would step on stage, strike a Jack Benny pose, and the spotlight would pick me up as the pre-recorded announcer said, "Ladies and gentlemen, Mr. Jack Benny!"

Many reviewers commented that it took a lot of confidence for me to show the audience footage of the actual Jack Benny, and then come onstage in his persona. All of them agreed that it worked, though. Someone who had never seen the show before once told me, "You know, to tell the truth,

Eddie as Jack Benny.

when that spotlight hit you, my first thought was 'He looks *sort* of like Jack Benny,' but then you did your walk across stage and said your first line… and you *were* Jack!" Well, you know, if you can get over the initial hurdle of that side-by-side comparison, then you have the audience rooting for you, and that gives an actor fantastic energy and assurance.

You might think it would be harder to cram myself into Jiminy's small frame, but thank heavens the animators took care of the physical appearance. As for the voice, each time I had a recording session for a Jiminy project I would pop an audiotape into the car stereo as I drove to the studio and speak along as Jiminy talked. When I parked in the studio lot, I was Jiminy. By this time I had done Jiminy so long that his verbal tics were second nature and I was totally aware of how he worded ideas, of his habit of dropping his *g*'s, his slight whistle as he pronounced *s*'s, the wispy quality of his breath as he spoke, and his Midwestern accent and phrasing.

Now that they came easily whenever I needed to summon them up, it was always an absolutely delightful experience each time I performed either Jack or Jiminy. I respected and loved both of those characters so much. I cherish the memories of all the times I performed as both, and whenever I need a little boost of confidence, I do what Jiminy recommended and give a little whistle.

But though performance opportunities came flooding in, the meteorological situation was a lot drier. Even that changed overnight. Southern California had gone through a decade of drought, but February and March of 1991 brought torrential rains, pouring down at an inch and a half every hour, a huge volume that the parched soil could not soak up, and the area saw historic flooding. Nothing could stop the deluge of water sheeting down off the higher slopes and into the valleys. Freeways had to close, and in the canyons around Hollywood, whole roads were simply washed away. With so many vital transportation arteries blocked, the entire city came to a virtual standstill.

Carolyn recalls, "Homes slid down hills. Debris washed all over town, especially in the San Fernando Valley where we live. We even saw cars floating down our street, every make and model from Cadillac, Mercedes, and Lexus on down. The water rose so high that mud clogged the engine compartment of Leland's Camaro and he had to have it cleaned out."

The flood had invaded the Carrolls' garage, which didn't fully dry out for months. That spring was a difficult one for everyone in Southern California, and for those whose homes were destroyed or damaged, a sad time as well. The Carrolls were resilient though, and they weathered the storms and saw it through.

As the floods passed, the water receded, and the debris was cleaned up, life began to return to normal. Though sometimes he had to take torturous routes while repairs were going on, Eddie resumed his trips in to the Disney Studio for his recording sessions as Jiminy. Then one Monday morning in June, Eddie received another momentous call, this one from his voiceover agent, Don Pitts, who led off by asking, "Would you like to go to Japan?" Here's how Eddie responded:

EDDIE CARROLL: I shouted, "Yes, we would *love* to go to Japan!" Don explained that when he'd arrived in his office that morning, he found a fax waiting from him from a Japanese company. It wanted to produce an educational project called "Red Light, Green Light," comprised of a book and video. The book would follow along with the video production and the idea was to offer English speech instruction to young Japanese children, helping them to deal with the L/R speech syndrome.

Later I learned from Japanese speech teachers that when children are young, they exercise certain muscles in their mouth and become accustomed to using only the ones required for their native language. In Japanese, the letters L and R aren't used, and when the students grow older and study English, they don't know how to form the sounds and have a hard time both producing the L and R sounds and distinguishing between them.

The Japanese company had asked the Disney Studio if they could license Jiminy to be the spokesman for the program. Jiminy was a very popular character already in Japan, though of course in *Pinocchio* and other appearances, either a Japanese actor had dubbed in his voice or else he had appeared with Japanese subtitles. The Disney Studio and the Japanese company reached an agreement for the loan-out of Jiminy's services, and now the Japanese company asked if I could come to Japan and record the track for the program. And they meant right away. We would need to fly to Tokyo that week!

Fortunately we had our passports ready, and we hastily made preparations for the assignment, which would last for a little over a week. Carolyn and I flew over, tremendously excited. As it worked out, I had to do only eight hours of recording, six on one day and two on the next. The English parts were easy — Jiminy would tell the students, "This is a *horse*. This is a *house*," but in addition, I also had the task of giving instructions in Japanese. Needless to say, I don't speak Japanese. Fortunately, a linguist wrote out the lines phonetically and stood by to correct my pronunciation. I had developed a good ear — I had to, of course, in my line of show business — and the linguist was often happy after one or two takes, a shorter time than they had anticipated. Because we wrapped up the taping so quickly, Carolyn and I had the rest of our eight-day stay to enjoy Japan.

Let me give you one piece of advice if you are considering a visit to Japan. Bring two suitcases. One holds your clothes and the other holds the money you'll need.

Believe me, it's worth it. The company treated Carolyn and me as if we were top-name stars, VIPs. They took us to enjoy a meal of Kobe beef cooked on a rock. We visited a farmhouse with an open-fire barbecue. We toured the picturesque countryside.

Now, here's what I mean by bringing a suitcase full of money: In a restaurant I ordered coffee, which came in a demitasse. An extra-small demitasse. That cost five dollars back then. Two seconds later, the waiter noticed my cup was empty and asked if I wanted a refill, and I said, "Yes, thank you." He poured the tiny splash of coffee and charged me another five dollars. I asked, "How much to leave the pot?" and he very politely answered, "You couldn't afford it." Luckily for me it was excellent coffee.

Now, you know that last part is not true. I'm channeling Jack Benny again. The real truth is that not only was the company very kindly covering our expenses, but I also received a paycheck for the work. It was a dream assignment, and once more I thanked that lucky star that another wish had come true.

The instructional video led to similar assignments. A project very much like the Japanese one was put together for China, but this time Eddie went to Boston to record it under the auspices of Harvard University. Then to help American children learn to speak Spanish, Jiminy was used as the narrator of "The Ugly Duckling," with the visuals in the story used to reinforce the Spanish vocabulary.

While in Japan, Eddie and Carolyn became close friends with a vice-president of the company that had hired Eddie, Guy Cihi, and his fiancée, Keoko. A couple of years later the two married and came to L.A. for a reception. While the Carrolls were in Japan, Guy saw to it that Keoko provided guidance and translation for Eddie and Carolyn as they toured the country. When Guy and Keoko came to L.A., the Carrolls were happy to reciprocate.

During the Carrolls' stay in Japan, on Eddie's recording days Keoko and a driver took Carolyn all over to visit the magnificent old temples.

Carolyn says, "I learned to wash my hands in a trough before entering and to sweep the incense toward me with my hands for healing."

She had a memorable meal with Keoko as well: "One day for lunch we went to a small restaurant and Keoko ordered for us. She chose large bottles of beer for our beverage. They brought the food to the table, and she politely turned her head away while taking off the porcelain lid cov-

Guy and Keoko Ciki's wedding reception.

ering a dish. I was given mine and saw that the bowl contained broth, a boiled potato, and tiny, wriggling things. I was glad I had the beer, because it helped me swallow whatever it was. I had no idea what I'd eaten and didn't want to upset Keoko by saying, 'What in the world was *that?*'"

Weeks later, back home in Encino, Carolyn was reading a spy novel set in Japan, and it described the very dish: baby eels. Carolyn says, "When I'm traveling, I love to sample the local food and if it's exotic, I try to be brave about eating it. In this case, I'm glad I didn't know and didn't ask what was swimming around in my bowl!"

Over the two days of Eddie's intensive recording sessions, Carolyn estimates she walked over thirty miles, visiting several historic Shinto temples and the beautiful Imperial Gardens. Though there are no street signs and the buildings are all high-rises, she never once got lost. Then when Eddie wrapped up the taping and joined her for sightseeing, he learned to rely on her instincts. "We were out seeing Edo, the old city," she says, "and Eddie turned right. I stopped him and said, 'No, we have to turn left to go back to the hotel.' He went along with me, and I had chosen the correct turn. Eddie asked, 'How in the world did you know which way to go?' I told him 'I don't know. I just had a feeling it was left.'"

As they had been a few years earlier with the Thais, again the Carrolls felt impressed by the politeness of the courteous Japanese. Once when the Carrolls were in a bullet-train station, trying to figure out a map of the routes, a Japanese gentleman noticed their struggle to understand the huge, complex map. He came up, gently touched Carolyn's elbow, and motioned for her to follow him. Eddie fell into line behind Carolyn, feeling a little bewildered and a bit startled.

The man led them to a ticket window with location names posted in Japanese and English and gestured for them to indicate their destination. Eddie did so, and the gentleman got the tickets for the couple, led them to the correct train, and saw them safely aboard. Imagine that happening in New York! However, it did happen in California, at least once. A few months later, Eddie and Carolyn were having lunch in an open-patio San Fernando Valley restaurant when they noticed a young Japanese couple at a nearby table ordering a meal with difficulty, speaking broken English. They then spread out a road map, bent over it, and murmured worriedly to each other in Japanese.

Eddie and Carolyn remembered the help they had received in Japan, so they went over and learned that the couple worked for a sporting-goods company and needed to get to Orange County, to the south. Eddie drew a colored line along the route, knowing how confusing L.A. freeways can be even to natives. The young man and woman thanked the Carrolls profusely, and Eddie and Carolyn explained how they had been helped in Japan. The couple was so grateful that they wrote down their address and invited the Carrolls to visit them the next time they came to Japan. Later, Eddie told Carolyn, "Doesn't it feel good to be able to give something back when you get a gift?"

Months after the Japanese trip, back in Encino, Eddie got another delightful call. The municipality of Rancho Cucamonga was planning to erect a statue to Jack Benny. "Hmmmm, what a coincidence," Eddie mused in his Jack Benny voice.

EDDIE CARROLL: It all went back to a famous routine on the Jack Benny radio program, which Jack later reprised many times on the TV version of his show. The great voice actor Mel Blanc, who spoke for all the Warner Bros. cartoon stars from Bugs Bunny, Daffy Duck, and Porky Pig to Yosemite Sam and Tweetie Pie was a semi-regular on the Benny Program, and in an often repeated bit, Benny and his gang would be in a train station ready to depart on a journey. They would stop their dialogue now and then to listen to the PA announcements.

Mel was the train announcer. His droning voice would come out of the loudspeakers saying, "Your attention, please. Train now leaving on Track Five for Anaheim, Azusa, and Cuc……….a-mongaaaa!" The break in "Cucamonga" got longer and longer, and just the silence between the first syllable and the next one became a sure-fire gag. That was Benny's genius, by the way: a radio comedian who got huge laughs from silence!

The gag first aired in a Benny radio broadcast done on January 7, 1945, and it became one of the standard jokes on the Benny show, so well-loved that audiences would begin laughing when Mel's first words came over the P.A. The three California cities in Mel's announcement are real, but no train route ever directly connected them. Mel's train ran on tracks that existed only in imagination, but the comic bit became so popular that it put the three cities on the map. Well, in gratitude, in 1947 Cucamonga threw a huge celebration for Jack Benny, who showed up in a Maxwell to be the grand marshal of a parade.

And now, many years later, the town had changed its name slightly and wanted to erect a statue in Jack's memory. They asked me to attend the unveiling of this statue, and I took great pride in accepting this honor. The statue is a life-sized replica of Jack, in one of his most familiar poses, done by the artist and renowned sculptor Lawrence Noble. It was thrilling to see how the people at the event loved the memory of Jack, and I knew that if I ever got the chance I would bring *Laughter in Bloom* to Rancho Cucamonga for a performance in his honor.

The trips to Japan and to the marginally less exotic Rancho Cucamonga gave Eddie wonderful new stories to tell, too. By this time he had found a favorite coffee and brunch spot, the Sportsmen's Lodge Coffee Shop on Ventura Boulevard. It was a venerable establishment. In the 1930s, the Lodge featured its own trout pond, and visitors could fish for a trout, catch it, and the restaurant would clean and cook it for them. It is in Studio City, not far from the old Republic Studio. Stars of Western films began to hang out there: John Wayne, Rex Allen, Gene Autry, and Roy Rogers all dropped in back in the old days.

Some of them were still showing up now and then when Eddie and his friends started a routine of Saturday brunches and coffee klatches. Eddie got to know Gene Autry, who in his later years needed to lean heavily on a cane to get around. Squeaky-voiced Pat Buttram had played Gene's sidekick in many a Western and he frequently showed up to reminisce about the old days with Gene.

Eddie remembered,

EDDIE CARROLL: Gene had some unusual canes. Once Carolyn and I were having brunch and Gene came in and sat with us. When we were about to leave, he looked around for his cane and couldn't find it. He said he must have left it in the men's room, and because he had some difficulty in walking, I told him I'd go look for it.

I found it leaning against the wall near the sink. It was dark brown, nearly black and when I picked it up, I was startled because it felt so light although it seemed sturdy. I turned it over and over in my hands, noticing that it didn't seem to have any grain in it at all.

So I took it back and handed it over and asked Gene what kind of wood his cane was made of. "Oh, that's not wood," he said. "They gave that to me once when I went to Spain. That cane's made of a specially-treated bull's urethra and penis."

We said goodbye to Gene, and wondering what the cane's *knob* was made from, I told Carolyn, "I'll be back in ten or fifteen minutes. I'm going to wash my hands for a *long* time."

On another occasion, Eddie noticed Pat Buttram coming slowly into the dining room. His head was down and he was barely shuffling along, taking painfully slow baby steps. Fearing he might have had a stroke, Eddie jumped up and ran to help him, asking, "Pat, are you okay?"

Buttram looked up, grinned, and winked. In his rusty-gate squeaking voice, he replied, "I'm fine. Gene's gonna be along later, an' I'm just practicin' so's I can walk alongside of him." Eddie could mimic Buttram flawlessly.

One good audience for Eddie's stories was the Barranco family, Carolyn's second family. Their son, Rob, had met Carolyn at a Junior Dance Masters Convention at the Ambassador Hotel when she was fourteen and he was seventeen. They became instant friends and are still close to this day. Rob served as Tina and Leland's godfather.

The best part of the friendship was that Carolyn's and Rob's parents liked each other as well. Rob's dad and mom, Tony and Toni, would get together with Carolyn's parents Glenn and Dorothy on weekends and they would all play cards — games which Rob and Carolyn usually won.

"They accused us of cheating," she says, "but truthfully we never cheated or signaled each other."

After the Carrolls married, Eddie and Rob became as close as brothers. The Barrancos loved to laugh, and Eddie was a never-ending source of entertainment for them as he would talk of his adventures and misadventures in show business.

Rob and Eddie enjoying their stories.

On one occasion, Rob — known professionally as choreographer and director Rob Barran — was staging *Ain't Misbehaving* at Harvey's in Lake Tahoe. Eddie suggested to Carolyn that they go to see the show, even though they already had reservations in Mazatlan, Mexico, for a warm-weather vacation. It worked out, though: Eddie got tickets for the morning after the Carrolls flew back home from Mexico. They came in straight from the tropical climate of Mazatlan, unpacked their bathing suits and shorts, and repacked with thermals, sweaters, and jackets, and caught an early flight to Tahoe the next morning.

It was bizarre, but Carolyn says it was also fun and silly. And as it turned out, they had a great time with Rob and loved the show. So choreographer Rob, who always enjoyed Eddie's show-business stories, actually became the star of one of Eddie's anecdotes.

CHAPTER 18

*Upheavals Good and Bad —
or Shake, Rattle and Roll*

In July of 1992, Eddie was asked to present another statue of Jack Benny, this one in the atrium of the Academy of Television Arts and Sciences. Though busts represent the other great celebrities, the only life-sized standing statues in the Academy are of Jack and Johnny Carson, who never made a secret of how much Jack had inspired him. Another full-sized statue is of Lucille Ball, seated on the rim of a fountain. The ceremony impressed on Eddie "how loved and revered Jack Benny still is today. He left a wonderful legacy."

Once again Eddie met Joan Benny, Jack's daughter whom Jack had loved deeply. Eddie had read *Sunday Nights at Seven,* the 1990 book that combines Jack's unfinished autobiography with chapters written by Joan, and the biography not only had helped Eddie deepen his understanding of Jack's personality but also had revealed how deeply father and daughter had loved each other.

Eddie also met another Benny biographer, Irving Fein, who had been Jack's manager for the last twenty-eight years of his life. From then on, Eddie and Irving lunched together whenever they could, and Eddie recalled many fabulous talks about Jack that they had. He also read Fein's hefty 1977 book, *Jack Benny: An Intimate Biography*, in which he found both insights and fun stories not well-known to the public.

Fein had also become George Burns's manager after Gracie's passing and supplied the push that persuaded George to accept the role in the film version of *The Sunshine Boys* that was to have been Jack's. After Jack learned he had pancreatic cancer, he had specifically asked Irving to make sure the part went to George — a good call, as the role not only won George an Academy Award, but completely revived his career, and after emerging from semiretirement Burns enjoyed an extraordinary second round of celebrity, thanks to his lifelong friend Jack. His

1977 appearance in the movie *Oh, God!* netted a Best Actor Academy Award for George, and his frequent movie and TV appearances won him a whole new generation of fans. He also became an author, cowriting with others many volumes of reminiscences, anecdotes, and advice about how to grow old either gracefully or disgracefully, depending on your preference.

Eddie and Jack Benny statue at Academy of Television Arts and Sciences.

Through Fein, Eddie met Burns: "I was in Irving's office and he introduced me to George, who with Hal Goldman was writing a book, *Wisdom of the 90s*. I felt like a fan — George fascinated me. He was a funny, warm, delightful man bubbling over with so many stories about his friendship with Jack, all delivered in that wry voice of his. I hung on every word he said, and I remembered his last bit of advice: 'Listen, kid, always have a reason to get out of bed in the morning.' And I took it to heart."

Carolyn confirms that "Eddie adored being with George partly because he always called Eddie 'kid!' He was in his nineties then, so to George most people were kids. When I knew Eddie would be meeting George, I could never wait for Eddie to get back home and share the stories George told with me. They were hysterical — and many of them shouldn't be printed, even now — but what I loved most was that Eddie would nearly collapse with upheavals of laughter when he was re-telling them to me. He incorporated several of them into *Laughter in Bloom*. You can tell which ones those were because when Eddie used them, he'd still laugh at them himself even on stage."

Eddie was turning sixty in 1993, but he was working harder than ever:

EDDIE CARROLL: Retire? I had no need to retire. Besides, retire to what? Playing golf, fishing, watching TV? I believe that people should retire only when they're no longer happy doing their jobs. As for me, I love what I do and it brings me tremendous fulfillment and joy. Carolyn and I like to read and the long airplane trips give us time to do that. As I toured more and more in *Laughter in Bloom*, literally barnstorming the country from West Coast to East and all stops in between, I learned to enjoy even the time on the planes.

I had asked Carolyn to take over officially as the overall producer and show manager, and she gave up her practice to do that. With the kids grown, we stayed together on all those long journeys. After every show, I go out into the lobby and chat with the members of the audience, and even in the early days of touring, they'd often ask, "How do you stand so much traveling?"

The answer is that we got that down pat years ago. In fact, it got to the point where the only really hard part was getting to LAX on the 405 parking lot. Well, it's supposed to be a freeway, but the traffic moves so slowly you feel you've parked.

When the economy tanked and theaters stopped flying us first class — and meals were no longer served in economy — Carolyn would pack turkey, bread, lettuce, tomatoes, and fresh fruit. When the attendants let us know we could lower the trays, we'd pull them down and Carolyn would wipe them down with an antibacterial cleanser — you can't risk getting the flu or a cold on the road — and then we would break out the ingredients and build our sandwiches. Attendants would watch in amazement at how deft we were, but that came with lots of practice.

By this time Lee had finished his pre-med studies and received an offer of a fellowship to Berkeley in cancer research — with pay! We were so happy and proud of him. Carolyn rode to Oakland with him to keep him company, thinking she would be dropped off at the Oakland Airport, but Lee suggested she might go with him to check into his hotel the group was to be housed in.

Carolyn takes up the story: "Boy, I'm sure glad I did. I wouldn't have missed it for anything. Lee checked in and the desk clerk handed him two keys — one to his room and another to the bathroom, which was down the hall. Lee learned from Eddie how to do a perfect deadpan take, and when he gave me that look, I started to laugh. We unlocked his room to discover that it contained a rusty sink, two twin beds, two small desks, one dresser, and a closet with room for twelve hangers. Not only was the room half the size of his bedroom at home, but he had to share it with a roommate.

"It had been a long drive, and I needed to use the bathroom, so down the hall we went. The bathroom must have been converted from an old broom closet. I had to stand in the shower stall to be able to close the door. Leland is six feet two, and he has long legs. When he was, well, seated, his knees jammed against the closed door.

"But it was Berkeley. Very prestigious, right? Then on the very first day of school, one of the students went to his classes wearing his backpack. That's *all* he wore, period. I was back home and while cooking dinner when I heard the news. They gave the name of the student, Andrew Martinez, and — you know moms — my first thought was 'Thank God it wasn't Lee!' Mr. Martinez later became somewhat famous, or maybe infamous, as 'The Naked Guy.' Eddie walked in and I was crumpled up from laughing. It took me awhile to get it together so I could tell him what I thought was so funny."

When they weren't touring with the show, Eddie and Carolyn found lots of activities to keep them busy. A few years before, Eddie had come home one night after a late meeting to hear country music pouring from the house. That surprised him:

EDDIE CARROLL: Nah, I thought, it must be coming from a neighbor's place. Country music wasn't a favorite of either Tina or Lee. But, to my amazement, when I walked in, there were Lee and Carolyn dancing, and he was dressed in Western gear and a great cowboy hat. They were doing the ten-step Country-Western dance in the living room. That particular kind of dance had recently become popular, and Lee had learned how to do it.

Left: Lee in his western outfit. Right: Lee and Carolyn two-steppin'.

Well, Lee led the whole family into it soon. We all became addicts and frequented Denim and Diamonds Restaurant, where they taught lessons in two-step, West Coast swing, and line dances. Eventually we even pulled in other family members.

From then on, Carolyn and I had a ball whenever we could go steppin'. For years we celebrated every birthday, anniversary, Mothers' Day and Fathers' Day at Denim and Diamonds. And years later, when the craze had faded and Denim and Diamonds was closing, Carolyn and I went there for the last night. Lee is still involved with West Coast swing at another club, and he's very good!

Another activity that kept Eddie and Carolyn entertained — well, maybe Eddie more than Carolyn — was horseback riding. Despite never managing to be cast in one, Eddie always loved Westerns, and of course

Ben Cooper had taught him to do a fast draw. Eddie had also become a terrific horseman, and even when he and Carolyn were courting, some of their more memorable dates were on horseback.

She recalls, "One day the horse I was riding decided to lie down, and my favorite Cricket talked me through the process of persuading her to keep standing on all fours. Just as my ride and I got things straightened out, Eddie's horse stepped backward and slid down the cement embankment of the Los Angeles River — not what most people would really call a river, but a concrete streambed that catches the runoff of rain and takes it to the ocean.

"Eddie's horse kept slipping backwards, and Eddie reined him to start up the slope for the top again. Somehow they made it safely, but after that time, I was done with horseback riding, though Eddie still enjoyed it and later Tina took it up and became very good with horses."

In turn, Carolyn loved snorkeling, while Eddie preferred to sit out her swims on the beach. He tried it, but he would always say, "I don't *want* to know what's under that water." Once in Cabo San Lucas, Carolyn went snorkeling, leaving Eddie reading under the shade of a palapa. Carolyn would wave to him every so often, and he would wave back.

Carolyn snorkeling.

Then she dived to take a close look at the reef. She grimaces as she recalls, "A moray eel stuck his head out of the rocks, a few inches from my mask! Now, I'd been told that they wouldn't bite, but had anyone told the eel? I know one thing: morays are not attractive or cuddly. Eddie said that that was the only time he had ever seen anyone in flippers run right across the surface of the water!"

And, perhaps because of Leland's scary experience, Eddie also wasn't crazy about Carolyn's venturing out on the boogie board. When she'd come riding in on a wave, she'd see him standing right at the water's edge, wearing his favorite white baseball cap with a gold Jiminy Cricket pin on the front. If she dived under a wave to avoid being tossed, as soon as she surfaced again, he'd yell anxiously, "Are you okay?" and she'd nod to reassure him.

A few times, when the water was calm, Eddie would venture out on his board, and he even enjoyed riding a moderate wave in to the beach. Carolyn didn't think Eddie should have worried about her so much: "My dad was a Safety Engineer, and I was taught always to practice safety first, which I did." She shrugs and adds with a smile, "Most of the time!"

Then something new came along. A friend of the Carrolls' was Randy Clark, a musician who did a perfect John Lennon in a show called *Beatlemania*, and he called one day to say he was going on a sky dive. Carolyn says, "Randy and I had talked about that a few times, and I was always looking forward to actually doing a jump. How fantastic it would be to enjoy complete freedom! But when I told Eddie, he couldn't even speak for a second — just gave me a look of horror. He finally asked me to promise on everything sacred that I would never attempt a sky dive even in tandem with an instructor. I gave him my promise, but I still felt disappointed. I was always more of a daredevil than Eddie, always wanting to see and do it all if morally possible."

Shortly into the new year, an upheaval of another kind occurred without warning, another natural disaster. This one, though, was sharper than the floods. Eddie vividly recalled what happened:

EDDIE CARROLL: At 4:31 AM on January 17, 1994, an incredible jolt awakened us. Carolyn was thrown completely out of bed, landing on a lampshade, and in a moment I fell to the floor, too. My first thought was that a bomb had gone off, but then we both felt the whole house shaking. The Northridge Quake, at 6.7 on the Richter scale, had just hit.

For what seemed like minutes we couldn't even get our footing. All around us we could hear breakage, creaking and ominous groans coming from the walls. I had never imagined such sounds could be possible. We had been advised to stand in a doorway for safety, but that advice assumes you can reach a doorway without being thrown flat on your face. Carolyn and I kept stumbling and trying to support each other, and we both got badly bruised.

It seemed to go on for an eternity before everything got quiet again. Quiet and dark. We were to learn later that the ground acceleration movement was one of the highest ever recorded in a North American urban area. No wonder it caused so much damage. We knew from the sound that we'd had a lot of breakage, but we were alive with only cuts and bruises.

All the power was off, and the phones. We had sneakers and sweats under the bed in case of an emergency, but the flashlights had rolled around and in the dark it took us a while to find them. When we did find a flashlight and got dressed, the damage we saw inside was just heartbreaking, the furnishings and pictures toppled and scattered all over the floor. We kept hearing a "thunk-thunk-thunk" coming from the backyard.

We checked and found out that the concrete block fence had partly collapsed, and more blocks fell out with each jolt of an aftershock. The pool had lost a third of the water, and waves splashed out with each tremor. When the sun rose and we had enough light to see the whole house, the damage was unbelievable. I went out to the garage and brought the huge trash bin and a shovel inside. "What are you going to do?" Carolyn asked.

"Shovel out the kitchen," I told her. The floor was literally six to nine inches deep in debris, and the same was true in the utility room and bathrooms.

Carolyn said, "That'll ruin the floors!"

I said, "What do you think the floors look like now under all that broken glass and crystal?"

We were grateful to be alive, and with Lee's help we set about trying to pick up the pieces.

Leland had completed his fellowship at Berkeley and was back home for the event. The Carrolls had a five-foot pyramid of beveled-glass shelves with keepsakes on it, placed behind their living-room sofa. The quake had devastated it, leaving nothing unbroken except for a six-inch porcelain angel that had been a gift sent to Carolyn from a grateful client. It was made of German porcelain and had delicate fingers joined in an attitude of prayer and lovely pointed wings. Carolyn saw the angel in sunlight and stooped to pick her up. Lee stopped her and warned her, "Don't reach into all that glass. If there's another tremor, you could get badly cut."

But the angel had made it that far, and Carolyn rescued her, placing her under a heavy quilt box to keep her safe. Over the next days, first Eddie and then Lee found the angel under the quilt box and, thinking they were doing Carolyn a favor, each of them put the figurine on top of the box. Carolyn put her back under it, where she would be sheltered. The angel is still in the Carroll home today.

As the family worked on the house, they started to smell gas. When they stepped into the yard, they heard a hissing coming from two doors down the street. Eddie and Leland hurried over to find the problem, while Carolyn discovered that the phones were working again and tried to call the gas company. Thousands of people in the city were trying to do the same thing, and although Carolyn got through to report the emergency, she remained on hold for 52 minutes before she finally was able to talk to a representative.

Eddie and Leland had discovered that a fence had fallen onto a neighbor's gas meter. Fortunately, the owners of the house were away, because they had workmen coming in to do some remodeling. Until the gas could be turned off, there wasn't much anyone could do, but at least they were able to get back and let Carolyn know what the problem was. Meanwhile they would have to be very careful.

And then Carolyn noticed that their next-door neighbors, who spoke little English, were stirring in their house. Their water heater had fallen over, and Carolyn saw the woman of the house lighting a candle — the electricity was still out. Carolyn hastily went over and mimed blowing out the candle to prevent an explosion and got the message across.

Carolyn thought of her sister Gloria, whose husband was away from home, off in Illinois visiting his family there. Gloria was alone, except for her two silky-coated dogs. Like the Carrolls, she had wakened in the dark and, trying to reach and comfort the terrified dogs, she had run into a half-closed door, badly gashing her eyebrow.

Carolyn says, "Trying to get to an emergency room was out of the question — there was so much damage to the streets, and many of the hospitals had suffered from the quake, too. The hospitals that were open were packed with emergency patients, many severely injured, and the hospital systems were barely working. Glo brought her dogs over and stayed with us for a few days."

Seeing the cut on his aunt's forehead, Leland put his medical studies to good use: "Lee used butterfly stitches to close Glo's wound. When she could get to a doctor, he took a look and, impressed, asked her who had applied the butterfly stitches to her cut. She told him it was her nephew, and the doctor said, 'He did a great job.' He left the stitches in place.

"Her poor dogs were so scared. When we let them outside, one of them ran blindly right into the pool and Glo went in after him. The other one cut the corner short and fell into the Jacuzzi — and I had to go in after her!"

The gas company eventually arrived and turned off the gas to stop the leak. Carolyn fired up the outdoor propane grill and boiled water on it and made instant coffee. That evening they cooked dinner by lantern light and candle light, the candles standing in bowls of water for safety reasons because the house was still constantly shaking. Fortunately, they had a water-purification system, so they had access to safe water, unlike many others who had to rely on bottled water for days or even weeks. Eventually the city asked all residents to place debris at the front curb for clean-up. That task took the Carrolls days, with lots of back-straining hauling. All down the street you could see a jumbled assortment of broken things: chimneys, water heaters, block-wall fences, furniture, mounds of broken glass and splintered wood. It looked like a scene from a disaster movie.

Still, the Carrolls felt lucky that no one had been seriously hurt. "We had that star shining over our house," Carolyn says, "and we gave many, many thanks."

Tina got in touch and wanted to come and help, but the freeways were still damaged and overcrowded, so Carolyn asked her to wait for a few days — and then when she and her husband were able to arrive from their home in Orange County, a swarm of tremors showed up at the same time they did.

Tina's husband Rick ran into the kitchen — the worst place to be in a quake — and they yelled for him to move to a safer location. Carolyn had thought about Tina and Rick during the initial quake when the crystal and dishes were crashing and shattering. Eddie and Carolyn's things had been wedding gifts back in 1963, and Tina's and Rick's wedding had been in 1992. Carolyn says, "I hoped the epicenter wasn't near their home so their lovely new things wouldn't be ruined, but as it happened, only a couple of small items fell at their house. I was so glad for that. When they came to our home, Tina, the artist, got together the broken pieces of one of our large statues and decided she would repair it, but at our house the ground wouldn't stay still long enough for her to put the pieces together. She decided to take it home with her and fix it there, and she did just that."

Aftershocks continued to rattle the house for days and nights, making it impossible to sleep. On the third night an exhausted Carolyn told Eddie and Lee she was going to bed early, at nine o'clock. As soon as she drifted to sleep, a tremor began and continued on and off for over half an hour. Carolyn gave up and went back to the den. Leland saw her coming and laughed. Mother Nature wasn't being very kind to the worn-out Carolyn.

However, the Carrolls remained resilient, and they had absorbed the self-reliant California spirit. They had earlier retrofitted the house to make it more earthquake-resistant, and now they had eleven-inch Simpson plates installed between the retrofit screws. Now the house is really attached to the foundation.

Slowly life got back to normal. Eddie and Carolyn knew how lucky they had been to get through the massive quake with only property damage to show for it. They still had the most important things in their lives: Each other.

CHAPTER 19

Jack and Groucho, Together Again

As life in Southern California returned to normal after the earthquake, Eddie decided that he and Carolyn deserved a reward, and because they both loved to travel they decided on another trip to London. They had visited the British capital before, finding it a fabulous place where Eddie said he always felt at home. On this trip Carolyn, with her love of history, suggested continuing from there to Greece, and so, as Eddie said, they were off on another one of Carolyn's Wonderful Adventures.

The extended journey was relaxing and helped them to regain a sense of calm, but Eddie always thought they had visited Greece out of order: "We had gone to Italy a few years before and toured the ruins there, which seemed ancient to us. Yet the Romans used to go to Greece to visit its ruins, which *they* considered ancient!"

When Eddie and Carolyn returned refreshed from the European journey, Eddie's work as the voice of Jiminy immediately picked right up again: "This time it was a series of fun, educational bits like the 'Encyclopedia' segments that Jiminy had hosted for the original *Mickey Mouse Club*. Cliff Edwards's Jiminy sang a catchy little song that taught a whole generation of kids how to spell *encyclopedia* and in the short cartoons he would present live-action footage, drawn from Disney's nature films and other sources, that taught as they entertained. The new Jiminy Cricket projects had him explaining to kids how the body worked from the inside: the eyes, the ears, and all the other sense organs. And at about the same time, Jiminy began to do Earth Day announcements to be played at the celebration of that holiday at Disneyland. Eventually Jiminy became Disney's official Ambassador of Environmentality and his likeness appeared on the napkins made from recycled paper and on all the trash cans at the park."

Environmentality was a Disney-coined word that meant, essentially, "think green." Years before those two words became a national slogan,

Jiminy was endorsing it, and quite naturally. After all, Jiminy really *is* green. Carolyn loved the idea that Jiminy would appear on the trash receptacles in the theme park. She says, "of course I took many photos of Eddie standing next to trash cans and holding a Jiminy recycled napkin! How many wives are proud of their husbands for appearing on trash cans? I sure was!" Eddie Carroll, star of stage, screen, and…trash bins!

At the same time, the other role in Eddie's performing life was offering more opportunities, too. Eddie found that his Jack Benny appearances were earning him a reputation as a scrupulously prepared, accomplished actor and that he was in increasing demand:

EDDIE CARROLL: The President of the Friars Club, Saul Burakoff, asked me to a luncheon at the famous Beverly Hills branch of the organization, which had been founded in 1947 by Milton Berle. Over the meal Saul told me he would like for me to perform as Benny in a show for the members of the club.

Eddie (as Jiminy, the Ambassador of Enviromentality) next to a recycling can.

Now, Frank Ferrante had established himself in an intimate limited-cast show by Arthur Marx, *Groucho: A Life in Revue*, in which he brilliantly brought Groucho Marx to life, acting Groucho at various times in his career from youth through his old age. I thought it would be fun to share the bill with Frank, and Frank was all for it. We were friends by that time, and he had seen me in *A Small Eternity with Jack Benny* when it had first run.

So with Saul Burakoff's blessing Frank and I planned *An Evening with Jack Benny and Groucho Marx* to be presented just once, at the Friars Club in October. I'll admit that both of us wondered if we could succeed before an audience largely made up of comedians. Sometimes it's hard to get laughs from the pros in the business — and at the Friars Club the members were all recognized performers — but we were relieved when the show went over well.

So well, in fact, that we booked a couple of local performing-arts theaters and we did encores of *An Evening with Jack Benny and Groucho Marx* several times. Frank and I had a terrific time doing it, and we developed a great respect for each other's talents. Still later on, we appeared together in several re-creations of radio broadcasts that Jack and Groucho had done in real life, and I always got a kick out of them, too.

Saul Burakoff, Steve Allen, Red Buttons, Frank Ferrante, and Eddie.

Frank Ferrante confirms and shares Eddie's fond memories of the occasion: "When Eddie and I played the Friars Club of Beverly Hills in exchange for memberships, it was quite an honor. Steve Allen hosted that night in 1994 and was extremely flattering regarding our tributes to Benny and Groucho. Red Buttons was in the audience as was my friend Arthur Marx, Groucho's son who wrote my New York show *Groucho: A Life in Revue*. Eddie opened with 45 minutes, then I followed with another 45. At the end, Eddie and I sang a duet as Benny and Groucho–a parody of "I Remember It Well" From *Gigi* in which we lovingly jibed each other. Buddy Arnold, who wrote the theme song for Milton Berle's *Texaco Star Theater*, penned the special lyrics:

> GROUCHO: Because of Rochester and Mary
>   You became a star —
> BENNY: You got laughs with that crouch
>   And that stinkin' cigar —

GROUCHO: I guess it worked;
   They liked our jokes.
BENNY: For all the laughs,
   We thank you folks.
BENNY & GROUCHO: Ah, thanks for remembering us well.

"The pairing was well received and led to some California bookings and eventually our extended run in *The Odd Couple* at the New Theater in Kansas City."

As for Eddie, becoming a Friar was a well-deserved honor for him and led to his meeting many idols in the business:

EDDIE CARROLL: As a result of our appearance at the club, I became an honorary member of the Friars Club of Beverly Hills, and to me it was a real honor to meet and talk to so many legends of show business there. They treated me very well, and it was such a joy to meet the great comedians who were members of the club. Red Buttons, especially, could always make me laugh just when I looked at him and he put on a comic expression. In turn, he was a terrific audience because he had such a wonderful laugh, and after our show he came up to me and warned me he was going to steal one of my jokes because it was the funniest one he'd ever heard.

And that reminds me of another Friar, the man who started the California branch, Milton Berle. One day at the Friars Club as he puffed on one of his signature cigars, which looked about a foot long, Berle started talking to me about Jack Benny. He said, "You know, they always kidded me about stealing jokes. They called me the Thief of Bad Gags. Well, I have to admit it was true. Television demands so much material that I had no shame about taking whatever would play, and I'd steal it from anyone and everyone. But here's a thing: I never once in my whole life stole anything from Jack Benny."

So I immediately became Jack Benny, crossed my arms, and put a hand to my cheek. To Berle, I said, "Ya know, Milton, I certainly can't understand *why* you wouldn't. I mean, 'Well!' and 'Gee!' aren't *that* hard to remember."

A surprised Uncle Miltie laughed so explosively that his cigar zoomed across the room like a missile. Actually, I knew exactly why Berle wouldn't steal Jack's material — it was because no one *could* steal it.

Other comedians based their whole acts on a string of gags, but instead of that, Jack based his scripts on personality and character. One secret of Jack's comedy was in his unmatched sense of timing and his delivery, which could make a hum-drum line or even a pause funny. Jack was involved in the writing of every show script and was the greatest comedy editor of all time. His writers told me how Jack was always happy to give the laugh lines to others in the cast.

"Lookit," he would say, "on Monday morning people at the water cooler don't say, 'Dennis Day said the funniest thing on the radio last night.' They say, 'Did you hear what Dennis Day said on the *Jack Benny Program?*' As long as they mention the name of the program, I'm getting the credit anyway, and it doesn't matter who gets the laughs."

Another reason why Jack was so popular was that he allowed himself to be the butt of all the jokes. In one routine on TV, Jack is at an airport waiting to board a plane. First he runs into Mel Blanc's little Mexican Sy, who nearly cracks him up with his monosyllabic answers to Jack's questions: "Are you waiting for the flight to Mexico City?" "Sí." "So you're going to Mexico City?" "Sí." "And your name is — " "Sy." "Sy?" "Sí." The routine doesn't read funny, but watching Jack trying to hold it together produced gales of laughter from the audience.

Next comes Jack's age, perennially 39: Frank Nelson announces on the airport PA that Jack's plane is ready to board at Gate 39. Jack murmurs, "Thirty-nine. Gee, what a coincidence."

Then Nelson jeers over the loudspeaker, "It's *really* 64! We have *our* little secrets, too!" and Jack is crushed. The people in the audience laugh.

They laughed because they sensed that the cheap, boastful, vain guy they heard on the radio or saw on TV wasn't the real Benny. Even with all his ego and stinginess, Jack's essential sweetness came through, and the audience were in on the best joke of all, that Jack was playing a character whom they recognized and loved as if he were an eccentric uncle.

When Jack was filming *To Be or Not to Be*, which is his best movie, he expressed some doubt about his acting ability to the director, the great Ernst Lubitsch. Jack confessed, "I don't know whether I can play a part like this. I'm not really an actor. I'm just a comedian."

Ernst Lubitsch's response was wonderful. He said, "Jack, you're a *great* actor. In fact, you're not a comedian at all. All your life you've been an actor who's *playing* a comedian, and I know your secret."

That was true. Jack played one role all his life: Jack Benny. And he played it superbly well and took great care in his preparations. To Jack, his writers were the real reasons for his success, and he was so generous in giving them their due. Long before other comedians, he gave the writing staff an end credit on all of his radio and later TV shows. And I agree with him — the writing is the keystone of any comedy, and Jack was always careful to find the most talented writers in the business.

That New Year's Eve found the Carrolls back in Vegas to celebrate. In the early years of their courting and then just after their marriage, when they were young newlyweds, they often didn't have the opportunity to enjoy New Year's together because one or both of them would be working, so now that they had the chance, Eddie and Carolyn always took advantage of the occasion to give each other the celebration as a gift. The New Year, 1995, looked bright and would bring new opportunities and new excitement into their lives.

Eddie remembered the first of these, when he received a chance to attempt something that had never before been done:

EDDIE CARROLL: In February, Frank Ferrante called me from Overland Park, Kansas, just outside Kansas City, where he was performing *Groucho: A Life in Revue* at the New Theatre. "Listen, Eddie," he said, "the patrons of the New Theatre just voted for their choice of a play to be brought in, and the winner was *The Odd Couple*. How would you like to be in that?"

It sounded good to me. Neil Simon's *The Odd Couple* was an institution by then. The original Broadway show had opened in 1965 and was an immediate success. It ran for about a thousand performances and swept in Tony Awards both for acting and writing. The rumor was that Neil Simon had based the play on experiences his brother Danny had when he divorced and moved in with another divorced guy, and also on stories told by Mel Brooks about the crazy things that happened when he was separated from his first wife and roomed with the writer Speed Vogel.

In the play, sloppy sportswriter Oscar Madison takes in his buddy, the uptight, neat-freak newspaperman Felix Ungar, when Felix's wife divorces him. In the first run of the play, Walter Matthau played Oscar and Art Carney, famous as Norton on Jackie Gleason's *The Honeymooners* series, was Felix.

As everyone knows, the play went on to inspire a successful movie with Jack Lemmon in the Felix role and Walter Matthau as Oscar, and then it became a long-running TV series with Tony Randall and Jack Klugman in the roles. [Randall's character's last name was spelled a little differently, though: Felix Unger.] In regional theater and off-Broadway, the play had been reworked and recast many times, with an all-black cast, an all-female cast, just everything you could think of.

I had already appeared in the show as one of Felix's and Oscar's poker buddies, and it would be fun, I thought, to take one of the lead roles instead. So I tentatively said yes when Frank asked if I'd like to be in it, and then I learned the rest. Well, Frank told me, the New Theatre owners, Richard Carrothers and Dennis Hennessy, wanted to come up with a whole new twist, and Frank's Groucho show gave them a bright idea. What if Frank portrayed Oscar — as Groucho? When they asked him the question, the first thought that ran through his mind was "Eddie has to play Felix — as Jack Benny!"

Frank waited for my reaction, and honestly the first thing I thought was "This sounds like an episode from *The Twilight Zone*!" Initially there seemed to be something just a little creepy about it.

But Richard and Dennis asked me to fly to Kansas the next weekend to consider the possibility, and an actor is never hasty to say "No." When I arrived, the wonderful, state-of-the-art theater impressed me. It's a beautiful place, the lobby, the entire theater, just a gorgeous gem. In those surroundings I felt a little more willing to consider the offer, so Frank and I sat down and did a table-read of the script.

Newspaper ad for "The Odd Couple."

And you know what? It worked! Truly, the fit of Marx and Benny with Madison and Ungar just amazed me. I honestly believe if the play had been written when Groucho and Jack were in their prime, they would have been the natural choices for the roles. The dialogue suited both of their personalities like a pair of snug, comfortable gloves. "I'll do it," I said as soon as we finished the read-through. Very soon the contracts were ready and Frank and I signed off on them.

We scheduled to open the play November 17, to run through February 11. Now, I had been in plays often enough before so the length of the run didn't bother me in itself, but here was the challenge: I was playing one character, Jack Benny, who was an actor playing another character, Felix Ungar.

In fact, both Frank and I had to act two roles at once. We sharpened everything up in rehearsals, and the show turned into a big hit. It was so successful at the New Theatre that the Nederlander Theater Company even explored the possibility of sending us on tour with it.

However, at that time Neil Simon was writing *The Odd Couple II* and didn't want the touring show to distract from the new work, so he turned them down. That was too bad, but the run in Overland Park was a wonderful experience, and Frank and I bonded, becoming close friends and sharing stories about our one-person shows.

Frank Ferrante agrees, and during the run of the show he came to be one of Eddie's reliable and close pals: "Working with Eddie on *The Odd Couple* in 1995 and '96 was a delight. Eddie was 30 years my senior, though it never felt that way. He had boundless energy and enthusiasm and a passion for show business. I learned a great deal from Eddie. I never said it to him but there was a period in which I felt we were bonded as father and son.

"Certainly, he was a mentor. I studied him. He was classic show business, always impeccably dressed and groomed. I wore a baseball cap and jeans. He gave useful advice. He once said to me, "Frank, do two things a day toward your career." Make the call. Send out the packet. I took that to heart and still do. Eddie knew how damn tough it was to exist as a comic actor. It could be discouraging, humbling, borderline depressing at times. But Eddie was relentless and a success. In his 70s he was still sending out those packets. I can relate.

"Sometimes I'd wonder how he felt about the meteoric success of peer Robert Goulet and friend Jamie Farr's lottery win with *M*A*S*H*. And then I'd contemplate Eddie's career. Eddie was a working character actor. For decades. He had a loving family, warm home and he kept it going. No easy task for a free-lancer. Show business is laden with bitter, cranky folk. Some of Eddie's peers were like that. Not Eddie. The beautiful part about Eddie is that he never lost his love of performing. He was open-hearted, kind and more than willing to share his story and encourage other performers. He was ageless to me. He was sentimental. I never heard him utter an unkind word about anyone. He was a true pro and always to took the high road."

No wonder Eddie found working with Frank such a delight. He was cheered, too, by visits from Carolyn, who on alternate weeks joined Eddie in the apartment provided by the theater, a two-bedroom, two-bath place that even had its own library.

She remembers the Kansas winter as being unbearably cold: "One day Eddie and I were watching the news as we ate, and a reporter wearing a parka with the hood closed so tightly that only his eyes were showing tossed a cup of hot coffee into the air, where it instantly froze and crystallized. I had to try that. We had a fresh pot of coffee, so I poured a steaming cup and went to the sliding glass doors. We were on the second floor, and the apartment had a balcony. I opened the doors — just a crack — and threw the coffee up into the air. We could hear it crackle and clatter down to the balcony as it froze and fell again."

Eddie morosely predicted that because of the frigid temperature he and Frank would play to an empty house that evening, but to his surprise it was practically a sell-out. The hardy Kansas folk had heard about the show and they came to see it regardless of the Arctic conditions.

As they worked together, Frank Ferrante learned that he and Eddie shared an approach to acting the role of a beloved star: "Eddie took umbrage to the word 'impersonator.' Many times he would say to me, 'Frank, we both approach these roles as actors. These are fleshed-out portrayals.'

"Eddie saw the importance of making that distinction. He had worked a lifetime as an actor and had worked hard. His Benny was far from mere imitation and Eddie really fought for his place on the one-man show pantheon. Every gig he got, or that I get, is hard-earned. We shared that understanding and experience. Eddie and I individually spent more than a decade playing one-nighters on the performing-arts-center circuit. I still do. Often following a show, the presenter/producer at the theater would ask if there was another show like mine that I could recommend. Without fail I would say, 'Yes. Eddie Carroll as Jack Benny.' He always did the same for me."

Though the Kansas winter could be brutal, Eddie particularly remembered Christmas that year:

EDDIE CARROLL: Leland flew into Kansas City to celebrate the holidays with us. He was astonished at the climate. This wasn't like the dry cold air of Tahoe, but a windy, bitter, biting chill that got right into your bones. The Arctic Pipeline for weather comes right down from the North Pole into Kansas! Tina couldn't be with us because she and her husband were spending Christmas in Chicago with her in-laws.

But we had put a tree up in our Kansas apartment, and when Carolyn had flown in she brought a whole suitcase bulging with our decorations from home. It made the holiday look much more friendly and inviting to me.

We managed to prepare our usual Ukrainian Christmas Eve dinner, but instead of family and friends we asked the cast members to join us. The next day we had our traditional family Christmas menu of turkey, and then, untraditionally, we took Lee to Harrah's Riverboat Casino. I gave him another Christmas present, forty dollars as his starter kit for gambling. He went off to find a poker machine while Carolyn and I played video Keno (we usually win a few bucks at this). After about forty-five minutes, Lee returns and hands me two twenties. I didn't want to accept them and I say to him, "No, that's for you to have fun."

Lee's face is glowing red. "Dad," he says, "I just won $250.00 at poker, and I'm finished with gambling for today."

I realized that two hundred and fifty dollars at that time was a windfall for our student-chiropractor son. But his warm glow didn't exactly last. The second we got back in the car, he muttered, "Dad, turn on the heater. I'm frozen." That's our Southern-California-raised son!

Christmas in Kansas City.

Carolyn had her beef with the climate, too. First, it made transportation iffy. In the mornings they had to use a turkey baster filled with hot water to thaw out the car-door locks before they could even climb in. Some days it would take a long time to persuade a chilled engine to catch, turn over, and fire up. One day the couple went to a video-rental place to return a tape, with Eddie driving. The temperature was low, and the winds were whipping. To prevent their being frozen out of their car, Eddie stayed behind the wheel and kept the engine and heater running while Carolyn dashed up to the video shop door to drop the videotape through the return slot.

She remembers, "It was incredibly windy, and I was wearing a long coat. I dropped the tape in the slot and just then a huge blast of wind hit me and I grabbed the handrail — fortunately. I'm not a heavyweight, and I'm not built low to the ground, and that gust of wind caught my coat and sailed it like a kite. My feet flew up in the air behind me, and there I was flapping like a flag! I got back to earth unhurt and pulled myself along the rail, hand over hand, until I got to the car. I was laughing my head off, but as I got in, Eddie said, 'That wasn't funny!' The sight had alarmed him, and his voice was even a little shaky. For a moment there, I thought I was the Flying Nun."

"The Odd Couple" cast in Kansas City at the New Theatre.

Because Carolyn was alternating, spending one week with Eddie in Kansas and the other back in Encino, at least she could occasionally go home and thaw out in the sunshine. She and Eddie saw in the New Year in Kansas, together with their new friends from the cast and crew:

EDDIE CARROLL: By then our run was winding down, but even as that production of *The Odd Couple* ended, Jack Benny found more work for me to do. That year I signed a five-year contract with Aetna/U.S. Healthcare Corporation to appear in commercials as Jack. These were so successful that in May of the next year the company sponsored a five-month tour of my *Jack Benny Tribute*. This was the time that I suggested (and politely asked) that Carolyn finally give up her therapy practice completely after twenty-three years to become my permanent road manager, traveling with me. The show eventually appeared in forty-seven cities across the country.

And more about their adventures on the road a little later. Frank Ferrante also regretted that he and Eddie were never able to tour with their version of *The Odd Couple*. Like Eddie, Frank is a meticulous performer who now does two Marx shows, *Groucho: A Life in Revue*, written by Groucho's son Arthur Marx and Robert Fisher, and the one-man show *An Evening with Groucho*, which Frank himself wrote. Arthur Marx personally chose Frank to represent his father on stage, and just as Eddie worked with the blessing of Jack Benny's daughter, Frank remained close to Arthur for the rest of his life.

Frank says of Eddie, "He was a thoroughly professional actor and a delight to work with. Audiences loved that show because of our chemistry on stage, and I know exactly why we were so good together. As Oscar I have that Groucho timing, quick and sly, sarcastic and absurdist, just jab-jab-jab, and Eddie's persona as Jack Benny in the role of Felix is just the perfect balance to that fast, clever manner. Like the real Jack Benny, Eddie's Felix had that great relaxed style, paced and deliberate and timed impeccably. His dry wit and measured comebacks built on the laughs that Groucho's mile-a-minute delivery generated."

Toward the end of the run of *The Odd Couple*, Jamie Farr arrived in Overland, Kansas. He had been booked to star in the next show coming into the New Theatre and of course he had to show up weeks early for rehearsals. During the run of a play, the New Theatre gave the stars a two-bedroom, two-bath and one-library apartment to live in, the one where Eddie and Carolyn hosted their Christmas Eve dinner and where Carolyn had made instant iced coffee.

Jamie, however, had to stay in a hotel until Eddie's show closed before he could move into the apartment, and so they established a pattern: Carolyn would cook dinner every evening in the apartment and Jamie would drop in as the Carrolls' guest. Jamie got so accustomed to these that when the Carrolls moved out, he asked the cleaning crew for a favor: Leave the spices and whatever was in the freezer for him.

Carolyn remembers the overlap, when Jamie and Joy Farr and the Carrolls were both in Overland: "Joy Farr and I had many laughs about the laundry room in the basement. For some reason, one of the walls had an enormous gaping hole in it, and through the hole we could see packed dirt. While we were doing laundry, we talked about what kind of monster might live in there. It's a miracle we didn't scare ourselves!"

In the middle of February, Eddie finally returned home to Encino, and he said, "After four months of being away, it felt so great just to sleep in my own bed again." Carolyn promptly told him that for the *next* four months, his job would be to open the mail and take care of the family finances, because she'd just had her turn, but of course they really shared the chores, as always.

Leland's good friend Chuck Magnus, whom the Carrolls always called TOS ("The Other Son" — in turn, to Chuck Eddie was TOD and Carolyn TOM, The Other Dad and The Other Mom), joined in

Eddie with the 1925 Maxwell.

the preparations for taking Jack on the road: "Chuck put up a website for us, and then when that attracted hits and generated interest, he stayed on to keep it running. He continues to be the webmaster and continues to hold a dear place in our hearts. TOS joins us for every family celebration and holiday, and he is invaluable to us in more than one part of our lives."

As for the coast-to-coast Jack Benny tour, Carolyn realized that she was sacrificing something as she took the full-time position with Eddie: "Eddie, my new boss, didn't tell me that I would not only be the manager, but also the tour arranger, travel agent, tech advisor, PR supervisor, stage manager, and key technician to set up the audio and light cues — and throw in secretary, too. And you could tell he was playing Jack Benny, because he hired me to do all that on a salary of nothing. It was a lousy contract, but it was a joy to share the road adventures with my honey."

Carolyn had exchanged her nice clean office for dusty tech booths. She sneezed her way through performances while Eddie got to take the spotlight and do his bows to standing ovations. However, he assured her that in reality she owned fifty per cent of everything he made. Carolyn, though, thought her best payment consisted of the laughter and fun they shared. Now that they were on the road not just occasionally but constantly, she concentrated on making their lives more comfortable and homey. She would bring small things from Encino to decorate the apartments or hotel rooms and was careful always to say "Let's go home" after a performance, meaning their home on the road.

Carolyn had signed on — and as it worked out, she had signed on for the long haul, for an extended career as Eddie's road manager that would bring both hard work and great rewards.

CHAPTER 20

Always Something New

By 1996, Jack Benny had been gone for twenty-two years, and yet he remained just as popular as ever. As Laura Leff, President of the International Jack Benny Fan Club *(www.jackbenny.org)* has often observed, Benny's brand of humor is timeless. It's difficult to follow the recordings of many radio comedies from the 1930s and 1940s. A Bob Hope show is riddled with machine-gun-paced gags, but half or more of them are topical references that not many younger people can understand and the jokes just don't work because of that.

With Jack and his gang, the humor is built on personality and character, and a 1945 broadcast is still just as funny a lifetime later. Today it's still just as easy to laugh at a stingy man's agony at paying one cent more than he thinks he should as it was for audiences to laugh at Jack in a 1940s sketch when he's vacillating over his choices for a Christmas present to give Don Wilson: Should he choose plastic-tipped shoelaces or the more durable but slightly more expensive type with metal aglets? The painful penny gag still teases laughter from listeners.

Eddie Carroll had a lot to do with Jack's continuing visibility in the public eye. As *Laughter in Bloom* was developing, another review-styled show came up for him almost immediately:

EDDIE CARROLL: Bill Kirchenbauer, a marvelous stand-up comedian and actor, got in touch with me and offered me a contract with BaldGuy Productions to perform in *Legends of Comedy*, a show in which various actors brought back to life great comedians of the past. Carolyn and I became good friends not only with Bill, but with all of the acts that appeared in the show. These included Marcel Forestieri as Jay Leno, Bill Sacra as Rodney Dangerfield, Chuck Fraher as George Burns, with my Jack Benny as the closing act. Sometimes when Bill was doing another show Johnny Dark and Jimmy Walker would stand in as emcee for the show. They were all great at what they did.

The contract called for four months at the Flamingo Casino in Laughlin, Nevada, ninety miles from Las Vegas. The countryside there is beautiful, with the Colorado River running through Laughlin and dividing Nevada from Arizona. As you look across the river into Arizona, you see a grand vista of mesas gorgeously layered with streaks of tan and red that glows in the light of sunset. The feel of Laughlin is much different from that of Vegas, a little more unhurried, a little more relaxed, not as brightly lit. I enjoyed working there.

At that time there were no stores in Laughlin, so to visit one you had to drive over a bridge to reach the airport and Bullhead City, AZ, which had a Wal-Mart. Carolyn was the show manager again — even Bill Kirchenbauer started calling her "boss" — but we arranged it so she could fly back to Encino every weekend to keep an eye on the home front.

For her birthday that year I drove across the bridge to get her something at the Wal-Mart. I remember it was 122 degrees Fahrenheit when I climbed out of the car. I made my purchases and last of all bought her a helium Mylar balloon with "Happy Birthday" imprinted on it. I took my purchases back to the car and climbed in with them.

The car had been standing in the sun, and in that heat you could have baked cookies in it. I rolled down the window until the air-conditioner could get up to speed…and the birthday balloon made its exit. I jumped out of the car and chased it partway across the lot, but it had a lead and altitude on me.

But a real man does not go back to his wife on her birthday without a helium balloon.

So I marched right back into the Wal-Mart and found they had one birthday balloon left. I bought it and was very careful not to let go of it until it was in the car and the windows were rolled up again.

Carolyn thought that was sort of a Jack Benny thing to do — trying to chase down a runaway helium balloon that he had just bought rather than lose it to the wind. She laughed, but she also made sure that Eddie hadn't put himself in danger by galloping across the hot parking lot in his futile pursuit.

She remembers one of the tasks she had managing that particular show was also managing her and Eddie's boss: "Bill Kirchenbauer was my boss, but he had a voice that carried, and he talked all the time, including when he was holding a hot mike and his voice was coming through the speakers. I was always having to tell him to keep his voice down or just hiss 'Shush!' at him, and he would take my orders."

On the trips back and forth to Encino, Carolyn flew in a tiny prop-engined Cessna, and the air, made turbulent by the desert heat, caused some rough landings. She remembers how steeply the little plane had to bank as it came in to the airport: "The Cessna literally turned sideways, with the desert straight down on the left and the open sky on the right. Davis Dam is just a couple of miles from the Bullhead International Airport, and it supplies electricity, with high-tension wires radiating out from it in all directions, so we had to come in low. I got used to it, but some of the commuting high rollers coming in to gamble would turn white when we banked in for that landing." She often reflected that Bullhead International Airport had a deceptive name — it was international, as it served planes coming and going from Mexico and other places, but she remembers it as "only one cement room."

Bill Kirchenbauer, producer of Legends of Comedy, *and Eddie.*

While Eddie was taking the last turn at the mikes in *Legends of Comedy* — as Jack, he always closed the show, sending the audience home laughing — his other career was continuing too. That year brought him another chance to return to Disney World in Florida:

EDDIE CARROLL: October 1996 marked the twenty-fifth anniversary of Walt Disney World, and the Disney Company flew Carolyn and me in for that. It was a fantastic celebration. Every night for a week one of the parks would close down to the general public, allowing only the celebrities to come into that area.

Epcot was wonderful, a place where we ate and drank our way around the world. Then every morning we character voices would go to a roped-off section where hundreds of DJs from all over the world were broadcasting by live link-ups to their home stations. I'd sit with one for a while and, as Jiminy, talk about the parks and all the things to do there. Bill Farmer might take my place to do a Goofy interview, while I moved on to another DJ. Radio stations literally from all around the globe had broadcasters there. It was really exhilarating, a magnificent event, and my only tiny regret was having to get up at 4:30 every morning to start broadcasting!

Susie Lum, the Vice President of Character Voice Development at the Disney Studio in Burbank, supervised the character broadcasts. We had been friends for some time, but Susie is absolutely charming, and before the end of that trip, Carolyn and I had adopted her into our growing extended family as another daughter.

Most of the interviews were cheerful and upbeat, but one particular DJ from New York decided to do everything he could to throw the performers off. With Eddie, speaking as Jiminy, the DJ suddenly interrupted him and asked, "Hey, is it true you're about to go to New York to the opening of *Stomp*! on Broadway?" And then he began pounding a book down onto the table, like someone trying to crush a bug.

Eddie didn't miss a beat. As Jiminy, he threw in warning yelps after every reverberating *boom*! of the book: "Watch out, now!" "Uh-oh!" "Hey, that was *too* close!" Eddie was always fast on his feet, and so Jiminy was, too. Susie Lum immediately came in, grabbed Eddie by the arm and moved him from the booth. In no uncertain terms she told the DJ to pack it up, because he was no longer welcome at Disney World. You don't tug on Superman's cape, and you darn sure don't try to stomp on Jiminy Cricket.

Eddie, during the radio show portion of "Laughter in Bloom."

As soon as the anniversary celebration ended, Jack Benny picked up. Eddie recalled,

EDDIE CARROLL: By this time I had done Jack in so many different vehicles, but *Laughter in Bloom* now started to gain momentum, with more and more requests for the show pouring in. I had never got the hang of the Internet, so I let TOS Chuck and Carolyn handle the website and take care of all the emails that were coming in.

Carolyn, always a careful planner, worked up a tech rider for the website that showed the theaters what they needed to supply. The set was simple, but there were a few things we absolutely needed: a projection screen and VHS or DVD projector for the excerpts from the Jack Benny TV show; a living-room set with a period rug, an armchair, a sofa or love-seat, a music stand, and an old-fashioned radio and microphone. Eventually, after flying with things like violins became more difficult, we also asked for a tuned violin, rosin, and a bow. Carolyn

Eddie during radio interview with a station from Belgium.

made a sketch so the theater people would know exactly what the stage set-up would be.

Of course the furniture was always different from venue to venue. Sometimes Jack would have a 1930s-style living room with a cathedral-style Crosley radio, or he might have a 1950s-style set up, and the radio would be an ivory-colored Zenith table model with pushbuttons. That made no real difference, but I could count on always knowing the stage layout and on having to adjust the blocking of the show only for the dimensions of the stage.

Chuck and Carolyn also designed posters and a program cover which bookers would download, customize with information about the times and places of the performances, and reprint, and she would coordinate things like telephone interviews prior to the show to get the PR out. And then during the show, she would be up in the booth overseeing light, AV, and sound cues. As we toured, I continually tinkered with the show, so the cue sheets had to be continually revised. Within a couple of years the show went from an hour and a half to two full hours. Then when I'd think of something new to add, Carolyn put her foot down: "Absolutely not! These people in the audience will be starving by the time it's over. Send them away happy, not hungry!"

Eddie gained fans just from the touring shows, and sometimes they surprised him. After one performance of *Laughter in Bloom*, a talented young prop designer, Charles Dillman, even crafted for him an authentic-looking 1930's-era ribbon mike, one of the diamond-shaped kind that you see in old photos of radio stars. It wasn't operational, but in the show Eddie used a lavaliere mike anyway, and the microphone became a prop that helped set the mood.

One of the highlights *of Laughter in Bloom* was Eddie's re-creation of a Benny radio broadcast. Using the recorded voices of Eddie "Rochester" Anderson, Mary Livingstone, and Dennis Day from two actual Benny programs, Eddie performed Jack's lines live, into the prop microphone. The bit was a masterpiece of comic timing. As Jack, Eddie complains to Rochester that there was no soap in the shower that morning, so he had to come down to the kitchen and get the bar that was on the counter, and it must have been all dried up, because it made hardly any suds.

Rochester says, "That wasn't soap. That was a peeled potato!"

When the laughter subsides, "Jack" says, "You mean I showered with a potato?"

Rochester's riposte: "Boss, you now have the skin that lamb chops love to touch!"

Later Mary enters, "Jack" gives her a kiss, and she suddenly develops a craving for lamb chops.

Carolyn had worked with a software program to clean up the hisses and pops and crackles from the old recordings, so all the voices sounded crisp and clear, not just Eddie's. It was all impeccably done, with Eddie's live voice work seamlessly merging with the recordings, and the ribbon microphone made the bit look, as well as sound, authentic. The hand-built prop microphone was a present to Eddie, given in gratitude for his performance, and it came not on Christmas, but appropriately enough on February 14, the anniversary of Jack Benny's birth.

Carolyn's unpaid position soon became a full-time job. Staying abreast of the emails, the scheduling, and the PR and updating the cue sheets and notes for the tech crews of the theaters kept her busy enough. She didn't need any extra work, not when she had to also do the cleaning and the family laundry. At times when the pressure stressed her, Eddie would take her out to lunch. Eventually they developed the habit of going out to lunch every day, just so Carolyn could enjoy a break from the computer, the phone, and the household chores. They also started to do crossword puzzles together, focusing on filling one out every day while clearing their minds. It gave them a little quiet time together when they could simply enjoy each other's company.

They also learned to split the entrees at lunch time. "We had to keep Eddie slim enough to fit into his tailored suits," Carolyn says. "It's hard to find Jack Benny-style suits that are wrinkle resistant! Anyway, I wanted to keep my honey healthy so he'd be with me longer." Soon Eddie signed another contract with BaldGuy Productions to perform as Benny at Trump's Castle (now Trump's Marina) in Atlantic City, a great venue. Once more Carolyn had to fly back and forth, but because there was no direct connecting flight that became something of a routing ordeal. January of 1997 was a chilly, blustery month in Atlantic City, snowy and extremely cold. Eddie and Carolyn kept in shape by working out in the fitness center, but eventually they got cabin fever and decided to go out for lunch one gusty, raw day to Harrah's Resort, just next door. It should have been a short brisk walk, but the weather threw them a curve ball.

Once more, Carolyn was wearing a long coat, and with the whipping wind right in their faces, she had a hard time gaining ground. Eddie, remembering how one blast in Kansas had lifted her right off her feet — like Dorothy, she had almost flown from Kansas to Oz — told her to walk right behind him, so he would provide her with a windbreak, and advised her to hold onto his coat. It was a little like two mountain-climbers roped together as they fought the wind to arrive at Harrah's. They laughed their way to lunch, and afterward, with the wind at their backs, they made the return trip in record time.

When the show's run ended, as always it was a bittersweet time. Eddie never met a stranger, and by the end of a run he and the crew were always friends. However, the cast of *Legends* would meet again and again. Eddie explained:

EDDIE CARROLL: I had been doing those health-care commercials for a year, but the executives of Aetna came to Trump's Castle and saw me in a full show, before a live audience, for the first time. They liked it and immediately booked me for several months of shows in the Boston area, the New York Metropolitan area, Washington, D.C., Virginia, and then the next year California and Florida. This was really gratifying. We got to see so much of the country and experience so much of U.S. history, and again our dreams were coming true.

The largest major city in whatever area the show appeared became our home base. We'd awaken every morning, and then get ready and go down to the lobby, where a limo driver would be waiting to take us to the show venue for that day. Just having the limo was such a blessing — we didn't have to worry about fighting traffic. Carolyn would have her tech bag, we would pack the wardrobe, and then we were off to the next show. Almost all the shows were matinees, leaving us with evenings free, and we would be back in the hotel for the night.

Larry Alten, the health care executive who was always with us, asked what we did on long trips. "We listen to books on tape," I told him.

He said, "My wife Barbara and I do that, but we listen to CDs of our favorite groups instead."

"Oh?" I asked. "I used to be interested in the music business. What groups do you like?"

"The Lettermen — " he began.

"Really? What's your favorite song of theirs?" I asked.

"We both like 'How Is Julie?' That was our song," Larry said.

"I wrote that one," I told him.

Larry chuckled, obviously thinking I was making a joke. "Yeah, sure."

"No," I said. "I really did write it." I went on to tell him how I wrote it when Carolyn and I were on tour when we first met. He got a kick out of it.

And then that night, I woke up from a sound sleep at three a.m. and jumped to my feet, standing up on the bed in our room at the Helmsley Hotel and screamed "CD!"

Carolyn leaped out of bed, thinking I had completely lost it. "What is it?" she asked.

I explained my thought processes: Larry and Barbara listened to "How Is Julie?" on CD. The last time I had received any royalties for "How Is Julie?" must have been 1967 or so. Back then there weren't even any audio cassettes, let alone CDs. So — where were thirty years of royalties?

The next day we squeezed in time to go to Tower Records just around the corner and check to learn whether "How Is Julie?" was actually on any CDs, and it was. Carolyn and I ran down the music-publishing company that currently held the rights to it: Warner/Chappell Music, Inc. I phoned and asked if they were holding any royalties for me.

The man at Warner/Chappell called it up on the computer and said, "Yes, we do. Where have you been?"

Well, we have only had four addresses the whole time we've been married, and I hadn't thought to send along any change-of-address forms to the music people. I'd thought the ride with "How Is Julie?" had ended many years before. This was a very nice surprise!

Later, when Carolyn and Eddie saw Tony Butala, she told him what had happened, and he asked, "Did you get the royalties? I sure hope so!" They had, and the royalties still continue to come in today. Carolyn says, "Thank you, Larry and Barbara!" Their good taste in music gave Eddie and Carolyn not only a great surprise, but a long-lasting gift.

After every show, Eddie loved to go out into the theater lobby and sign autographs, chat, or pose for pictures with fans. Once in a while he would get entangled. Outside Philadelphia, he did the show and then the Carrolls had to get very quickly to the airport to fly to Maryland. In the tech booth, Carolyn packed up the bag and double-checked to make sure she had everything. Then she went down to the car, expecting that Eddie would be along right behind her after having met the fans.

But Eddie came out of the stage door and immediately an elderly female fan latched onto him, talking a mile a minute: "It must be so much fun to travel. I'd love to be in the show. I'm a party girl — "

Eddie politely tried to get away, but the lady clung to him like a limpet. Carolyn got out of the car and came over to say, "Excuse me, but we have to leave for the airport right now."

The fan, obviously thinking that Carolyn was just the tech manager, turned on her and snarled, "Just give me a minute!"

The limo driver had become a friend of the Carrolls' who stood six-two and who could look menacing, came to the rescue. He rumbled, "Mrs. Carroll, let me take care of this for you."

The fan backed off as this towering man unfolded from the car, and Eddie made it into the limo. "At my age I've got groupies," he said. "Who knew?" But it was a real concern, and from then on Carolyn made sure that some form of security would be on hand, especially when Eddie played casinos.

As the tour continued, the Carrolls pursued their on-the-road hobby of exploring history. Eddie said:

EDDIE CARROLL: We ventured into every museum in Boston, Philadelphia, Washington, Baltimore, and New York. We could never decide which one had the best dinosaur display, because they were all phenomenal.

We loved touring the historic landmarks of New England, the marvelous parks, and the monuments. Once when we were on our way to Union Station in Washington, D.C., the police stopped us and asked us to walk in another direction because they had received a bomb threat. There was no explosion, but we took advantage of the detour to look at the historic buildings in the area.

In Pittsburgh we stayed at the Sheraton, which was a converted train depot. The lobby of the station had become a lovely restaurant, and all around the complex ran a real train. It was a brilliant idea, a good way to preserve a bit of American history.

And in New York we had time to see all the shows on Broadway and off-Broadway. We loved it. It was wonderful to me to be part of the audience for a change! Carolyn and I both enjoyed New York's fast pace, and I think that's when we started our routine of daily power walking together.

After returning to Encino for a bit of rest and a spell of catching up on the home front, Eddie and Carolyn decided they would visit Carolyn's cousin Sandy, an artist in New Orleans. "I'd never been to New Orleans," she says, "and all I knew was that she covered the park at Jackson Square — I didn't have her address or phone number."

But the Carrolls strolled the Jackson Square area, asking everyone they met whether Sandy the artist worked there. Finally someone pointed out her cart, which was unmanned, and said, "She'll be back in a few minutes."

Though Carolyn and Sandy had not seen each other since Carolyn was about eleven, they recognized Sandy at once when she came back. There was a strong family resemblance. Sandy was surprised and overjoyed at the reunion, and she was impressed by the detective work that Eddie and Carolyn had put in to locate her. From then on the Carrolls had a grand time enjoying the Southern hospitality of New Orleans with its music, food, and warm smiles.

After the New Orleans trip ended, they went back to Encino, but hardly had time to set foot in their house. Eddie remembered:

EDDIE CARROLL: Two weeks after returning home, we were back in New York City for the Disney Radio Christmas show, *A Very Merry Christmas* with Dan Aykroyd. Dan is also a Canadian and he and I had fun with that. Most often when we do character radio shows, we record them in the Burbank studio. That's always fun because as a rule, when we're recording for an animated project each of us is alone in a studio booth. Being on the radio means that Jiminy can interact with Mickey, Donald, Goofy, and the whole gang, live and in person.

In the New York studio, the whole Disney gang was there: Mickey (Wayne Allwine), Minnie (Russi Taylor), Donald (Tony Anselmo) and my dear adopted family member Goofy (Bill Farmer). We had a ball together, and after the recording session we went to the Carnegie Deli for a bite to eat.

The cast of the Disney Christmas Radio Show, "A Very Merry Christmas," starring Dan Aykroyd.

They put us in a small back room away from the main area — maybe we were a little too loud for New York, or maybe the occasional burst of Goofy "a-hyuck" laughter or Donald squawk or Mickey's "gosh, fellas!" was too much. We had a wonderful time, but when Russi and Wayne each ordered a whole sandwich Carolyn and I exchanged a look. When the waiter brought out two of those enormous deli sandwiches, Wayne and Russi could only gasp at the size of them.

We had been in New York only a month before, but now it was the Christmas season, and New York is spectacular for the holidays. We visited Rockefeller Center, where the outdoor sitting area had been transformed into an ice rink. I asked how long it took to make the change and freeze the ice. The total time was forty-five minutes. What a set change!

At an age when most people are thinking of retirement, I found myself busier than ever, and delighted to be so busy. Years of hard work were paying off, and I treasured it all. Happiness is doing what you love and loving what you do, especially when the love of your life shares it all. What a joy it is to work and travel with Carolyn!

In February, the show played Calgary and then Edmonton, my home town. Oh, how special that was, playing the show I loved for my friends and family. Carolyn and I were housed in a two-bedroom apartment, so we had family and friends come by to visit, catching up on each other's lives, reminiscing about our shared times, and having grand reunions. I wouldn't have missed it for anything, and my chief memory is laughter, laughter, laughter.

From Canada, it was off to Florida and California for the continued U.S. Health Care tour. We spent more time with friends in California, then with Carolyn's parents in Florida. When the show played Punta Gorda, FL, we visited my old high-school friend Marilyn Dingle, which is her real name, though she is also Marilyn Thorndycraft and her husband Murray. She and I had acted together in the Orion Theatre back in the 1950s, when she and her sister billed themselves — no fooling — as "The Dingle Sisters." We had a fantastic time, again reminiscing and catching up. Once more I felt the universe had handed me a great present.

Lots of laughter: Eddie with long time friends Senator Tommy and Ida Banks.

Carolyn remembers a show where things all at once got seriously off track: "My parents came to the show when we played Tampa, because they live only about an hour away. The matinee audience was mostly made up of elderly people, and in the middle of the show an urgent announcement broke in over our audio system: *Whoop! Whoop! Whoop! This is an emergency! Leave by the nearest exit! This is an emergency! Whoop! Whoop! Whoop!*"

The recorded announcement kept repeating, drowning out everything else. Carolyn's dad was one of the best safety engineers in the country and had been President of the National Safety Council. Carolyn could see from the booth that the Springers, sitting right down front, stayed in their seats. She didn't smell smoke, and there was no trace of an electrical short. Carolyn jumped out of the tech booth, grabbed a phone, and called the theater office.

"There's no emergency," the manager told her. "We were just doing an electrical check and triggered the warning accidentally."

A routine electrical check — *during a show?*

Barry and Sarah Vogel, Carolyn and Eddie, Senator Tommy and Ida Banks.

Carolyn acted quickly, racing down to the theater floor, where a frightened throng of people were stampeding, very slowly, many of them using walkers or in wheelchairs. She yelled up to the booth, "Get me a hot mike!" They tossed her a cordless one, she fielded it, and then overrode the announcement: "There is no emergency! It's a false alarm! Please return to your seats!"

The annoying recording was switched off, and most of the audience returned for the rest of the show. Eddie was on stage just vamping and chatting. Later he told Carolyn he wasn't worried — "I knew you'd take care of the problem." Carolyn's parents never moved, and as long as her safety-expert dad Glenn wasn't worried, all was well.

The audience settled down again as Eddie gave his long-suffering Benny look. As soon as it was quiet, he crossed his arms and said, "Now, where was I?" and got a laugh, and people yelled to him the story he had been telling and the show was back on track.

Back in California, Leland had completed his studies and would graduate from the Cleveland Chiropractic College of Los Angeles, becoming a Doctor of Chiropractic and Kinesiology in April, 1999. Leland had always won high honors in school, and a couple of weeks before his graduation Carolyn asked if he were preparing for his graduation speech. He gave her a deadpan look and said, "What, to thank everyone for giving me graduation gifts?"

Then at the graduation ceremony before everything got underway, Eddie and Carolyn looked through the program and couldn't find Leland's name until finally Aunt Gloria spotted it. The name was on the

Leland's graduation from Chiropractic College as Summa Cum Laude and Valedictorian.

front page with three asterisks next to it. He was Summa Cum Laude and Valedictorian of his class. With his family, godparents, and friends looking on, Leland graduated, and there wasn't a dry eye in the house — at least not in the Carroll section.

Just before the march into the huge auditorium, Carolyn went to the restroom, which was near the place where the graduates gathered. She picked Lee out at once because he towered above the others and went to hug him, misty eyed. He had a big grin, gave her a bear hug and lifted her off the floor, and said, "Nice surprise, huh, Mom?"

Carolyn whacked him on the arm with the program, but in fact it was a glorious surprise. Eddie threatened to bust some buttons as his chest swelled with pride. On stage, Leland was in the back row, but his height made him easily visible. The Dean made an introduction, and then Leland, in mortarboard and gown and looped with cords showing his numerous achievements, made his way to the podium. His first words over the microphone were, "Boy, if they'd told me I'd have to do that long walk, I might not have agreed to this."

His speech was clever, humorous, and smart, though on the first two or three jokes the audience tried to hold in its laughter — this was a solemn occasion. But Leland was the son of performers, and soon the audience was roaring and applauding. The following graduation party was another high point.

Another year, another decade, and another century were ending, and Eddie was enjoying every minute:

EDDIE CARROLL: The Ameristar Casino on the Missouri River in Council Bluffs, Iowa, booked *Legends of Comedy* for New Year's Eve and New Year's Day. It was going to be fun welcoming in 2000 working with my friends. But then the airline misplaced my luggage with my wardrobe. Somehow I couldn't see going on stage as Jack Benny while dressed in a turtleneck sweater and jeans — Jack was always a sharp dresser and had been voted the Best-Dressed Man in Hollywood more than once. The airline could only assure us they were trying to find our baggage.

But by the next day I was getting nervous. It was a holiday, and there was no place open where I could rent or even buy a suit that had that tailored look. I was beginning to feel frantic, and then, barely three hours before the show, our lucky star twinkled and the suitcase showed up. That was the last time I checked the suitcase with my wardrobe in it!

The show played to sell-out crowds, and we loved celebrating the holiday. The theater even catered our dinners, and Carolyn and I discovered that there's nothing — *nothing* — that can beat the taste of an Omaha steak.

On New Year's Day, Carolyn noticed that the tech crew had not been served dinner and were sitting rather forlornly in the open tech booth. The servers were just bringing the dessert cart out, and she took the cart and served each crew member two desserts of their choice. She always liked and always respected the crews and was always protective of them. "These are the people who can make or ruin a show," she said. So she was like a mother hen to them, always keeping a sense of humor even when there was an *oops!* in the technical part. There's no second take in live theater, but that's part of the excitement of doing a live show.

The booking was superb, a perfect way to end the nineties and begin the year 2000. The casino ushered in the new century with an awesome fireworks display. Carolyn and I had so much to look back on and to be grateful for, and so much to look forward to. We couldn't wait to see what would unfold next in our lives.

CHAPTER 21

Life on the Road

The new millennium found Eddie busier than ever. *Laughter in Bloom* had taken off, its popularity fueled by word-of-mouth praise and by the website. In nearly ten years of performing it, Eddie worked sixty-four theaters and six casinos, and at the same time Disney kept Eddie hopping as Jiminy with tons of new projects. Occasionally Eddie still found time for performances on television.

In 2000, Eddie made a guest shot on an episode of *Frasier* called "The Bad Son." First, as usual, Eddie read through the script with the cast. He was playing Lee, a character who was supposed to be the same age as Frasier's dad, Martin (John Mahoney). At the first read-through there was little time for small talk, but in rehearsals the cast and Eddie warmed to each other and had a relaxed, enjoyable time preparing for the shoot. After five days of rehearsal, Eddie went to the makeup department, where they sprayed his hair white and put wrinkles on his face with make-up.

Eddie recalled, "When I went back into the room for the final read-through, no one said hello or gave me a second glance. They were just sitting around talking to each other, but they ignored me. I felt frozen out for some reason, and I started to wonder what I had done. But when I read the first lines from my script, David Hyde Pierce sat back and said, 'Oh, I didn't recognize you!' The whole cast started to giggle, and then our warm relationship was back. Whew! I didn't realize what a difference the make-up made!"

The plot of the episode involved Frasier's taking his dad, Martin, to inspect an assisted-living home, mainly because Frasier wanted a chance to ask the attractive director of the place for a date. Eddie's character, Lee, knew Martin and when he mistakenly thought Martin would be moving in, he said, "Good! We need a fourth hand for poker!" Though Martin has no plans to move into the home, he does sit down with Lee and his cronies later on to play poker. When Frasier is ready to leave, Martin objects, "These guys are the worst poker players I've ever seen!" and doesn't want to go until he's cleaned them out. However, Lee is not quite as bad as Martin thinks…

As the crew prepared for a scene in which Eddie, the Jack Russell terrier, was to perform, there was a bit of a pause as the stagehands put up a screen around the living-room set. The star of *Frasier*, Kelsey Grammer, is a huge Jack Benny fan and in 1995 hosted a TV special, *Kelsey Grammer Salutes Jack Benny*. During the lull, Eddie was introduced to the audience and the producer told them, "Mr. Carroll does a fantastic two-hour theatrical show about Jack Benny's life."

He handed the microphone to Eddie, in full old-age makeup. Eddie glanced backstage at Carolyn, who was laughing hysterically. He said, "Carolyn was thinking the same thing as I was: How am I going to do the fastidiously dressed Jack Benny in an old man's sweater and snow-white hair?" Gamely, though, just as he had done in a similar situation with Lucille Ball, he turned to the audience and greeted them as Jack: "Hello, everybody, and welcome to the show." He did a few jokes about working with a youngster like Kelsey Grammer and the wonders of stage make-up that could turn a thirty-nine-year-old into an old man, and he did a great job of warming up the audience prior to the taping of the Jack Russell's scene. Frasier was a nice opening act for Eddie's Jack Benny bit.

Eddie as Lee in an episode of Frasier.

After the taping, Eddie decided to keep the make-up on for a little while. He and Carolyn drove back home, where Lee was in the process of taking a garbage bag out to the trash container as they turned in at the driveway. Lee greeted them with "Hi, Mom, hi, Dad" — and then looked up and yelped in laughter when he saw Eddie. He was so surprised that he dropped the garbage bag, but fortunately it landed in the container. Carolyn insisted on taking a photo — "So we can see what Eddie will look like in fifteen years." Leland has fond memories of the teasing they gave him.

As demand for *Laughter in Bloom* increased, Eddie and Carolyn agreed to be choosy about bookings: "We always made it a practice to find places where we could find something interesting to visit — historical sites near the city, landmarks, little treasures that we could discover. This was a reward we gave ourselves, and we always added extra time to each trip just so we could enjoy ourselves."

Around this time casinos began asking for the show, but they were happier with a shortened version, so Eddie edited the two-hour version down to a more casino-friendly length. Jack Benny had worked Las Vegas, and Eddie took material from some of his shows there that were a little more adult (though certainly not dirty — maybe "mildly risqué" is a good description) and incorporated some of these stories into the presentation. The Tropicana Resort and Casino was the first to book Eddie for black-tie banquets given especially for the high rollers, and the show went so well that he was to do return engagements there, getting to know the resort employees and staff well.

One memory Eddie had of his first appearance at the Tropicana involved transportation: "I remember Carolyn and I laughed out loud the first time we saw a stretched-Hummer limousine on Ventura Boulevard in Encino. Who would be so extravagant as to use a silly thing like a Hummer for a limo? But then when the time came for us to return to the airport after the shows, the resort called and said a car would be waiting at the hotel entrance to take us. We went down, and of course there was a long stretched Hummer. The two of us in that huge car! I think it was a little larger than the hotel room that Tommy Banks and I shared when we first came to Hollywood."

As the decade began in a casino, so it ended. Eddie signed a contract with BaldGuy Productions to once again be the closing act for a revue at the Frontier Hotel and Casino in Las Vegas. Carolyn, already at ease in the control booth, was asked to direct the other three acts that preceded Eddie's Jack Benny closing, and as usual the schedule was tight: two shows a night, six nights a week, for two solid months. Still, Carolyn recalls this as a good time with old friends. Once more she made their temporary apartment as homey as possible, bringing things from California to decorate it and make it familiar and comfortable.

Their routine was to make dinner before the first show, then return between shows to clean the kitchen and have coffee. Because the show was dark on Mondays, they ventured out each week to a different hotel, where they had lunch and then went on a date, maybe seeing a show or movie, and then having dinner before going back to their apartment home-away-from home.

Because they had Christmas week off (though that translated to five days off, really), Eddie and Carolyn returned home to Encino for the holiday, where Leland and his girlfriend had already decorated the house and put up the tree. Before the show run had started, Carolyn had prepared and frozen many of the traditional Ukrainian Christmas dishes, and as Eddie drove back home, Carolyn wrapped presents in the car. They pulled off another miracle, and the Carrolls treated friends and family to another annual Ukrainian Christmas, their regular tradition.

Then back to finish the run. The New Year's Eve show ended at ten

Taa-Daa! It's the Ukrainian Christmas Eve feast.

minutes before midnight, and the cocktail waitresses brought into the showroom champagne for the crew and cast. Carolyn closed the tech booth and put their two glasses of champagne on the floor under the tech panel, and she and Eddie ran through the casino to enjoy the fireworks display bringing in 2001. The finale, with all the casinos shooting off brilliant, multicolored fireworks at the same time, was thunderous and memorable.

However, when Eddie and Carolyn returned to the showroom, their two glasses of champagne were missing. Someone had sneaked a little extra cheer. The cocktail waitresses replaced the champagne, and Eddie and Carolyn toasted in another New Year while giving thanks for everything the old one had brought them.

After a two-month engagement at the Frontier Hotel, the very next day Eddie and Carolyn flew to Chesapeake Bay for a performance. Carolyn remembers the food: "we had the best crab cakes we had ever eaten!" And it was the year the Baltimore Ravens went to the Super Bowl, with Baltimore aglitter with fans rooting for their team. Downtown buildings had lights spelling out "Go Ravens," and banners and signs hung all over. On January 28, the Ravens did win the Super Bowl, adding to the general euphoria that accompanied Eddie's performance there.

Ramada Express ad from Laughlin, Nevada.

From Baltimore, the show toured the Midwest and then California, then the Spirit Lake Casino in Devil's Lake, North Dakota. Surveying the flat landscape, Eddie said, "If your dog ran away from home here, you could still see him three days later."

Carolyn found the location intriguing: "A casino named Spirit Lake Resort in the middle of Devil's Lake!" At that time, the Carrolls noticed that beneath the waters they could see houses. The locals explained that starting in the 1990s the area had received unprecedentedly high rainfall. The lake has no natural outlet, and so each rainstorm made it overflow more and more. As the lake waters rose, people moved their houses back from the shore until finally they had to abandon their homes altogether as the lake covered them, even the roofs. Eddie and Carolyn both sensed and shared the sadness of this long-term flood. It was a town that needed laughter.

Next, in October the show was booked for a week's engagement twice a year for the Ramada Express Resort and Casino in Laughlin, Nevada. The resort had a railroad theme: the swimming pool was shaped like a locomotive, and a real antique train took guests on rides around the complex. Guests were called passengers, and the staff dressed as engineers. The Ramada Express became one of Eddie's favorite places to work, partly because most of the lounge acts were old friends with whom the Carrolls enjoyed spending time. The talented pianist twins Mark and Clark, whom they knew from Atlantic City, were there. One night they showed up in the audience for Eddie's show, both wearing Benny-style horn-rimmed glasses. The Laughlin engagements continued twice a year for four years, always a high point of Eddie's tour memories:

> EDDIE CARROLL: It even gave me a little taste of celebrity. You know, no one recognizes me as Jiminy's voice. Maybe they were expecting someone taller, I don't know. And because in *Laughter* I take on Jack Benny's look and mannerisms, I don't think I'm that recognizable when I'm offstage. So in Laughlin when I wear my normal glasses and a baseball cap, I think I'm pretty much incognito.
>
> Well, think again. The first time I appeared there, my photo was on the cover of the *Laughlin Entertainer* magazine, and every twelve or fifteen feet in the resort you'd see a 24-by-30 inch poster of me. And there were long banners all over town advertising *Laughter in Bloom*, so it wasn't easy to go unrecognized. That was probably the first time since I'd been a page at NBC that so many people came up to me just out of the blue and asked for an autograph.

One year Chuck, TOS, came to Laughlin so the Carrolls could celebrate his birthday with him. Chuck had become the Carroll website's official webmaster, and after they had the celebratory dinner, Carolyn asked him if he'd like to help set the stage for the show and turn on the showroom lights and walk-in music. Off they went.

It was the first time that Chuck had ever walked onto a stage, and he frankly found it a little spooky, standing there with the lights on him and looking out over a thousand seats waiting for a crowd to come in and fill them. The Carrolls also taught TOS about their favorite gambling game, video Keno, and he won two small jackpots. To this day Carolyn wonders if that was a good thing to teach him! As for the Carrolls, they had their usual good luck at the game. Once Carolyn put in twenty dollars, marked seven numbers, and all seven came up on the first play, netting her a jackpot of $1750 and attracting other players — who instantly recognized Eddie and engaged him with reminiscences of having seen Jack Benny himself in performance. Eddie didn't mind at all. He found such moments wonderful.

Laughlin is in the desert, and the Carrolls worked there each October and January for four years. One year in October, the air conditioning was cranked up so high as they played Keno at the Ramada that Eddie ran up to the suite to get their sweaters. While he was away, Carolyn won another jackpot, and when the host verified it, he announced over the loudspeaker, "Mary Livingstone, Mrs. Jack Benny, just won a jackpot of $2,350 on video Keno!" The casino brought her a bouquet of balloons and a little Teddy bear, which she sat on the machine. When Eddie returned, he saw the balloons and asked, "What did you *do*?" The staff brought the cash, and Eddie saw what she had done. It was good PR for the show,

Chuck Magnus, the other son, *in Laughlin, Nevada.*

and from then on when the couple was playing Keno and having no luck, one would say to the other, "Go get the sweaters!"

The security that Eddie had once never worried about began to come in handy. Carolyn says, "At the Laughlin we always had the beautiful 'Broadway Unlimited' suite. The first time we worked there, after dinner we went back to the suite, brushed our teeth, and Eddie lay down for a quick nap while I headed to prepare the showroom for the audience to enter. Two huge security guards waited outside, and one of them said, 'Ma'am, we're here to assist you and Mr. Carroll down to the dressing room.' I already knew the back way to the dressing room, down through the kitchen to the backstage area, and why did I need a guard? Who knew me? However, when we went down with Eddie, people standing behind the corded-off area kept reaching out to grab his arm and speak to him. Then I got it!"

The show usually ran flawlessly in Laughlin, but on one Tuesday performance, after the show was dark on Monday, Eddie's lavaliere mike died. Carolyn caught it in the pre-show check, but the audience members were in their seats and it was show time, so she had a stagehand pass Eddie a cordless microphone. It was a problem for Eddie: Jack Benny gestured extravagantly as he talked, and the mike hindered that, and at the end of the show he needed both hands free to play the violin. To let the audience know what was going on, Carolyn said over the PA, "Mr. Benny! Mr. Benny, we're having an audio problem, and we need you to use a hand mike."

Before long the crew found and fixed the problem, and Carolyn came back on the PA from the tech booth: "Mr. Benny, you are now double miked. Put down the hand mike, and thank you. Now on with the show."

Not long after that a casino executive took the Carrolls across the street for dinner, and while Carolyn was away from the table for a moment, a fan came up to Eddie. Carolyn returned, and Eddie said, "This is my wife, Carolyn."

Carolyn said, "Nice to meet you."

The delighted fan said, "Oh, I recognize your voice! You played the manager in the show!"

Carolyn replied, "Oh, you saw the show Tuesday night!" Eddie and Carolyn let the fan believe that Carolyn wasn't a real stage manager — she just played one in stage shows!

In addition to touring *Laughter in Bloom*, Eddie also began to receive invitations to perform as Jack Benny in a variety of Old Time Radio conventions, usually re-creating a Benny broadcast. At the same time, he was celebrated as the voice of Jiminy in a whole range of Disney events in California and Florida, where he regularly appeared at the Disneyana conventions, enthusiastic gatherings of friendly, young-at-heart people who love and treasure Disney characters and memorabilia. His autograph on reproductions of Jiminy's film scenes was in high demand, and he always enjoyed chatting and reminiscing with fans of his Disney work.

A new recording area opened for him, too. Disney had ventured into the video-game market, most notably with a series called *Kingdom Hearts*, an adventure game that transports the player to a world where the Disney characters are real and interact with him or her. The game's complex storyline allows each player to take on a personality of one of the game characters and to make decisions and form strategies that will lead to different outcomes. In the role of the wise advisor, Jiminy appears at intervals in the game to caution the player about dangers ahead or to gently suggest re-thinking some potentially harmful decision — still playing the role of a conscience!

At a Disneyana Convention. Top row: Terry Hardin, artist and actress, Minnie and Mickey. Bottom row: Carolyn, Eddie, and Margaret Kerry, model for Tinker Bell.

The Disney Channel also developed a new TV series called *House of Mouse* in which the classic Disney cartoon characters appear in somewhat updated versions. The House of Mouse is a dinner theater club co-owned by Mickey and Donald and managed by Mickey and Minnie. Eddie voiced many Jiminy appearances in the show, including one in which Jiminy became a *naughty* conscience — he thought it was a lot of fun to be cast as a villain, so out of character for the normal Jiminy. He also had a memorable speak-singing bit, a recitation to music in which he cautioned everyone not to make the kind of mistakes that Disney characters are prone to — You should never trust a guy named Foulfellow, he suggests, because he's got the word "foul" in his name, for crying out loud!

In the summer of 2002, Jack Benny's home town of Waukegan, IL, planned "the Benny Bash," a great celebration in the comedian's honor. Among other things, a larger than life-sized statue of Jack was to be unveiled, with Jack posed as he so often was with crossed arms and a hand to his cheek. The granite base included etchings of Benny-related people and things: a violin, Mary, a pair of glasses, the lock of Jack's vault, and other memorable items. As a part of the celebration, Eddie and Carolyn agreed to bring a version of *Laughter in Bloom* to Waukegan, where Eddie would also participate in a live re-creation of a radio script organized by President Laura Leff, with other members of the International Jack Benny Fan Club assisting.

At the Jack Benny Center for the Arts Eddie did the cut-down version of *Laughter in Bloom* as a dinner show on the evening of Friday, June 7, to great applause. On the IJBFC website, Laura Leff wrote, "As an introduction, some videos from Jack's TV shows were shown. At some point I turned and looked out toward the foyer. I could see a person's silhouette, which gave me a small gasp. It looked exactly like Jack Benny in one of his favorite poses." At the end of the show, Eddie received a standing ovation.

On Saturday Eddie and Carolyn were taken to the Waukegan Yacht Club for lunch. On the way there, as Jack, Eddie asked, "Yacht club? How many yachts do you have here? One boat?" However, the club proved to be lovely — and it had many beautiful boats and terrific food.

Meanwhile, the IJBFC team rehearsed the radio re-creation. Laura had chosen a vintage Benny radio script from September, 1951, when Lucky Strike Cigarettes had been the sponsors, with the often repeated tagline "LS — MFT! Lucky Strike means fine tobacco!" In this particular episode, Jack and the gang do one of their parodies of a popular film, in this case *Captain Horatio Hornblower*, with Jack playing the dashing English sea captain from the days of the Napoleonic wars (Gregory Peck played him in the film) and Mary taking the role of Lady Barbara Wellesley (Virginia Mayo in the film).

Chuck Schaden, legendary Chicago radio personality, was there to record an episode of his nostalgia show "Those Were the Days" that would incorporate clips from the re-creation. The cast of Eddie's show included Charlie Willer as the sound-effects man and Mel Blanc; Dan Leff as Rochester; Bill Powers as Don Wilson; Eric Brolund as Phil Harris; Tom Trethewey as Dennis Day (who sang an *a capella* version of the lively "Clancy Lowered the Boom," one of Dennis's familiar Irish numbers); and Maria Scarvelis as Mary Livingstone.

When show time arrived, Eddie warmed up the audience as Jack, speaking about the times that Jack had revisited Waukegan and previous recognitions: Waukegan had named a school for him and in 1939 had even hosted the premiere of his movie *Man About Town* in the Genesee Theatre (under renovation in 2002). Once the city had also planted a tree in Jack's honor, but it died. Eddie repeated the quip made by Fred Allen (supposedly Jack's radio enemy, but in person his great friend): "No wonder. How can the tree live in Waukegan when the sap's out in Hollywood?"

Then Eddie and the cast went into the re-creation with verve and a gusto that charmed the audience. Early in the show, Jack has one of his many minor squabbles with announcer Don Wilson over the terms of the new contract that Don has just signed. When Don says, "This contract isn't so different from the old one. I've always worked week to week," Jack shoots back, "Well, *this* time you're working from word to word! I can fire you between LS and MFT!"

As Don announced the movie parody sketch, one of only two prerecorded sound effects played: an orchestra giving a rousing rendition of "Rule, Britannia" to set the scene. The plot called for a South American dictator, El Supremo (Dennis Day), to come aboard Hornblower's ship, but when Phil Harris ordered the crew to fire "an eleven-gun salute" to welcome him aboard, there was a sound miscue. Instead of cannon fire, the soundman played "Rule, Britannia" again, to the visible surprise of the cast members, but Eddie stepped in with a quick in-character save. As Jack, he turned to the sound-effects man and said accusingly, "And *you're* working from sound effect to sound effect!" It was an ad-lib that brought down the house — and caused members of the orchestra and the onstage cast to break up as well. The re-enactment concluded to cheers and wild applause.

Later, the group attended the formal unveiling of the bronze Benny statue, diagonally across from the Genesee Theatre, and there Eddie met and talked with Jack's three grandchildren: Joanna and her husband Brad Meiseles, Maria Rudolph, and Bobby Blumofe with his beautiful fiancée Cynthia Breazeal, an expert on personal robotics at the Massachusetts Institute of Technology.

All of them have the warmest memories of Eddie and his performances as Jack. Bobby was glad that Cynthia was with him: "Of course, she entered my life long after granddad had died, and though through her life with me she's gotten to know more and more about him, this was one of the few times that she's been really able to experience directly why it was that audiences so loved him." And Bobby adds another reason: "I, in fact, had very little opportunity to be part of a live audience reacting to granddad's performance. I saw him a couple of times in Las Vegas, but I was young and remember very little of it. For me, watching Eddie was as close as I could get in my adult life to that experience. Performers often say there's nothing like a live audience, and I can see why. I found it

Joanna Meiseles (Jack Benny's granddaughter), Eddie, Maria Rudolf (Jack Benny's granddaughter), Joanna's husband Brad and Maureen Finn.

profoundly moving to be part of a live audience reacting in the moment with such joy and laughter to Eddie's performance — or was that my granddad's performance?"

Joanna, too, found *Laughter in Bloom* a joyful but deeply poignant experience. She says, "My memories of my grandfather are somewhat fragmented and scattered, because I was only nine years old when he died. It makes me a little sad that I didn't know him better, but one thing most kids can't say is that because my grandfather was famous, I've had the opportunity to get to know him even after he passed away. I've watched tribute shows, his old shows, and his movies, and of course I read my mom's book, so I've learned a lot about him and even how he felt about me through those things. But what really brought him back to life was watching Eddie's shows. It was truly amazing to have that in my adult life,

Eddie with the Jack Benny statue in Waukegan.

thirty years after my grandfather died. I felt like I could actually be with him, not just learn about him. Eddie gave me a special gift! I remember one time we saw Eddie's show when my sister, who is eight years older than I am and remembers grandfather better, started crying, really bawling, sobbing uncontrollably. I whispered to ask her what was the matter, and she replied through her tears, 'It's like he's here.' It was a surreal experience for me and a very emotional one for Maria. How many grandkids get that kind of memory? Eddie gave that to us!"

Maria adds simply but from the heart, "We, as a family, were very lucky to have Eddie keep Granddad alive for so many years. So many people were exposed to Granddad's career because of the work that Eddie did."

Everyone, fans and family alike, admired the bronze statue of Waukegan's favorite son, and of course everyone had to be photographed with it, including Eddie, his pose matching the statue's. A week later, Eddie also received an honor that not even Jack himself had been given. The Mayor, Richard H. Hide, presented him with a formal resolution that ended,

> "NOW, THEREFORE, BE IT RESOLVED, that the Mayor and City Council of the City of Waukegan recognize Eddie Carroll as HONORARY MAYOR of the City of Waukegan."

Eddie and Carolyn received an embossed copy of the resolution, a source of quiet pride for Eddie, proof of the high esteem Jack's home town felt for him and the respect the citizens of Waukegan had for Eddie's honest, painstaking effort to bring Jack back to the stage. Betty and Tom Kennedy sent him a congratulatory letter: "You and Carolyn must feel on top of the world after the last few months of your lives! You certainly deserve to feel such…the official proclamation of Eddie Carroll as Honorary Mayor of the City! Jiminy Crickets! Does it ever end?" The Kennedys warmly concluded, "Betty joins me in congratulating you and your gorgeous Production Director, Carolyn, on your accomplishments and sure-to-follow encores!"

Eddie had always been so accomplished that he could follow hard acts with no qualms. He had followed Cliff Edwards with talent and aplomb. In that summer, he followed the hardest of them all, Jack Benny, in Benny's own home town, and he had done it with such grace and style that the performance reflected beautifully on both Eddie and Jack.

CHAPTER 22

New Places, New Faces

The National Fantasy Fan Club (NFFC), now the Disneyana Fan Club, is made up of multi-talented people from all walks of life and from all over the world who have in common a devotion to all things Disney. Eddie became a favorite guest at their conventions during the early 2000s, and he won a "Disney Legend Award" from them posthumously (though he knew he was going to receive it before he passed away). Eddie loved associating with the members of the club and attending the conventions at Disneyland and Disney World, where he signed autographs and heard hundreds, if not thousands, of stories from people who loved the little cricket he voiced so well.

In turn, the fans found Eddie approachable, friendly, upbeat and always cheerful. He *was* Jiminy (somewhat larger than life sized), and collectors, fans, and friends adored him. Eddie had a real knack for making friends, as one of us can attest.

BRAD STRICKLAND: In real life, I am a Professor of English at North Georgia University in Georgia, but in my *other* life, I'm a writer primarily of fantasy and science fiction. In the summer of 2002 I was signing books at a conference, and next to me at the autograph table was Tim Hollis, author of many fascinating volumes about the past, including *Hi There, Boys and Girls! America's Local Children's TV Programs*. As Tim chatted with me, I mentioned that I loved old-time radio and the Jack Benny program in particular.

Tim said, "Oh, then you must know Eddie Carroll." I didn't, and he told me about Eddie's one-man show as Jack Benny. We exchanged business cards, and that would normally have been the end of it.

However, Tim talked to Eddie not long afterward and told him what a big Jack Benny fan I was. He passed my telephone number along, and one day that fall as I was sitting in my office at Gainesville State College (as the University then was), the phone rang. When I answered it I heard that unmistakable voice: "Is this professor Strickland? This is Jack Benny talking."

The penny dropped after a moment, and I said, "Eddie Carroll! You do a great Jack Benny!" We talked for half an hour, and after the first five minutes it was like conversing with an old and dear friend. Later on we phoned each other frequently just to chat about this and that and to

Yarmy's Army gathering: Shelley Berman, Chuck McCann, Henry Gibson, and former Los Angeles Mayor Richard Riordon.

catch up with each other.

Quite soon, I knew I had to see *Laughter in Bloom*. I checked Eddie's website and discovered that in the following spring's tour it came no closer to Georgia than ... Pomona, New Jersey. However, my wife Barbara knew how much I wanted to go, and so we made a special trip, saw and loved the show, and spoke briefly to Eddie afterward. "We have to have you come to our college," I said, and with the help of the Gainesville State College Drama Department and the Gainesville Theatre Alliance, we did, two years later, in March 2006.

During all the time I knew him, Eddie was always warm, open, and friendly — even when, toward the summer of 2004, he was briefly sidelined with an illness that kept him from getting out as much as he wanted to. When I called him, not knowing he was home recuperating until he told me so, I apologized and said I wouldn't bother him.

"Oh, no, you don't," Eddie shot back. "I've got cabin fever. Tell me how your kids are doing!" He was always interested and always remembered the names of our children, Jonathan and his wife Rebecca, and our daughter Amy, a puppeteer by trade. They, in turn, had a chance to meet Eddie when the show came to our town, and like Barbara and me, they felt they had known him for years after one meeting. And we weren't the only ones.

Richard Riordon and Eddie doing Benny at Yarmy's Army.

That friendliness created and continually expanded Eddie's vast, extended family of fans and colleagues, as did his association with old-time radio groups, the International Jack Benny Fan Club, and other organizations. To take a great example, Eddie was also a member of Yarmy's Army. Dick Yarmy was the brother of Don Adams (of *Get Smart!* fame), and Dick was a man with a sharp sense of humor and great talent as both an actor and director. He and Eddie met in the 1980s when they worked on a gas-station commercial together, and they routinely ran into each other at auditions for sitcoms or commercials.

In the early 1990s Dick was diagnosed with lung cancer. He told everyone who visited him, "If you came to tell me a joke or make me laugh, that's great. Just don't feel sorry for me or be depressed." Eddie was among the many writers, actors, and comics who visited and cheered up Dick Yarmy, and in honor of him they formed a brotherhood, Yarmy's Army, dedicated to keeping up the spirits of all those who need laughter.

They still carry on the tradition today, and when Carolyn needed cheering up, the group was there for her.

The initial group included Pat Harrington, Ronnie Schell, Howard Storm, and Hank Bradford. The Army grew over time, coming to include Shelley Berman, Bill Dana, Gary Owens (the familiar announcer and voiceover artist from *Rowan and Martin's Laugh-In*), Jack Riley, Peter Marshall, Harvey Korman, Louis Nye, John Rappaport, Chuck McCann, Kerry Ross, Jack Sheldon — a whole roster of multi-talented and caring people. Eddie fit right into the group. They got bookings as Yarmy's Army and did (and continue to do) performances and raise money to help those in need.

Thanks in part to his work with Yarmy's Army, Eddie developed a routine that he greatly enjoyed of meeting his coffee buddies every Wednesday and Saturday mornings — when he wasn't on the road, of course — first at the Sportsmen's Lodge in Studio City and then when that watering hole closed for renovations at Jerry's Famous Deli.

The gang would talk shop about upcoming jobs or what had happened on the last one, they would tease each other unmercifully but with good humor, and they would exchange excruciating puns. The group developed a tremendous camaraderie and eventually included not only the Yarmy's Army gang but also Randy Kurdoon, Jim Vidor, Arnie Kogen, Bob Mills, Steve Landesberg, and confetti-tossing comic Rip Taylor. After a session with these guys, Eddie would return home for lunch elated, still laughing over something that one of the wits said during coffee.

Once when chatting on the phone to Brad Strickland in Georgia, Eddie mused that it was a small world and told this story:

EDDIE CARROLL: You know, it's funny how you'll run into someone now and then when you haven't seen them in a while and you'll take right up where you left off. Rip Taylor somehow drifted away from the coffee meetings, and I hadn't seen him for, gosh, six months or so, though Carolyn and I have known him forever. Then we had a booking for *Laughter in Bloom* in Fredonia, New York, and Carolyn and I decided that after the run of the show we'd plan to spend a few days in Manhattan, as we hadn't been there for some time.

Well, we were going to fly out of L.A. on Wednesday. The Monday before that, Carolyn was tired, so we decided we'd have dinner out, and we went to one of our favorite restaurants. I'm sitting in the booth, and I hear a familiar voice behind me, and I turn around. There sitting in the booth literally inches away from me is Rip Taylor. I greeted him, we talked and caught up on what each other had been doing, and it was nice.

So the *next* night, Carolyn and I thought we'd eat out again because we had to catch an early flight the following morning. We went to a different restaurant, and as the waiter brought our menus, I glanced over, and two tables away, there sat Rip Taylor — remember, I hadn't seen him in half a year up until the night before, and here two nights running we meet him randomly. So I walk over and we talked about what a coincidence and so forth.

Carolyn and I flew to New York and we did *Laughter in Bloom* in Fredonia, and we had good audiences, the show was a success, and we were happy. Then we drove into the city and checked into a hotel. That evening we went to Elaine's for dinner, and almost as soon as we were seated, I saw Rip Taylor sitting across the room. I got up and did my Jack Benny walk over to his table, posed there, and in my best Benny voice, I said, "Oh, Rip — we've *got* to stop meeting like this!"

And you know, without even looking up, Rip motioned a waiter over and in a fussy voice said, "You have to move me to a different table. This strange man is bothering me!"

The capper? All right, a couple of days later Carolyn and I get up to go to the New York airport to catch an early flight back to California. So we decide to grab something for breakfast at the coffee shop down near the lobby, and when we walk in — there's Rip Taylor having coffee! We found out we had been staying in the same hotel and didn't realize it. Now, isn't it a small world?

Even smaller than Eddie thought. Brad told him, "You won't believe this, but the day after tomorrow I'm going to the DragonCon media convention in Atlanta, and one of the guests is Rip Taylor!"

Eddie laughed. "Oh, my goodness! Well, don't make a special effort, but if you run into him, be sure to tell him Carolyn and I send our best wishes."

Brad did find Rip at the convention, went up and introduced himself, and said, "Mr. Taylor, Eddie Carroll asked me to give you a message: He and Carolyn went to dinner last night in Hollywood, looked all around the restaurant, and didn't see you. They miss you terribly."

A surprised Taylor laughed so loud that everyone around had to hear the whole story, which Rip told with great glee, not neglecting to inform everyone of how talented Eddie was. Brad called Eddie to tell him about the payoff, and Eddie thought it was fantastic. Then, not a week later, Eddie phoned Brad to say,

EDDIE CARROLL: You're not going to believe this. This morning I went to have coffee with my usual gang, and they started telling stories. I piped up with, "This is the strangest coincidence. You all know Rip Taylor. Well, I know this guy in Georgia, of all places, and — "

I broke off because they were all grinning and looking past me. Just then someone tapped me on my shoulder. I turned around and looked up, and there stood Rip Taylor. He made a dismissive gesture, flapping his hand at me and informed me, "No, no. I'm going to tell it. *You'll* just mess it up!"

What a small world it really is!

In January, 2003, Eddie signed with a new booking agency, Gurtman and Murtha. Jim Murtha and Bill Weir were enthusiastic about representing Eddie's show, and they became good friends. Immediately *Laughter* began to be booked into more and more venues, with Gurtman and Murtha often managing to route a tour to concentrate on one area of the country at a time. Eddie was busier than ever, but because he and Carolyn were always together on the road, they enjoyed each other's company and had a blast visiting towns they had never seen before.

Also in 2003, Eddie met another old friend again. *Laughter in Bloom* was in production in the San Fernando Valley at the same time that a touring company was putting on *South Pacific,* starring Robert Goulet. The ads for the two shows appeared on the same day on the same page of the same newspaper, but Eddie's ad was not only larger, but placed above Robert's ad. Eddie sent a copy to Robert with a note teasing him about Robert's finally getting second billing to Eddie. The next weekend, both shows had a matinee and an evening performance, and after the matinee, Eddie and Carolyn returned home to find a message on the phone from Bob. Eddie returned the call and asked, "How were you able to call me? We both had matinees today!"

Goulet replied, "I've got a stand-in performing for me today, because I've got a sore throat."

"A *stand-in*?" Eddie asked. "You know, I don't have one of those. It's just me!" Within minutes the two old friends were laughing and joking as if they were still seniors in high school.

As Eddie continued to tour with *Laughter in Bloom* over the next few years, he gained a deeper appreciation for America's beautiful theaters. Many of the old Fox and State theaters that had survived the wrecking balls became valued landmarks and transformed themselves back into live-performance venues, coming full circle. Eddie admired the gorgeous carvings in some of them — often bits of architectural splendor that had spent decades concealed behind drywall. Old opera houses, too, were being remodeled to accommodate state-of-the-art equipment.

One that fascinated Eddie was the Cheboygan Opera House in Michigan, which seemed to have led a charmed life: "It was originally built in 1877, and then rebuilt after a fire in 1888, and again after a second fire in 1903. Now the grand old structure contains the city hall, the police headquarters, and the fire station — now, that was a great idea, considering the theater's history!"

When Eddie played Cheboygan, he and Carolyn had to venture over to Mackinac Island, a ferry ride away. It was said to be one of the most beautiful islands in the world. No motor vehicles are allowed there, just bicycles and horses. There is no automotive pollution (though behind the horse-drawn carriages men with wheelbarrows and shovels take care of another kind of exhaust), no engine noises, and as Carolyn observes, "You awaken each morning to the sound of hooves on cobblestone streets. It's so quaint, and the people are so friendly." The Carrolls spent a couple of days there and returned home with a box of their world-famous fudge.

Eddie and Carolyn in Pella, Iowa.

Another wonderful opera house that Eddie played is in Pella, Iowa, the city where Pella Doors and Windows is headquartered. The Pella Opera House on Franklin Street was built in 1900 and its architecture reflects Dutch heritage. Its façade represents Dutch houses, with tulips and other flowers in abundance, and not far away is Vermeer Mill, the only working wind-powered gristmill in the United States. As in Holland, Pella has bridges arching over canals, though everything was frozen solid during Eddie's run there.

More than once Eddie and Carolyn took the show to the Poconos or the Berkshires during autumn, when the fall color is glorious. Carolyn thinks everyone should make the trip just to see the turning leaves. The show played Denver in the winter, when Colorado was a true winter wonderland. Eddie enjoyed playing Myrtle Beach, South Carolina — even if he was a bit confused because the theater was the Alabama. He later learned that the music group Alabama actually created it. He thought the St. Louis Arch was amazing, learning that it had been built from two bases up to the top, meeting perfectly at last. He found Seattle's

George Takei, Fred Travalena, Eddie and Carolyn.

Space Needle awe-inspiring. When Eddie played near Amish country, the Carrolls' confetti-tossing friend Rip Taylor asked them to bring him back some Utz potato chips, but though they searched, the stores were all sold out. Eddie reflected that Utz chips must be delicious — or maybe, crumbled, they make fantastic confetti.

All these locations, and so many more, enriched Eddie and Carolyn's life, giving them extraordinary opportunities to visit scenic and historic places that they both loved. Carolyn remembers Old Sacramento especially: "Old Sac was a grand week for us. Eddie was there to do signings for an art gallery, and they put us up on the Delta King, the riverboat that is the sister — or brother — vessel of the Delta Queen. Both are paddlewheel steamboats built in 1926, and staying on one was like taking a step back in history. Today both the Delta King in Old Sac and the Delta Queen in Chattanooga, Tennessee, are hotels with elegant dining rooms and lounges. Once more, Eddie and I thanked our lucky star — and Jiminy, and Disney — that we got the chance to experience all this."

Eddie was invited to act the role of Jack Benny for the Lily Ball campaign for Easter Seals in Louisville, Kentucky, where he and Carolyn met new friends, including Fred and Lois Travalena. Fred, the man with a thousand voices, was one of the best impressionists in America, not only duplicating the voices of celebrities, but approximating their faces in his act. Tom and Betty Kennedy were there, too, together with

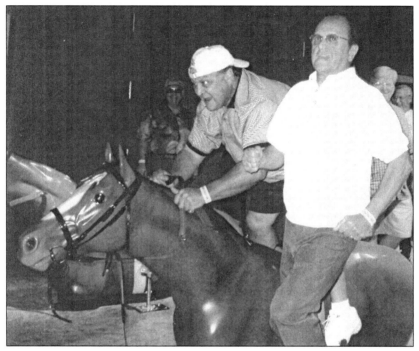

Eddie racing Ed O'Ross on mechanical horses.

Ed O'Ross, who is usually a tough bad guy on screen but is a funny, witty man in private, plus actor Conrad Bachman and his wife Kate. The whole gang visited Churchill Downs, where they fed peppermint candy to the horses — "They love it!" Carolyn reports. They also toured the Louisville Slugger baseball-bat factory and museum, and two weeks later FedEx delivered to Eddie and Carolyn personalized bats with their names etched in the wood.

Louisville is also famous for bourbon, and the show promoters arranged a bourbon and bourbon-containing food tasting in Eddie's honor. He expected something like a wine tasting, with a spoonful in a glass, but when he walked in, he and Carolyn each received a full glass of Maker's Mark. One sip and Carolyn was off in search of ice. They went from booth to booth sampling foods that all included bourbon as an ingredient, and by the time they left, they were glad a limo was there to return them to the hotel.

About a week after they had returned to Encino, the Carrolls heard a knock on the door. A delivery man had arrived with a box containing eight bottles of bourbon, and as Eddie signed the receipt, the poor guy dropped

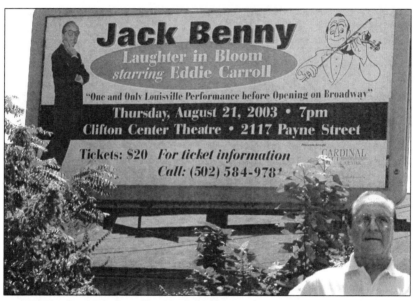

Eddie with a billboard in Louisville, Kentucky.

the box on the tiled entryway. Two of the eight bottles had broken — the only two "Special Reserve" bottles, the best of the best. For the next few days, the Carroll house smelled like a distillery.

As in Laughlin, in Louisville Eddie's face was everywhere: billboards advertised the show, and during their daily walks the Carrolls saw buses with Eddie's picture on the sides. Eddie bought another baseball cap as a partial disguise. Carolyn remembers that their room boasted a four-poster bed. In the middle of the night, she got up to visit the bathroom, but it was so dark that in feeling her way down the bed she smacked into the foot post hard, taking most of the blow in the center of her forehead. The next morning she discovered that she had an angry red circle right in the middle of her forehead, and from then on she remembered to be careful in navigating her way around the room in the dark. After that, she always packed two small nightlights in her travel bag, one for the bedroom, one for the bath.

Of course Eddie's Jiminy assignments continued too, coming in sometimes almost daily. He did more educational recordings, more bits for TV and the parks, and always, always protected the dignity of Pinocchio's small conscience. If men were measured by kindness, maybe it's true that Ebeneezer Scrooge would be a tiny speck of dust.

Eddie, though, would be as big as all outdoors.

CHAPTER 23

Clubs, Recognitions, and Awards

In January 2004 Eddie and Carolyn, at the urging of Bill Weir of Gurtman and Murtha, attended a convention specially designed for show and theater presenters from around the world. It took place at the Hilton in New York and proved to be a good conference to visit, because the promoters often decide to book a show based on presentations at the convention. It was a crisp New York winter at first, and then it grew really frigid. Carolyn remembers, "Our room had a window seat with a beautiful view of the city. Just outside the window was a tall thermometer, and the reading just kept dropping until it reached twenty below zero at midnight. We closed the drapes not only to keep out the cold but also because we just didn't want to watch it get any lower!"

Now committed power walkers, the next day Eddie and Carolyn rose and decided they would at least venture outside for one walk around the block. They bundled up with gloves, scarves, hats, and long faux-fur coats and then went out to meet the Arctic morning. They didn't even make it around the hotel, but went out the front entrance, turned at the corner, and immediately came back inside via the side entrance. Carolyn remembers, "The tears in my eyes had frozen! I couldn't even blink." Fifteen minutes after they got back into the warmth of the hotel, Carolyn's tears began to flow and wouldn't stop — her eyes watered for another hour. "After that experience," she says, "I always wear my sunglasses outside, even in the freezing cold."

Almost immediately after the convention, Eddie and Carolyn signed a contract for a seven-city tour in Ontario, Canada, with theaters in St. Catherine's (on the Canadian side of Niagara Falls), Barrie, Chatham, Oakville, Kitchener, Brampton, and North Bay. Then Gurtman and Murtha added another city, Bellville, and then one in Fredonia, New York, and one in Sellersville, Pennsylvania: ten cities in twelve days for *Laughter in Bloom!*

It was a flood of engagements, and Carolyn sat at her computer in the Carrolls' guest bedroom, working on the road and theater arrangements. She spread the contracts and the technical rider information sheets on the bed, together with the cue sheets and the rehearsal times for each theater. Another stack contained hotel reservations. As Carolyn began to sort them into order by the appearance dates, Eddie came into the room and stood there holding a sheet of paper. When Carolyn glanced at him, he said, "Honey, when you have time, can you fax this for me?"

Oh, you've got to be kidding, Carolyn thought. She said to Eddie, "No, because I just quit!" But she couldn't keep from laughing.

Eddie joined in and then asked teasingly, "What if I gave you a raise?"

"How much?" Carolyn asked.

Eddie went away and came back a moment later…with a stepladder.

Jack Benny had always loved a visual gag, too.

Eddie took Carolyn's hand and said, "What if I took you to lunch?"

They went to lunch, and when they returned, the phone rang. It was Bill Weir, who started giving Carolyn information on yet more requests for the show. Carolyn said to Bill, "I just quit!"

She heard him gasp, and then there was a pregnant pause wide enough for two Mack trucks to go through side by side before Carolyn relieved Bill's anxiety by confessing, "I'm kidding."

She explained that she was just a little punchy from all the paperwork, and then they went on to the new show dates. Not long after that, the Carrolls' friend Rob Barran came over and heard what had happened. He immediately proclaimed himself Carolyn's agent and told Eddie, "We want a raise!"

Eddie spread his hands and said, "She already gets 50% of everything I've got!"

Rob came back with, "She wants 60%."

Eddie didn't say anything, partly because he was laughing too hard, and partly because, like Jack Benny being held up, he was thinking it over.

Later, reminiscing about the moment, Rob said, "Edd is all wonderful: understanding, caring, talented, giving, reliable, dedicated, dapper, and funny as hell. Edd could brighten any situation by his humor and saneness." Audiences didn't see as much of Eddie as Rob did, but they would agree with that assessment as the *Laughter* tours continued.

The Canadian tour was exciting, but the Carrolls soon discovered that the towns were scattered all over the enormous province. Eddie said, "It's like somebody took a handful of darts and just flung them at the map of Canada." Eddie and Carolyn packed as lightly as they could, considering they had only one day off following the Chatham engagement. There they were lodged at the Wheels Inn Resort, which offers laundry facilities, fortunately for Eddie and Carolyn. She remembers, "By that point we were down to bathing suits!" That attracted no attention, because the resort includes a water park, but it did mean that doing the laundry was high on the list of necessities.

So, taking lots of change with her, Carolyn took their clothes to the laundry room, intending to swim and use the Jacuzzi while the laundry was in the machines. However, she discovered that no coins she had would fit into the washing-machine slots. She went back to the room and told Eddie about the problem, but he had no idea what was to be done about it.

Carolyn says, "So, wearing my bathing suit and my gauze cover-up, I ran to the front desk, which was a long way off. The clerk there informed me that Canada has a one-dollar coin called the 'loonie' and a two-dollar one called the 'toonie.' The washers and dryers took loonies. I exchanged my coins for a supply and did the laundry. When I got back to the room and told my Canadian husband about the currency, he was surprised — he hadn't even heard about the loonie-toonie Canadian money." Carolyn was just glad that she had the water park and Jacuzzi to relax in while the clothes were being washed and dried. As Eddie commented when she brought the clean clothes up the stairs and to the room, "That's show biz!"

The widely scattered venues meant that Eddie and Carolyn skimped on sleep. They tried to make up for that by napping in the limos — when the driver was quiet. However, limo drivers, like everyone they met, enjoyed talking to Eddie! When they went to North Bay, they had to fly in, because the drive time was five hours through rough terrain. They discovered they had a choice of two airlines, either Bearskin or Jazz. Carolyn the dancer decided they'd take the Jazz, not try to fly on a bearskin. After a matinee in Brampton, they flew out of Toronto to North Bay, nestled in a picturesque bay of Lake Nipissing. As the plane banked in, they could see whitecaps on the water, whipped up by gusts of wind.

The Jazz plane landed, Lee Kools, the hostess who took wonderful care of them while they were in North Bay, met the plane, and almost immediately they rushed to the theater for the tech set-up and cue-to-cue run-through. Then came the show, and only twenty-one hours from the time they landed, the Carrolls were aboard the same plane flying to Toronto, which gave them a sense of *déjà vu*.

Next they were off to Windsor, where 44 years earlier they had performed *A la Carte from Las Vegas*. In 1961 they had played the Elmwood Casino, but now Eddie performed in the Capitol Theater. As they talked with the manager there about the tech requirements of *Laughter in Boom*, Carolyn mentioned that earlier show and the manager laughed. "The Elmwood is a drug and alcohol rehabilitation center now," he said. Eddie and Carolyn recalled their tiny rooms at the Elmwood, like monastery cells, with a sink in each, but the showers and kitchens at the ends of the hall. If anything could sober a person up, they decided, living in a place like that would do it.

From Ontario, the tour went on into the American Midwest. At one theater, the tech booth was in the open at the rear of the auditorium. Jeff, the local sound tech, was helping Carolyn close up after one show, packing up the CDs and the DVDs and making sure the board was shut down, when a tiny, elderly lady came up to the booth opening and asked Jeff, "Excuse me, young man, but may I ask you a question? Why do you keep turning the lights on and off and changing the colors?"

Surprised, Jeff did a double take and then politely responded, "We do it to change the mood or the setting of a scene."

The little old lady snorted. "That's the dumbest thing I ever heard!" And she flounced off.

Jeff shrugged and said to Carolyn, "She doesn't get out much, does she?"

In a gorgeous theater in Kansas, Eddie as usual went out to the lobby to pose for photos and sign autographs, and as the crowd cleared out, a gentleman staggered out of a bar adjacent to the lobby and came up to Eddie, who detected the aroma of Jack Daniels.

The man said, "I — I wanta to see — see your show tonight, but I — I got held up. Could I have yer autograph?"

Eddie, always polite, said, "Why, certainly," and signed a program *from Eddie Carroll as Jack Benny*.

The gentleman tried to focus on it. "So, so you play the clarinet?"

Surprised, Eddie said, "No, I play the violin as Jack Benny."

The man seemed genuinely bewildered. "Benny Goodman, an' you sign your name Eddie Carroll as Jack Benny? Geez, you don't even know who you are!" And he staggered away, still trying to figure it out.

Laughter in Bloom played a return engagement in Sherwood Park, a suburb of Edmonton, and the Carrolls took advantage of their visit to host a family and friends reception in a banquet room adjacent to the theater — with the number of each that Eddie had, it was the only way to get them all together in one place. Eddie enjoyed himself immensely and in a curtain speech introduced his 92-year-young Aunt Rose Starsuk, a lady with a wonderful sense of humor and a beautiful outlook on life. She had only one complaint: until Eddie announced her age, everyone thought she was younger! "People look at you differently when you're only in your eighties," she explained. Eddie also introduced many friends of long standing from school and from the Orion Theatre: Senator Tommy Banks, the Honorable Chief Justice Allan Wachovich, Attorney Practice Advisor Barry Vogel, and many others. Eddie, who cherished family, carried warm memories of the event for the rest of his life.

Aunt Rose and Eddie.

Back in California, Eddie had the pleasure of performing his one-man show in a brand-new theater complex in Rancho Cucamonga. Eddie had been an honored guest at the unveiling of a magnificent fifteen-foot statue of Jack Benny by the renowned artist Lawrence Noble. Now, with the building of the theater, the statue was moved to an alcove in the spectacular lobby of the Lewis Family Playhouse. After the show, fans lined up to have their picture taken with Eddie in front of the statue. The photography went on and on, but as it began to tail off, the Carrolls' friend Wende Doohan and her adorable six-year old daughter Sarah came up to Carolyn. Sarah explained that her dad was a huge Jack Benny fan and that the two of them would listen to his old-time radio show collection. She never heard a bedtime story — she preferred to listen to a Jack Benny program!

She knew all the characters in the show, and as Eddie finished posing for the last photo with a fan, he came over and heard Sarah talking about the radio program. "Would you like to have your picture taken with me next to the statue?" he asked.

Sarah nodded, and as they posed, with an incredible grin, she put her hand to her cheek. It brought a lump to Carolyn's throat, because not very long before Sarah's father, James Doohan, known to and loved by *Star Trek* fans as Scotty, the engineer of the starship *Enterprise*, had passed away.

Oh, the conversation with Sarah about the cast of the Jack Benny show revealed that her favorite among all of Jack's regulars was Dennis Day, "because he's so charming."

Another engagement at Newburyport, just north of Boston, brought Eddie a deep personal memory. Before a performance there, he got word that some special audience members would be Jack's granddaughter Joanna Meiseles and her husband Brad, with their two oldest children, Brandon and Ben, and Jack's grandson Bobby Blumofe with his lovely wife Cynthia (who had just given birth to their third child). In a curtain speech, Eddie surprised them by introducing them from the stage as the lights picked them out — and then Joanna surprised Eddie by bringing a beautiful bouquet of flowers up to him. The Carrolls enjoyed meeting the children, and Carolyn immediately began to call Ben "Ben Benny." Though the great-grandchildren never knew the real Jack, they were enthralled with Eddie and took posters from the wall and asked Eddie to sign them. Today both are college guys, attending Duke University. Jack would have been as proud of them as Eddie, Carolyn, Joanna, and Brad are.

Eddie and Sarah Doohan with Jack Benny statue in the theater at Rancho Cucamonga.

Two more especially memorable engagements: Eddie loved playing the Thousand Oaks Civic Arts Plaza, a beautiful area just outside Los Angeles. Again family and friends flocked to see the performance, and the first show sold out so quickly that the Plaza immediately added a second one. In the tech booth, one of the crew commented how impressed he was because "so many stars" were in the theater. Carolyn said, "Those stars are all our friends."

Then Chuck Schaden, host and historian of the *Those Were the Days* radio show, decided that after 39 years he was ready to retire. To commemorate the occasion, Chuck organized a live farewell broadcast, and as a special favor he asked Eddie to appear in *Laughter in Bloom*. Eddie readily agreed. After all, thirty-nine years was a perfect tie-in with Jack Benny! It was a festive night, filled with nostalgia and ending with a great dinner with Chuck, his lovely wife Ellen, and some of their friends. Eddie kept them laughing with his stories about Jack Benny.

The time was very hectic, and it had its downs as well as its ups. One was a serious health scare for Carolyn in 2007: "On the night before Thanksgiving in 2007, I had found a lump at the bottom of my left breast. After two weeks of tests we knew we were dealing with cancer. I chose to have a lumpectomy and thankfully the lymph nodes were found to be clear, as were the margins around the removed tumor. I had a seven-week pro-

Chuck Schaden's Farewell, the crew in Chicago. PHOTO BY DON POINTER

gram of radiation, and today I am coming up on being a five-year survivor."

Worried and frightened, Eddie still kept up Carolyn's spirits during the whole ordeal, and no one was happier than he was when the oncologists announced the good news that the procedure had been successful. After some rest and recuperation, Carolyn was once again ready to go.

Among the many, many performances of his one-man show, Eddie continued to do special appearances as Jack Benny — and he also began to collect dozens of awards. His office in the Carrolls' Encino home soon held shelf after shelf of plaques and certificates attesting to Eddie's talent, humor, professionalism, and generosity.

The International Jack Benny Fan Club, the Disneyana Fan Club, the SPERDVAC (Society to Preserve and Encourage Radio Drama, Variety, and Comedy) old-time radio club, and the Pacific Pioneer Broadcasters all enjoyed hosting Eddie. He performed in re-creations of radio shows at their conferences, and not always Jack — sometimes he was Al Jolson, and once he was Peavey the pharmacist in a script from *The Great Gildersleeve*. Eddie also gave many interviews on their programs and regularly would do telephone interviews for upcoming theater appearances, always gracious with his time. He was a perfect interview subject who could equally well handle being Jack Benny or Jiminy Cricket!

Eddie presented with the PPB Diamond Circle Award by Chris Thomas.
COURTESY OF PPB PHOTOGRAPHER

The radio re-creations that Eddie performed in took place at conventions of old-time radio enthusiasts, including *39 Forever*, a convention sponsored by the International Jack Benny Fan Club; SPERDVAC in Los Angeles; Radio Enthusiasts of Puget Sound in Seattle; Friends of Old Time Radio in Newark; and other venues. Live radio was always unpredictable, and so were these re-creations. One, duplicating a Benny

REPS Convention, re-creation of Pinocchio *and Jack Benny, LSMFT.*
COURTESY OF REPS

broadcast that parodied the movie *Treasure of the Sierra Madre*, proved difficult to stage. First a co-star had a time conflict, necessitating a rescheduling, and then a scheduling conflict developed with the room. And when the final rehearsal was underway, the script called for a sound effect of horse hooves galloping across the desert.

Nothing. Everyone looked at the soundman, who said helplessly, "The *Lone Ranger* re-creation next door is using the hoof beats!"

As Jack, Eddie complained, "Oh, great. Now the *horse* has a conflict!"

That was only one of many times that Eddie, without breaking character, came to the rescue of a show suffering a miscue. Many times the audience thought it was all part of the show, a testimony to Eddie's professionalism. Too bad that Eddie never had the chance to re-enact the "Drear Pooson" moment...but then such moments, like Eddie's ad-libs, come spontaneously, and planning a fake flub destroys its effectiveness.

Frank Ferrante recalls a late re-creation that reunited his Groucho and Eddie's Benny: "In June, 2009, less than a year before Eddie passed away, we were reunited as Benny and Groucho. The Radio Enthusiasts of Puget

Sound brought us together to enact the Jack Benny program that featured a parody of Groucho's *You Bet Your Life*. I hadn't seen Eddie for a while, and it was glorious rehearsing with him. I admired his focus and specificity. Such a pro. The intimate audience in Bellevue, Washington, seemed to enjoy our collaboration. It was sheer joy and when I want to relive that day I watch our performance on Youtube. What can I say? It makes me

Gloria McMillan with her talented grandson Sean Uminski.

laugh." And it did the same for the audience, who truly appreciated the effort both men made to entertain them.

Pacific Pioneer Broadcasters is a group of professionals who have twenty or more years of experience in radio, movies, and television. It was launched in 1966 by announcer Art Gilmore, ventriloquist Edgar Bergen, Jim "Fibber McGee" Jordan, and Ralph Edwards. Jeanne DeVivier Brown, the chairman, is a miracle worker who plans the five luncheons yearly and who oversees the ceremony recognizing each year's honorees. Usually the ceremonies are a gentle kind of roast. Eddie was on the Board of Directors from 1999-2008 and even served as president — for twelve hours. Then when he received the dates of the next board of directors meetings and luncheons, he realized he would miss more than half of them because he would be on the road with *Laughter in Bloom* and regretfully had to withdraw. However, in 2008 Eddie did receive the prestigious Diamond Circle Award for Many Distinguished Years in Radio and Television from PPB.

In Seattle for a REPS re-enactment, Eddie met a talented young man, only eleven years old at that time, who took the stage with him and the cast of a radio re-creation. His name was Sean Uminski, grandson of Gloria McMillan, who co-starred as Harriet Conklin in the radio show *Our Miss Brooks*, and Sean vividly recalls what happened: "It was right after Eddie and I and my grandmother, Gloria McMillan (we call her Grand'Mere) and some other great radio/voice actors had finished a show. That night on stage Mr. Carroll took my by the shoulders, looked me straight in the eye, and said, 'You have what it takes to be an actor. You have the sensitivity, the timing, and the stage presence.' At that time I knew that Eddie was the voice of Jiminy Cricket for Disney and that he also did a one-man show as Jack Benny. To get such a compliment from a man of such importance in the entertainment business was awesome! Eddie encouraged me to continue studying acting and pursue a voiceover career. He gave me one of his secrets: 'Every day of your life, do three things to further your career.'"

Eddie's encouragement and interest in Sean's talent was genuine and deep. That kind of warmth, that kind of caring, is why to those who met him, Eddie was always, in a very real sense, a shining star.

CHAPTER 24

The Shining Star Begins to Dim

CAROLYN CARROLL: Looking back now, I realize that little signs began to signal that something was not right with Eddie, but these were very slight, and only now can I recognize them. In September, 2009, during four days at D23 (Disney's first international Expo), when Eddie was speaking continually to fans while autographing, I saw his energy was draining and he slowed down a bit. The event used the entire Anaheim Convention Center, and it was huge. Eddie met people from all over the world that had made the trip to California just to attend the Expo: people from China, Australia, Ireland, even Iceland. The attendance was somewhere over 10,000 and perhaps as many as 20,000. Eddie talked himself hoarse chatting with fans over the four-day period, and at first I thought he was just tired.

But there were other little troubling signs. A few times as he signed things for fans, he misspelled his name, signing Eddiie and Carrolll, and when I caught those I asked him to redo those autographs. However, these were long days and Eddie was giving lots of energy to the fans because that was what Eddie always felt they deserved.

The day following the Expo we went to Jamie and Joy Farr's home for Joy's birthday. Joy and Jamie didn't notice anything different about Eddie that night. Speaking of Eddie, Joy said later, "Some men are hard to talk to, or when talking to a woman they try to come on too strong, but with Eddie, what you see is what you get. He really was like family to Jamie and me, and he made me feel like his sister. Eddie had the best manner with women of any man I ever met. I mean he was so easy to talk to, and he showed women the greatest and sincerest respect. He was always such a perfect gentleman, and he was so warm and caring, and that was him. That was Eddie, and he was just the same as always that evening."

But then on the way home we came to an emergency closure of the ramp leading to the freeway, and Eddie lost his sense of direction and began driving us the wrong way, even though we had lived in Encino so long he knew the route as well as our own rooms at home. He also drove much too close to the parked cars, just missing some of the side mirrors. I thought maybe it was the martini. I asked him if he could please pull over so I could drive us home. He did, I set the GPS, and got us home safely, but I wondered about his erratic driving. That was so unlike him.

The next morning we left for Cabo San Lucas for a restful, relax-

Eddie at D23, Disney's first international Expo.

ing week on the beach, a well-deserved vacation after a full spring and summer of work. Driving wasn't a problem, because a service picked us up to take us to the airport and upon our return would bring us back home again. In Cabo we laughed, swam, read, rode our boogie boards, chatted with the other vacationers, and walked the beach.

In the evenings we broke out our favorite word game, Boggle. We had been playing it for years and usually were very close in our scores. On Cabo, though, I would find 29-32 words, while Eddie was only getting 8-10. He said, "I just can't wrap my mind around this game. Too much mañana maybe!" So we laughed and boxed up the game, though in retrospect I can read more into what he said than I did at the time.

The day before we were to return home, Eddie began walking into doorjambs and hitting his shoulder, knee, or toes on his right side only. I was afraid that he might have had a stroke, so as soon as we arrived home the next day, the evening of October 6, 2009, I immediately called the Motion Picture Health Center to make an appointment for Eddie to be checked out the next day. I was extremely worried but tried not to show my concern to Eddie.

Our primary doctor examined Eddie first, and he, too, thought the cause might be a minor stroke. The test is the same exercises you've seen on TV for a sobriety test. On the heel-toe walk, Eddie made right turns. With the finger to the nose test, he completely missed the tip of his nose. To nail down the diagnosis, we began the rounds of specialists and tests. A week later, on the morning of October 13, I got the horrible phone call. We were facing the toughest battle of our lives: it was a brain tumor called Glioblastoma Multiforme.

After seeing the shape of it on Eddie's first MRI, I named it Oscar the Grouch. From the tumor there were three tentacles that I called the Oscarettes, while Eddie joked that it looked like a flying saucer had landed on his brain. We were determined to win this battle as we had so much to do in the future and marvelous things to look forward to accomplishing. We had struggled hard to get to this time in our lives, and we were so much looking forward to the future.

We had reasons to hope. After all, just two years earlier I had been through breast cancer and a lumpectomy. Though my diagnosis had scared him, throughout my own struggle Eddie gave me unfailing support and comfort and always tried to cheer me up. We had faced it together and I had come out cancer-free.

After my radiation round was completed, we had gone on to a week-long booking in Cambridge Springs, Pennsylvania. The Riverside Inn was built in 1885, and at that time its grounds boasted mineral hot springs, said to have healing powers. We learned the hot springs were no longer running when we got there, but it is a beautiful, tranquil place to heal, and the staff became good friends. We enjoyed a fun relaxing time and I had my energy back and we were well rested. Eddie glowed with relief and love and the feeling that the time had come to charge forward again!

So now, of course, when Eddie was diagnosed we knew he would win this one too. After all, we had won my battle, and Eddie had always been a fighter from the time he was a sickly boy. We fought his disease with everything in the arsenal: chemotherapy, radiation, Avastin infusions, alternative supplements plus the best brain specialist, Keith Black, his expert team, our son Leland, radiation oncologist Mary Lou Ozohan, and our primary physician, Gerald Michaelson. All are highly respected doctors in their fields and good, caring people.

But this kind of cancer is terribly aggressive and had reached Stage Four by the time symptoms began to appear. So sad to watch the depletion of this warm, fun-loving, brilliant man I loved so deeply. Still, we held on to a belief that Eddie would beat this disease. We kept humor at the forefront as we always tried to do in our lives, along with our faith in being positive.

I hid Eddie's car keys so he wouldn't even think of driving after the possibility of the diagnosis of a minor stroke. And now Eddie began to have absent seizures during which he would just vacate in his mind and go blank, not responding to anything. After the first couple of weeks he gave me a smile while asking me, "Would you trust me to drive to the post office?"

To that I quickly answered, "Absolutely not! But I would trust you to sit in the passenger seat while *I* drive you." With that he grinned, knowing that he was going to mail some PR material off to a theater because we knew he would kick this stuff out of his system. He was a trouper and the show must go on!

In November, Pacific Pioneer Broadcasters planned an event celebrating Yarmy's Army that Eddie deeply wanted to attend and participate in. I was concerned and scared, because the treatments were beginning to take a toll on his balance. Seven members of Yarmy's Army were to sit on the dais. Eddie's scar from the biopsy was apparent and we had his head shaved by that time. So he went into his old army duffel bag from the garage and found his garrison cap and became "Colonel Jack Benny," and he marched in with the rest of the other six and up the stairs to his seat on the dais.

Yes, I was scared and nervous and Eddie could not do his best Benny, but he performed his part and received great applause. The organizers had planned to give him a table microphone so he could do his bit sitting, but being Eddie, he rose and went to the podium just like the rest of the group. Peter Marshall told me five months later that at the luncheon he wasn't aware anything was off with Eddie. This was the last time he performed, and he was so courageous that, as usual, he amazed and awed me.

At home about a week later Eddie lost his balance and we both went down. I grabbed the back of his head while we were falling (and don't know how I did it). Somehow I only had two swollen knuckles, but Eddie had a broken tailbone. That made him even more uncomfortable, and yet he joked about now being a "real pain in the ass." Humor was the glue that held us together and was our salvation while going through tough times. Better to laugh to release the fear and tension than sink into depression.

Depression is a waste of time, and we didn't have time to waste, because it's something we can't buy or get more of in our lives.

The falls really began to happen more regularly. The corticosteroids prescribed to stop the swelling (edema) in the brain created weakness in Eddie's thighs, shoulders and neck. The upper arms and legs become thinner, losing muscle tone and that makes getting up and down from

Yarmy's Army at PPB luncheon. Eddie, Thom Sharpe, Howard Storm, Arnie Kogen, Gary Owens, Jimmy McGeorge, Peter Marshall, Jeanne DeVivier Brown, PPB Chairman. COURTESY OF PPB PHOTOGRAPHER

a sitting and lying position difficult and shaky at best. At the same time the face, feet and abdomen become puffy. These are not anabolic steroids, but I would teasingly ask him if he was ready to hit a homerun for me. We would giggle while praying that day would come.

Eddie fell more often, too, because he couldn't remember that his legs wouldn't support him. We would go through the same dialogue each time. I always said, "Honey, are you OK?"

He would smile up at me while sprawled on the floor and reply, "Come on honey, you've *got* to laugh. This is funny!"

With my hands on my hips I would say, "No, it is not!" But even at those times he gave me such a grin that I had to smile as I tried to figure out the best way to get him up on my own. Most of his falls happened in the middle of the night, and I didn't want to wake the neighbors by calling 911, bringing the EMTs and their sirens in to disturb the whole street. If I couldn't get Eddie up I would just throw the pillows on the floor and a blanket over us, lie next to him, and get help the next morning.

Our great neighbors Skyler, Sanford, Nora, and Caitlin would help us if Tina wasn't there.

As the Christmas season approached, Eddie wanted to go shopping every day, so after a radiation treatment or doctor's appointment we would visit a mall. He would take my right arm and I would squeeze his hand and forearm to my side to remind him to match my cadence, and off we would go.

Though chemo weakens the immune system, that winter Eddie never came down with a cold or flu. He was healthy except for Oscar and the Oscarettes. We ate lunch out every day, sometimes meeting up with Jamie and Joy at our favorite Chinese restaurant. Just being around Jamie and Joy always perked Eddie up so much, for they were his dearest friends. Joy remembers that even when he was obviously ill, Eddie never once lost his sense of humor or his love of life. "He was just the greatest guy in the world," she says. "To Jamie and me, Eddie is always family. And our hearts just went out to him. We wanted to help him in any way we could, and we both hoped he would beat the cancer." As time went by it became more difficult for Eddie to go out, so Jamie and Joy would bring the food to us. We would eat family style and they would stay with us all the way. What good Midwest stock they are!

The steroid Decadron also increases blood sugar levels, so Eddie became a drug-induced diabetic and regularly I had to check his blood sugar and give him an insulin shot in the stomach fat four times a day. Every time I would laughingly tell him, "Give me the finger and show me your belly!" I tried to make light of the situation, hiding how close I was to trembling. I don't like to hurt anything, let alone giving my darling those four injections a day. Smiling, he would give me his finger to check the sugar levels and then lift up his sweatshirt for the shot of insulin. We got on with the procedure, and Eddie never ever complained about it.

The first week in December the Disney fan club Laughing Place held their Golden Doobie Award ceremonies at Downtown Disneyland. Eddie was supposed to speak from our booth where we were sitting, but being Eddie, he rose and slowly walked up to the front of the room, always the professional and so congenial. He wore a Santa Claus hat to cover his scar, yet was open about this battle with cancer we were fighting. This was the last public appearance Eddie would make. He posed for pictures and even gingerly held an adorable baby for a photo. It was a lovely sight.

When the event ended, a wonderful gentleman, Bjorn Storness-Bliss, escorted us through downtown Disneyland back to our car. We had just met him for the first time that day and he was so kind and so gentle with Eddie. When we had Eddie secured in the car I gave Bjorn a hug thanking him for his help and he said to both of us, "I love you." This is the type of wonderful people that are the heart of the Disney Fan Clubs. They are what make it the happiest place on earth.

Mark Evanier, a writer/producer/director and popular Internet blogger at newsfromme.com, later wrote movingly of Eddie at this time. Mark

Eddie holding Gideon Moseley during the Doobie Awards at Disneyland.

is a tremendous fan of Jack Benny (and other classic comedians), and he loved and promoted Eddie's *Laughter in Bloom*. The last he saw of Eddie, he wrote, was when Eddie and I were walking away, hand in hand, like newlyweds in love. He was one hundred per cent right about that. Nearly fifty years of marriage had not changed that feeling. We were still so very much in love.

Eventually Eddie found that a walker was absolutely necessary, and the physical therapists explained to us how to get up when your legs are weak: Place your hands on the wheeled walker with the brake on, put your face over your feet and push with your arms and chest. So I would tell Eddie,

"Nose over toes, butt in the air, and up he goes!" The therapist's name was Yul, but Eddie couldn't remember his name. That was unlike Eddie, but the effects of the disease were beginning to show. I always tried to get him to think through the fog. My hints were, "I am the King of Siam" as I spread my feet and put my fists on my hips or sing "I Whistle a Happy Tune," and especially because I am a terrible whistler Eddie would laugh. I could never do Jiminy's song "Give a Little Whistle."

Eddie enjoyed our Christmas Eve and Christmas Day more than he ever had before. I placed a bar stool by the stove so he could sit and stir the wheat berries for the kutja and participate in the preparation of the food. Even though we saw in the MRI that Oscar and the Oscarettes had shrunken and thinned, Eddie wasn't sure about that. It went unspoken between us, but I know him well.

We had family and friends for the holidays as we always had done. Eddie smiled through the whole Christmas Eve and completely enjoyed the evening, but it took a toll on him. On Christmas Day we ended up visiting the Motion Picture Health Center for hours. That evening we planned to have a turkey dinner for ten people. Eddie was run through a myriad of tests all day, and as it got later, I called Tina and she prepared the whole dinner and everything was ready when we finally returned home. She was a Christmas blessing.

One day after lunch Eddie did his getting-up routine, nose over toes, butt in the air and up he goes. I had put a gait belt on his waist to help me guide and lift him. He got up holding onto the wheeled walker, and I was grasping to his gait belt, but his head and shoulders got ahead of his feet, and his feet were going faster and faster. It reminded me of the Roadrunner, his favorite cartoon. Eddie kept accelerating, laughing hysterically and having a great time. The Olympics were on TV, I remember, and as I tried to keep up with Eddie, I yelled, "Slow down! You're going too fast!"

By this time we had raced through the kitchen into the dining room. The only room left was the den, which has a window at the end of the sofa looking out over the pool deck.

Tina heard me, but she thought I was yelling at a bobsled or luge team on the TV until I screamed, "Honey, stop!" The walker knocked over the nesting coffee tables just as Tina came running into the den. Using the gait belt, I was trying to twist Eddie onto the sofa. We had only about six feet before hitting the window.

Tina realized what was happening and tackled Eddie from the side as I threw him sideways with the gait belt. We all three landed in a dog pile on the sofa, and Eddie was still laughing. That was the most fun he had in a long time. Tina and I were shaking, but because Eddie was so tickled, we all ended up hugging and laughing together.

Eddie saw an advertisement for Las Vegas on television and decided he wanted us to go for Valentine's Day. He was very excited about just the thought of going. Knowing how tough it would be to take care of him on the trip just by myself, I made some phone calls and the Monte Carlo gave us a handicapped suite — on the house. I checked with the medical team, and they all felt a change of scenery would be uplifting for him.

Just getting Eddie on the plane in Burbank was a new experience. The airport doesn't have jetway boarding tunnels, so Eddie, sitting in his wheelchair, was put in a crane elevator and lifted in through the galley. We placed him in the seat next to me in the front row with the wheelchair stored in the luggage department. When we arrived in Vegas, there the wheelchair was waiting for us in the jetway. Upon our landing an airline employee pushed Eddie in the wheelchair to pick up our luggage. After all the times we had worked in Vegas the people there knew us and treated us with good care. Bless the Monte Carlo for sending a limo for us, because I couldn't have pushed Eddie and rolled the luggage at the same time. The driver was a Godsend, and he hoisted Eddie up into the limo like a feather.

While we were in Vegas the Olympics were still on, and I agreed to take Eddie just for a change of scenery even if we only could watch the games on the two big screens in the suite. We took a nap and then visited the casino to play video Keno, which Eddie always enjoyed, but he couldn't remember how to play. He looked so cute, as excited as a child in a candy store. I put in a twenty, but the anti-seizure medication had given him tremors, and he had difficulty in pressing the numbers, so I asked what numbers he wanted to play, entered them, and had him push the start button. His eyes sparkled like a child's on Christmas morning. He won five or six $100 jackpots while we were there and I was so busy watching him that without realizing it at first I won $1,175. The alarm went off, and Eddie asked, "How did you do that?"

"I don't know," I confessed. "I wasn't paying attention!"

After playing Keno for an hour, we went to dinner, and I could tell that he was getting tired. We had only one fall while there, in the middle of the night. I called Security. Two of the guards came up to the room, picked him up, took him to the bathroom and helped me get him back into bed. I thanked them profusely. I told them, "Eddie is probably the only guy that hasn't had a drink in four months ever to fall down in this hotel." The guards laughed at that and insisted that I wasn't to hesitate to call them at any time if we needed any help at all.

Tom and Betty Kennedy had become very close friends of ours. Tom is best known as a game-show host, most notably of *Name That Tune*, though he and his brother Jack Narz were also game-show creators. Both Betty and Tom have a tremendous gift of humor. Every other day a nurse came to the house to take Eddie's vital signs, but one day we were blessed to have a special substitute nurse appear. Tom came dressed in drag as a nurse to take Eddie's vitals. Betty and their daughter, Courtney, came in first, and I was wondering where Tom was when I saw him walk around the back of his car. I laughed hysterically, the best laugh I had had in weeks.

It took Eddie a while to catch on because Tom played it all the way with chart and clipboard and stethoscope and uniform. Of course he wore a wig and spoke in a high, feminine voice. And I can't forget the long black socks that accompanied the uniform. This was wonderful! We loved it and I still enjoy the video of a performance by Tom that very few will ever see. It was so priceless to see Eddie laughing at this wonderful gift Tom gave us at a time when humor helped him so much.

Until you or a loved one is wheelchair bound, there are quite a few things you just don't think about. When you are out in public and need to use a rest room, what do you do? I couldn't take Eddie into the men's room, passing the urinals that are just out in the open. Our only alternative was the women's handicap stall, with us taking turns. On our way to the stall I would tease him telling him to close his eyes so the ladies wouldn't be embarrassed. Of course he would do that.

I was surprised at how many women came over to me while we were washing our hands to offer help or to tell us they did the same thing with their dads or husbands. It was so nice of them to share that with me, because until it happened, I had never thought about that situation. Another problem is simply going in and out of a place when the doors are shut. If someone doesn't open and hold the door for you (and a surprising number of people do offer), you need to back the chair through while your tush or foot holds the door open. I am so aware of someone in a walker or wheelchair now, and I run to hold doors for them.

In late February Laura Leff, the president of the International Jack Benny Fan Club, called to say she was coming into town, and we planned to have dinner together at our house. After a full day of radiology, a doctor's appointment and Avastin infusion at Cedars Sinai, Eddie's blood test came back showing he needed another blood transfusion. We needed to cancel the dinner, but I didn't know the hotel Laura would be staying while in Los Angeles, so I called her husband in Oakland to have Laura phone me because we weren't home and the time was already late. She returned my call and came right over to Cedars where Laura, Tina, Eddie and I laughed and reminisced until after midnight. Laura mentioned how she had an emergency surgery a while ago, telling us how much she enjoyed lying in the bed while staring up at the ceiling after a dose of morphine.

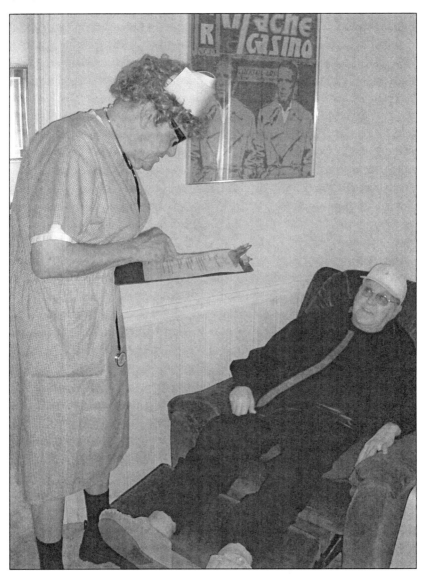

Tom Kennedy dressed as Eddie's nurse.

Doing Jack Benny, Eddie quipped as he looked up to the ceiling, "Oh, Nurse…morphine for *everybody*!" We all broke up laughing. I knew Eddie was feeling better because of his quick comeback with the line, and his color and spirits improved a lot. As we put Eddie in the car, Tina and I complimented Laura on her new lovely slim figure. She had lost some weight and looked terrific. Laura gave Eddie a goodbye hug and kiss and we all said, "I love you." We planned a do-over dinner for April 10, when Laura would be back in Los Angeles next. But it was not meant to be.

I had to begin canceling the theater dates for 2010, though I told Eddie I was only postponing them. Some were theaters that he had longed to perform in for years: the Genesee in Waukegan, the McCallum Theatre in Palm Desert, the Edmunds and Columbia Theaters in Washington State, and the Rialto Square in Joliet, along with seven others. When I told Eddie that I had postponed them, he just looked down and nodded, while I was crying and shaking yet trying not to show it. I knew how much he wanted to perform in these theaters and how hard he had pushed to get those contracts. The light went out of his baby blue eyes. But we both knew he was not able to remember two hours of his script, let alone stand for those two hours, even if the MRI showed the tumor was shrinking.

We had so many friends and fans that would drop by and spend time with Eddie. They would just talk and reminisce about good memories. This would cheer Eddie and our friends up. They were also kind to sit with him while I went on my errands. Friends are so needed at that time.

The treatment had taken its toll on Eddie. He fought a great fight, hung in there and was still a champion. He almost won the battle and will always be my hero, never complaining about everything we put him through and thrust upon him. He was not eating or drinking as much as he should, so I was even feeding him junk food that I never had before. Eddie always called me an alien because I just don't enjoy sweets! He loved them, and anyone who didn't like cake or candy was foreign to him.

When that didn't work, the oncologist asked him if he had ever smoked marijuana. In a shocked tone, Eddie replied, "No, no!"

I asked seriously, "Do they sell marijuana at Cedars?"

The doctor said, "No, but it does come in a pill form." So we tried the pills, but unfortunately they did not increase his appetite, but just made him mellow. Under their influence, Eddie would sleep for twenty-two hours a day. After three days, I took the pills back to the pharmacy so they could dispose of them. Eddie needed to eat and exercise not just sleep all day.

About two weeks before Easter, Brad Strickland called from Georgia. He had helped produce *Laughter in Bloom* when we took the show to Gainesville, Georgia, and he and Eddie had become phone buddies, calling each other every few weeks to catch up on the news. We also got together with Brad and his wife Barbara whenever we could. Brad was one of Eddie's greatest fans and best audiences, coming to *Laughter in Bloom* time after time and laughing at Eddie's off-stage stories, too. That evening Eddie and Brad talked for about twenty minutes on the phone, and Brad tried to get Eddie to promise to eat a hamburger — they both loved them — as a favor to him. He was surprised and hopeful at Eddie's upbeat tone as they joked back and forth. Even then, he told me later, he thought Eddie surely had the tumor beaten.

But I had to admit that it was not to be. At the close of *Laughter in Bloom*, Eddie always made a curtain speech, then the spotlight went out and he walked down from the stage and back through the aisles of the theater to the lobby. I decided that when Eddie took his final exit through the audience without a spotlight, I would throw him a party to celebrate his life, accomplishments and share it with his fans, friends and family. I began planning it in my mind, never once mentioning it to Eddie. This would be a fond remembrance and a tribute to his marvelous talent but more importantly to the love and kindness he shared with those around him.

Much too quickly the illness reached the point I had been dreading since that phone call back on October 13. The disease reached the stage where I was no longer capable of taking care of Eddie. He wouldn't eat or drink. We had been to the Motion Picture Health Center earlier that day, in late March, and Dr. Michaelson was well aware of the problem. When Eddie pushed his plate away from him at dinner without even a bite and put his head down on the table, it was time to check him into the Motion Picture Hospital, whose motto is "We take care of our own." They sure do a great job of it. I called our doctor and the hospital had everything waiting for us to check Eddie in when we arrived.

We in the immediate family had a meeting with the award-winning palliative care hospital team a couple of days later to discuss the future of Eddie's care. We both had made directives spelling out our final wishes. Jamie was there, and I asked him if he could sit with Eddie until we got back from the meeting. Eddie had been restless, pulling the IV out of his arm. I thought the meeting would be about half an hour or so, but it ran for almost two hours. When we came into Eddie's room Jamie was still holding his hand. He looked up at us and said, "This is the first time a man's ever called me *honey* and *sweetheart* when I wasn't in drag!" That gave us a badly-needed laugh. What a delight our Jamie is to my family. Of course, he and Joy are part of our family and always will be.

The doctors gently told us the battle we had fought was nearing the last siege. Our adventures were on the last chapter. Our good friends and relatives rallied around, creating an enormous support system for us during that last week. Gloria, Jamie, and Joy brought food for us as well

The Eleniak brothers: Dale, Eddie and Bob.

as for the visitors and the nurses. They brought in wine, and I put Eddie's favorite Jiminy baseball cap with the gold Jiminy pin on it on his head.

The palliative team asked me to go home quickly and retrieve things that made him feel good. Joy and Jamie pulled up as I was leaving and Joy jumped into my car and asked what we were doing. I shakily said it was the time we feared and I had to go home and get back as soon as I could. She asked me what she could do and I asked her to tell me if I was staying between the white lines. I was so frightened and couldn't believe Eddie wasn't going to make it. No, no no!

Eddie's favorite publicity picture was the one of him with the Jiminy Cricket cutout, and Joy and I quickly retrieved it from our home. We also grabbed his favorite big-band CD and back at the hospital placed his picture on the nightstand and played the tracks from the CD for him.

The Motion Picture Hospital had no visitor or time restrictions, so Eddie always had a gathering of friends and family. Tina and Lee were given the room next to ours and were there for me day and night. I slept in the lounge chair next to Eddie, never leaving his side except to shower or use the restroom. I always held on to his hand or his arm as if I could hold him here. He wanted me to sleep next to him, but I was concerned that I might stop the flow of oxygen or morphine.

On Saturday afternoon, knowing the end was near. I suggested all

Niece Erika and our grandniece Indyanna.

twenty of us make a toast and then each of us tell a fun fond memory of Eddie. We did, and hearing these stories put smiles on our faces yet with tears in our eyes. Erika's daughter, Indyanna, age four, came over to me and asked if she could hold Uncle Eddie's hand. I told her, "Of course you can. He would love it." Fifteen minutes later Indy came back over to me asking, "Auntie C, can I kiss Uncle Eddie?"

I replied, "All you want." She is an old soul and extremely brave for her age. Erika has done a marvelous job with raising her. On Easter, we repeated the same ceremony with another full house.

The last night as I was holding his hand, with tears flowing from my eyes and falling onto his cheeks, I gave Eddie permission to leave because I didn't want him to hurt anymore. That was one of the hardest things I ever had to do in my life. At that moment he came out of the morphine-glazed look and stared directly, clearly into my eyes without blinking. Then he did blink and looked deeper even, almost into my very soul. And he gave me a tremendous gift: The corners of his mouth went up to form a beautiful Eddie smile and those gorgeous blue eyes were clear for a minute. Gloria was crying with me as she saw the whole thing and then the whole room was in tears. I will hold that precious memory dear to me forever.

Laura Leff called a while later with another present for Eddie. As Laura wrote, "Carolyn and I continued to touch base frequently. Knowing how beloved Eddie was to so many International Jack Benny Club members, I wanted to give everyone a chance to send their best wishes to him. After my broadcast e-mail on Sunday (Easter), April 5, within 24 hours I had over 50 e-mails of well wishes. I called Monday evening, and Carolyn put the phone on speaker so they could both listen as I read through one e-mail after another, pouring out so much love and adoration to them through the words of others. Finally we were all tired and Carolyn's phone battery was almost out, so I wished them a good night. About seven hours later after this verbal standing ovation, Eddie took his last bow and sneaked quietly out the stage door, leaving a peaceful and beatific smile on his face." Thank you, Laura, and thanks to the IJBFC, including all the members, for the devotion and support they showed for Eddie's portrayal of Jack Benny.

Later that morning when Leland, Tina and I pulled into the driveway of our home, we saw waiting for us on the stoop a majestic yellow double orchid plant arrangement. Attached to a leaf by a straight pin was this note: "Dear Carolyn-We will be forever grateful to Eddie for keeping our Grandfather's name alive. He will be greatly missed. Signed Mike, Maria, Bobby, Joanna and most of all, Joan."

The flowers were from Jack's grandchildren and his daughter. There is a marvelous story about Jack's devotion to his wife Mary. The first year after Jack died, she received an unexpected red rose on their anniversary. Jack had secretly arranged with the florist to send one every year on that date "to my Doll." The orchids came from the same florist. This touched our children and me deeply and we are filled with tremendous gratitude for the Benny family's appreciation of Eddie's love and respect of the giant icon, Jack Benny.

About a week later while going through Eddie's desk, I came across some unsigned cards next to cards I had given to him over the years. These new cards were for Valentine's Day, Easter, a Ten Rules for Staying Happy with the One You Love Anniversary card, Mother's Day, and finally a birthday card that ended with, "At last I thought of something that is all the things I wanted: it won't ever wear out, you can't use it up, it will last forever, and you can take it with you everywhere. It's something no one else can give you: my heart, my love."

Though Eddie hadn't signed them, the cards were meant for me. I showed them to Tina, and we could not figure out how Eddie could have bought them because he had never been out of my sight for six months.

Laura Leff after a re-creation of an interview of Hedda Hopper with Jack Benny. COURTESY OF REPS

Yet the cards were in chronological order of the events to take place. I had signed an anniversary card for him at the hospital, but the day never arrived when I could give it to him. He passed the day prior to our 47th anniversary.

Finally I told Tina, "The only time your dad could have bought these cards for me was when we bought our holiday cards in November. He asked me to leave him for a moment so he could choose a Christmas card for me. I went to the cashier and explained my dilemma. She understood and I gave her the credit card and went outside. The cashier kept an eye on Eddie (as did I from the glass door), and he was so pleased when he saw me leave the store. When he left the register with the bag in his hand, I got him safely to the car and went back in to sign the credit card slip. That had to be the time that, thinking ahead, he purchased all the cards for the next six months." Even unsigned, these are the most precious cards I ever received.

The celebration and tribute to Eddie Carroll, "A Life in Bloom," was held six weeks later. This was the party I had planned in my mind and heart in the months following the diagnosis. The banquet room was supposed to hold 400, but the count was 611 in attendance. What a wonderful party it was too, lasting two hours and forty minutes! I asked the twenty that were to speak about Eddie to have fun and make it a true celebration of Eddie's life and all he stood for.

They told wonderful stories, and though there were plenty of tears, the room was also filled with laughter. There were game show hosts, singers, club presidents, agents, comedians, authors, a producer, radio personalities, a casting director, Fan Club Presidents, Eddie's brother Bob, and Jamie of course. Many years of relationships filled that room with lots of love and laughter of happy memories. Frank Ferrante couldn't be there because he was filling in for Eddie at an engagement in Longview, Washington — a final gift from Eddie to Frank. In a note to me, Frank said, "When I tour now I take Eddie with me. I think of him before I go on. I find myself humming "Love in Bloom" as I warm up…Eddie lives in so many ways." Peter Marshall sang Eddie's favorite big band songs. It was a beautiful salute and a final standing ovation by the fans, friends and family.

Eddie was aware he was to receive the *Disneyana Fan Club Disney Legend Award* in July. After he passed, Gary Schaengold, the President of the Disneyana Fan Club, called me to ask if I would accept the award for Eddie. I responded that of course I would, not realizing it would be in front of an audience with an interview to follow. Though the event was two and a half months after Eddie's passing, I was still emotionally raw and didn't think I could get through the presentation. I didn't. Being a program director, I took four DVDs with me so whenever I lost it I could cut away to a video. That saved me. I had a mike in one hand and a handful of tissues in the other during the forty-minute interview. When I went to the tech booth to collect the videos, I mentioned that I really was overcome many times answering the questions that brought back such a rush of memories. The crew told me they were also in tears.

I was so proud of Eddie's achievements as Jiminy, and I was filled with pride upon being presented the prestigious award. I treasure it. Gary wrote, "Eddie and his wife, Carolyn, were great friends of the Disneyana Fan Club. Eddie passed away April 6, 2010. He will always be in our hearts." Thank you Gary and Anita Schaengold, along with all the Disneyana Fan

Club and all that you represent. We feel the same way; the Disneyana Fan Club will always be in my heart.

Eddie was very much Jiminy Cricket within himself; his caring and devotion to all that this little cricket stands for in our lives is a wonderful example for us all to admire. In a sense Eddie lived those traits in his own life. He enjoyed guiding those around him to fulfill their dreams. He also wished upon a star and believed his dreams would come true, and they truly did.

After Eddie's passing, many of Eddie's radio interviews were pulled out of the archives and rebroadcast. Emails poured in from all around the world. His passing was in newspapers, and was picked up by API internationally and reported on news broadcasts. So much love flowed in for him from so many diverse people and places around the world. Eddie is admired and loved on all continents. On stage and in person he touched people's hearts.

I am so proud of Eddie. What an honor it is for me to have been married to this dedicated, talented man for just one day short of forty-seven years. The times and memories we had together will take me through the rest of my life. Our shared voyage of adventures hold me up when I feel weak and allow me to fall asleep at night and give me my reason to get out of bed in the morning.

Thank you, my darling!

Edward Eleniak, better known as Eddie Carroll, wished upon a star and his dreams did come true. And as he always told his fans, "Yours can too."

Eddie's closing speech in the performance of "Laughter In Bloom." COURTESY OF DON POINTER

CHAPTER 25

Eddie's Farewell

When Eddie's show *Jack Benny: Laughter in Bloom* came to an end, Eddie as Jack spoke a few parting words to the audience.

Eddie, it's time for your curtain speech.

EDDIE CARROLL: Ladies and gentlemen, I want to leave you with one thought: No matter who we are, we all go through the same three stages of life: youth, middle age and "you look *wonderful!!!*" And you know you've reached that stage when you bend over to put on your shoes and wonder what else you can do *while you are still down there*! But honestly folks, it is so important for you to laugh every day. And if you find something to laugh at every day, I guarantee…you will not only look better…you'll feel better…and you will all stay 39 forever. Thank you, ladies and gentlemen, and God bless.

When we look up into the night sky, each of us can find a star shining, one that will always be bright and will always stand ready to fulfill our hopes and dreams.

And when we look into our memories, for all of us who knew and loved him, there shines Eddie Carroll.

Index

39 Forever (convention). *See* International Jack Benny Fan Club
ABC (American Broadcasting Company) 100, 104
Academy of Television Arts and Sciences 195-196
Academy Theater (NY) 163
Adams, Don 251
Adams, Nick 89
Aetna Insurance Company 215, 225
Ahmanson Theater 156
Alabama Theatre (Myrtle Beach, SC) 256
Alberta, Canada 19-22, 31, 34, 178
Allen, Fred 137, 245
Allen, Gracie 195
Allen, Rex 192
Allen, Steve 207
Allwine, Wayne 173, 180, 229, 301
Alten, Larry 226
Ameristar Casino (Council Bluffs, IA) 233
Amsterdam, Morey 148
Anaheim, CA 192, 273
Anderson, Eddie "Rochester", 135, 137, 185, 207, 224, 244
Anderson, Maxwell 87
Anselmo, Tony 229, 301
Arnaz, Desi 154
Ascuagas, John 1165-166
Atlanta, GA 69, 162, 253
Atlantic City, NJ 150-152, 176, 225, 240
Auerbach, Artie 137
Autry, Gene 192-193
Aykroyd, Dan 166, 228-229
Bacharach, Burt 76-77
Bachman, Conrad 257
Bachman, Kate 257

Bakalyan, Dick 71
Baker, Kenny 136
Baker, Mike, Dr., 314
Baker, Ray 113
Baker's Dance Studio 73
Ball, Lucille 16, 152-158, 195, 236
Baloo the Bear (cartoon character) 175
Baltimore Ravens 2239
Balzer, George 149
Banks, Ida 116, 230, 231
Banks, Tommy 31, 33-34, 35-37, 40-41, 116, 230-232, 237, 265, 309
Barnett, Mike 82
Barran, Rob (Bobby Baranco) 73-74, 116, 193-195, 262
Barranco, Tony and Toni 193-194
Belushi, John 166
"Benny Bash" (Waukegan celebration) 244-248
Benny, Jack 15-16, 25, 60, 84, 103-104, 107, 135-141, 143, 152, 153-160, 167, 175-176, 185-186, 191-192, 195-196, 208-210, 219, 224, 233, 237, 240, 242, 244-248, 266, 270, 293
Benny, Joan 147, 195, 288, 308, 309
Bergen, Edgar 270
Berkeley 198, 202
Berle, Milton 74-75, 154, 206, 208
Berman, Shelley 250, 252
Bernie, Ben 136
Billboard (magazine) 63
Birnkrant, Gloria Springer 76-82, 91, 132, 203, 232, 286, 288, 308, 309
Bixby, Bill 72
Black, Keith, Dr., 275
Blanc, Mel 137, 191, 209, 244

295

Blocker, Dan 1126
Blumofe, Bobby 245-246, 266
Blumofe, Cynthia Breazeal 245, 266
Bogart, Humphrey 32
Borge, Victor 76
Borgnine, Ernest 55-56
Bowery Boys 32
Bradford, Hank 252
Brenerman, Allan 74
Brolund, Eric 244
Brooke, Sorrel 115
Brooks, Mel 68, 210
Brown, Jeanne De Vivier 270
Brynner, Yul 92, 280
Buddingh, Curt, D.C., 134
Bugs Bunny (cartoon character) 73, 75, 137, 192
Burakoff, Saul 206-207
Burns, Allan 164
Burns, George 76, 137, 195-197, 219
Busey, Gary 172
Butala, Tony 74, 77, 83-84, 227, 309
Buttons, Red 207-208
Buttram, Pat 193
C.M. Schulz's Goodtime Theater 151-152
Caesars Atlantic City 150-151
Calgary 19, 31, 230
Campbell, Glenn 83
Cantor, Eddie 47
Cape Cod, MA 161
Capitol (recording company) 82-83, 85
Carnegie Deli (NY) 229
Carney, Art 210
Carroll, Carolyn Springer 9-10; meets Jamie Farr 71, 76; early career and education 73-74; opens for Milton Berle 74-75; and Burt Bacharach 76; and *A La Carte from Las Vegas* 77-83; meets Eddie Carroll 77; and Tony Butala 82-85; Eddie's courtship 77-88; engagement 88; California wedding 93-97; Edmonton wedding 93; Chinese wedding 178; with Eddie on *Hollywood Palace* 101; birth of daughter Tina 104-105; difficult second pregnancy 109; birth of son Leland 110; assists Eddie with autosuggestion 111-112; finds dream house 113-114; commitment to family time 123-124; work with Hesby Street School PTA 125, 127, 129; earns doctorate in psychology 128; conducts motivational seminars 128, 215, 218; Tai Chi 128; karate 128-129; and home improvements 132-133; and Tina's skating 134; helps Eddie prepare to act role of Jack Benny 139-140, 145-146; and Joan Benny 147; with Eddie in Las Vegas and Atlantic City 151-152; at taping of *Life with Lucy* 158; in Miami Beach 158-159; in Boston and Cape Cod 160-162; in Toronto 161-162; and Eddie's bout with Lyme disease 162-163; in New York 163-164; helps choreograph "Blues Brothers" tribute 165; vacation stories 167-170; nieces Cami Elen and Erika Eleniak 170-172; begins to direct *Jack Benny: Laughter in Bloom* 177; trip with Eddie to Asia 177-179; and Disneyland 180-181; celebrating mother's birthday at Walt Disney World 181; and Bill and Jen Farmer 181; daughter Tina's wedding 183-184; and floods of 1991, 187-188; trip to Japan with Eddie 188-191; helps Japanese couple in California 191; and Rob Barran 73, 193-195, 262-263; son Leland attends Berkeley 198; and Western dancing 199; horseback riding 200; swimming 200-201; and Northridge Earthquake (1994) 201-204; and *The Odd Couple* (Overland, KS) 210-216; gives up practice to become Eddie's permanent show manager 215, 218; with Eddie in Laughlin, NV 230-231; Walt Disney World 25th Anniversary 231-233; and publicity for *Laughter in Bloom* 223-224; in Atlantic City 225-226; discovers royalties are owed Eddie for "How Is Julie?" 236-237; visits her cousin Sandy in New Orleans 238; Christmas in New York 229-230; solves show emergency in Tampa 230-231; son Leland graduates from Chiropractic College 232-233; Eddie surprises Leland in old-age makeup 236; routine for tours 237-239; works with Chuck Magnus on website and on tours 217, 240; microphone failure in Laughlin 242; in Waukegan for "Benny Bash," 244-248; and story about Rip Taylor 252-254; Touring with *Laughter in Bloom* 234-256; Lilly Ball campaign (Louisville, KY) 257-

INDEX

258; Canadian tour 261-264; and Wende Doohan 265; and breast cancer 267, 275; Eddie's final illness 273-288; and Eddie's passing 288; finds Eddie's cards 289-290; hosts "A Life in Bloom" tribute 290; accepts Eddie's Disneyana Legend Award 290; appreciation 291

Carroll, Earl 153

Carroll, Eddie (Eleniak) ancestry 19-21; birth 22; childhood illnesses and accidents 23-25; first sees *Pinocchio* 13-15, 25-26, 119-120; first performance at school and stage fright 26-28; birth of siblings 27-28; story of Mr. Wong 28-30; St. Joseph High School 30-34; classmates Robert Goulet and Tommy Banks 31-34; Orion Musical Theatre 35-37, 40-43; attends Radio College of Canada 37-38; works for Western Geophysical Oil 38; contracts polio 38-40; works as page for NBC in Hollywood 45-47; drafted into U.S. Army 47; Army service 47-53; meets Ben Cooper 49; becomes actor in Hollywood 55; rooms with Ben Cooper 55-60; meets Gary Cooper 59; recurence of kidney stone 60-61; changes name to Eddie Carroll 61; stars in comedy album 62-63; best man at wedding of Ben and Pamela Cooper 65-68; meets Don Rickles, Mel Brooks, Paul Frees 68-69; meets Jamie Farr 10-11, 69-71; stage work 70-73; meets Carolyn Springer 73-78; performs in *A La Carte from Las Vegas* 78-82; writes "How Is Julie?", 82; song accepted and recorded by the Lettermen 83-85; courtship of Carolyn and Eddie 87-89; Jamie Farr and *The Greatest Story Ever Told* 89-91; Eddie gets role in *Taras Bulba* 90-91; Eddie works in commercials 92-93; Eddie and Carolyn's wedding 93-97; *Hollywood Palace* appearances 100-101; parts in TV sitcoms 101-102; meets Don Knotts 101; appears in *Jack Benny's Birthday Special* 102-104; partners in Carroll-Farr Productions 104; birth of daughter Tina 104-105; works with Bob Hope, Bing Crosby, and Dorothy Lamour 105; costars on *The Don Knotts Show* 105-107; produces *Man to Man* TV show 107-109; birth of son Leland 110; becomes "King of the Commercials," 111-112; buys house 113-114; Jamie Farr joins the cast of *MASH* 114-115; auditions for Disney Studios 116-118; first recording session as Jiminy Cricket 118-120; guest appearances on TV and work for Disney 121-123; vows to play the Strip in Las Vegas 124; and Hesby Street School 125; home life with the children 125-129; and Screen Actors Guild strike of 1980, 131-132; home improvements 132-133; auditions for *A Small Eternity with Jack Benny* 135-141; performs in *A Small Eternity with Jack Benny* 143-149; difficulty with violin 144-145; meets Dennis Day and Joan Benny 147; impresses Frank Ferrante 148; reworks script with George Balzer 149; meets Laura Leff 149-150; cast as Benny in *Legends in Concert* 150-152; cast in *Life with Lucy* and meets Lucille Ball 155-157; plays *Legends* in Miami Beach 158-159; performs in Boston 159-161; ill with Lyme disease in Toronto 161-162; struggles to regain health 162-163; performs Benny in New York 163-164; plans to write *Jack Benny: Laughter in Bloom* 164-165; tours San Francisco and Sparks, NV 165-166; trips with family 167-170; nieces Cami Elen and Erika Eleniak 170-172; performs Jiminy in *Mickey's Christmas Carol* 173-174; pefroms on D-TV 175; meets Bill Farmer 175; acts with Frank Nelson 175-176; tries out *Laughter in Bloom* 176-177; trip with Carolyn to Singapore, Thailand, China, and Hong Kong 177-179; work for Disney parks 179-181; story of "the Curse of Goofy," 182-183; Tina's wedding 183-184; early runs of *Laughter in Bloom* 185-187; 1991 floods in Los Angeles 187-188; as Jiminy in Japanese educational program 14, 188-191; as Benny at Rancho Cucamonga 191-192; stories about Gene Autry and Pat Buttram 192-193; and Rob Barran 194; meets Irving Fein and George Burns 195-197; Leland enrolls at Berkeley 198; and country-western dancing 198-199; and horseback riding 199-200; and swimming/snorkeling 200-201; 1994 Northride Earthquake 201-204; as Jiminy in Earthday and Environmentality bits 205-206; performs Benny with Frank Ferrante as Groucho Marx at Friars Club 206-208; Milton Berle story 208; on Jack Benny's humor 208-210; Eddie and Frank Ferrante as Benny and Groucho in *The Odd Couple* 210-216; first coast-to-coast tour as Jack Benny 217-218; Bill Kirchenbauer casts Eddie as Benny in *Legends of Comedy* 219-221; celebrating the 25th anniversary of Walt Disney World 221-222; *Laughter in Bloom* tours with Carolyn 222-225; healthcare commercials and Benny performances for Aetna 225-226; royalties for "How Is Julie?", 226-227; touring 227-228; radio show for Disney 228-229; playing Calgary and Edmonton 230; Tampa performance interrupted by emergency signal 230-231; Leland graduates from college 231-233; guest shot on *Frasier* 235-236; casino versions of *Laughter in Bloom* 237-240; playing Laughlin, NV 240-242; as Jiminy in *Kingdom Hearts* video game 242-243; in *House of Mouse* 243; as Benny at the Benny Bash in Waukegan, IL 244-248; Disneyana Fan Club 249; Eddie and fans 249-253; Eddie and Yarmy's Army 251-252; Rip Taylor story 252-254; signs contract with Gurtman and Murtha Agency 254; reunites with Robert Goulet 254; touring with *Laughter in Bloom* 255-256; at the Lilly Ball campaign for Easter Seals in Louisville, KY 257-258; Canadian tour of *Laughter* 261-265; Eddie and his Aunt Rose Starsuk 265-266; meets Wende and Sarah Doohan 265; meets Jack Benny's grandchildren 266; Carolyn diagnosed with breast cancer 257; Eddie hosted by International Jack Benny Fan Club, Disneyana Fan Club, SPERDVAC, and Pacific Pioneer Broadcasters 267-268; radio re-creations 269-271; advises Sean Uminski 271; first signs of final illness 273-274; diagnosed with brain tumor 275; last performance as Jack Benny 276; attitude during struggle with illness 277-278; accepts award from Laughing Place fan club 278; last Christmas 280; trip to Las Vegas 281-282; visits from Laura Leff, Toma nd Betty Kennedy 281-202; enters Motin Picture Hospital 285; passes away 288; posthumous gift of cards to Carolyn 288-290; "A Life in Bloom" tribute 290; posthumously receives Disney Legend Award 290; curtain speech from *Laughter in Bloom* 293.

Carroll, Leland 16, 110, 116-117, 125-134, 151, 164, 168-172, 183, 187, 198, 202-204, 213, 231-233, 236-237, 275, 288, 308, 309

Carrol, Tina, *see* Monti, Tina Carroll

Carroll-Farr Productions 104, 107-109, 115, 123

Carrothers, Richard 211

Carson, Johnny 195

Carter, Jack 147

CBS (Columbia Broadcasting System) 70, 89, 104, 140, 154

Cedars Sinai Hospital 282

Centers for Disease Control (CDC, Atlanta, GA) 162

Charlie Brown (cartoon character) 181

Cheboygan Opera House (MI) 235

Chiropractic 134, 214, 231-232

Christmas Carol, A, (Dickens) 173

Churchill Downs, KY 257

Cihi, Guy 189-190

Cihi, Keoko 189-190

Clark, Randy 201

Clooney, George 118

Coca-Cola 88, 92, 163

Cole, Nat "King", 76

Cole, Tommy 74

Columbia Theater (Washington State) 284

Conrad, Michael 126

Cooper, Ben 49-53, 55-58, 65-68, 93-94, 97, 200

Cooper, Gary 59

Cooper, Pamela 65-68, 116

Crawford, Joan 55, 100

Crosby Brothers 76

Crosby, Bing 82, 100, 105

Cruz, Brandon 72

Curtis, Tony 92

D23 (Disney International Expo) 273

INDEX

Daffy Duck (cartoon character) 192
Dailey, Dan 76
Dana, Bill (José Jimenez) 37, 52, 252
Dangerfield, Rodney 219
Dano, Royal 55
Dark, Johnny 219
Dasha Shaw Goody 35, 40
Davis, Bette 87, 100
Davis, Sammy Jr., 74, 77
Davis-Elen Advertising Agency 170
Day, Clarence 49
Day, Dennis (Eugene McNulty) 136, 146-147, 176, 209, 234, 244-245, 265
de Cordova, Fred 104
DeRolf, Paul 79-80
Desilu 154-155
DeVorzon, Barry 83
Diamond Circle Award 268, 271
Dickens, Charles 173
Dietrich, Marlene 76-77
Dillman, Charles 224
Dingle Sisters 230
Disney Channel, The 122, 175, 243
Disney Legend Award 249, 290
Disney Sing-Along (video series) 14, 175
Disney, Walt 25-26, 173
Disneyana Fan Club 180, 242-243, 249, 267, 290-202, 307
Disneyland 127, 179-180, 205, 249, 278-279, 307
Donald Duck (cartoon character) 121, 173, 229, 243
Doohan, James 265
Doohan, Sarah 265
Doohan, Wende 265
Dreyfuss, Richard 158
"Dueling Pianos" (Musical act, Mark and Clark) 150-151
Duke University (Durham, NC) 266
Earth Day 205
Eastwood, Clint 62, 107
Economou, Michael 158
Eddie (Jack Russell terrier), 236
Edmonton, Alberta 20-21, 25, 28, 30-37, 47, 93, 146, 178, 230, 264
Edmunds Theater (Washington State) 284
Edwards, Cliff ("Ukulele Ike") 13, 25-26, 116-117, 205, 248
Edwards, Ralph 270

Einstein, Albert 148
Eisner, Michael 104
Elen, Bob (Eddie's brother), 22, 27-29, 127, 170, 286, 290, 308, 309
Elen, Cami 127, 170-171
Eleniak, Dale (Eddie's brother) 22, 27-29, 121, 170, 286, 309
Eleniak, Erika 170-172, 207, 308, 309
Eleniak, Indyanna 287, 308
Eleniak, Ivan (John) 20
Eleniak, Jerry (Eddie's brother) 22, 27-28
Eleniak, Marie Starcheski (Eddie's mother) 21-26, 28-29, 61, 144, 146
Eleniak, Peter (Eddie's father) 21-26, 28-29, 45, 144, 146
Eleniak, Steven 21, 309
Eleniak, Wasyl 19-20
Elmwood Casino (Windsor, Ont.) 81, 263-264
Engemann, Bob 82-84
Environmentality 205
Evanier, Mark 279, 308, 309
Fagott, Noni 145
Farah, Jameel. *See Farr, Jamie*
Farmer, Bill 116, 175, 181-183, 229, 309
Farmer, Jen 116, 181-182, 309
Farr, Jamie, 9-11, 69-72, 76, 88-91, 93-94, 104, 107-109, 111, 113-116, 123-124, 134, 212, 216, 273, 285-286, 290, 308, 309
Farr, Joy, 9, 88-94, 115-116, 123-125, 216, 273, 278, 286, 308, 309
Fein, Irving 195, 197
Ferrante, Frank 148, 206-208, 210-213, 216, 269-270, 309
Ferrigno, Lou 72
Fisher, Eddie 47
Fisher, Robert 216
Flamingo Casino (Laughlin, NV) 220
Flynn, Errol 87-88, 171
Ford Ord 48-51
Forestieri, Marcel 219
Four Preps 63
Fraher, Chuck 219
Fredonia, NY 252-253, 261
Frees, Paul 68-69, 175
Friars Club of Beverly Hills 206-208
Friends of Old Time Radio 290
Gabriel, Roman 1107
Gainesville Theatre Alliance. *See* North Georgia University

Gelbart, Larry 115
Genesee Theatre (Waukegan, IL) 245, 284
Gilbert, Johnny 107
Gilmore, Art 270
Gleason, Jackie 210
Goldman, Hal 197
Goodman, Benny, 264
Goody, Dasha Shaw 35, 40
Goody, Joe 35
Goofy (cartoon character) 116, 173, 175, 181-183, 221, 229
Gorcey, Leo 32
Gordon, Gale 153, 155, 157
Goulet, Robert 30-32, 35-37, 151-152, 212, 254
Grammer, Kelsey 236
Great Lakes Naval Station 136
Grey, Zane 58
Griffith, Andy 16, 70, 101-102, 110
Gurtman and Murtha 254, 261
Hackett, Buddy 76
Haley, Jack 153
Hall, Huntz 32
Hanna-Barbera (animation studio) 10, 111
Harrah's 51, 75-76, 244-245
Harrington, Pat 252
Harris, Phil 137, 174, 244-245
Harvard University 189
Harvey's (Lake Tahoe, NV) 76, 194
Haunted Mansion (Disney attraction) 69
Hawaii 124, 167-169
Hayden, Sterling 55
HBO (Home Box Office cable network) 1107
Hearn, Chick 103
Hearn, Sam 137
Hell's Kitchen (New York) 167
Hennessy, Dennis 211
Herb Alpert and the Tijuana Brass (musical group) 100-101
Hesby Street School (Hesby Oaks School) 125, 127-129
Heston, Charlton 92
Hi There, Boys and Girls! America's Local Children's TV Programs (Hollis) 249
Hide, Richard H., 248
Holbrook, Hal 148
Hollis, Tim 249
Holly, Buddy 150
Hollywood Plaza Hotel 33

Hollywood Professional School (HPS) 73-74, 82
Hong Kong 177, 179
Hope, Bob 105, 108-109, 219
Hudson, Rock 107
Huey Lewis and the News 161
Hunter, Evan 69
hypnotism 112, 148
Imperial Gardens (Japan) 190
International Jack Benny Fan Club (IJBFC) 116, 138, 149, 165, 219, 244, 251, 267, 269, 282, 288, 307
Jack Benny: An Intimate Biography (Fein) 195
Japan 14, 70, 188-192
Jason, the Underwater Robot (animatronic figure) 178-179
Jerry's Famous Deli 252
Jiminy Cricket (cartoon character) 13-16, 25-27, 116-122, 124-125, 127, 129, 132, 134, 143, 158, 167, 173-175, 179-183, 185, 187-189, 200, 205-206, 221-222, 229, 235, 240, 242-243, 249, 256, 259, 268, 271, 280, 286, 290-291, 307
John Ascuaga's Nugget Casino (Sparks, NV) 165-166
Jolson, Al 268
Jones, Tommy Lee 172
Jordan, Jim 270
Junior Dance Masters of America 73, 193
Karaoke 132-133
karate 128-129
Keaton, Buster 82
Kennedy, Betty 116, 248, 257, 282
Kennedy, John F., 100
Kennedy, Tom 116, 248, 257, 282-283
Kingdom Hearts (video game) 15, 242
Kirchenbauer, Bill 19-221
Klinger, Maxwell Q. (character) 115-123, 134
Klugman, Jack 148, 210
Knotts Berry Farm 151-152
Knotts, Don 16, 101-102, 106, 110, 126
Kogen, Arnie 252
Korea 48, 70
Korman, Harvey 252
Kosslyn, Jack 62
Kubelik, Jan 136
Kubelsky, Benny. *See* Jack Benny
Kurdoon, Randy 252
Lake Nipissing, Ont 263

INDEX

Lake Tahoe, NV 71, 76, 112, 124, 127, 151, 167, 169, 194, 213
Lamour, Dorothy 105
Landesberg, Steve 252
Laughing Place (Disney fan club) 278
Lawford, Peter 107
Leff, Dan 244
Leff, Laura 116, 138, 149-150, 165, 219, 244, 282, 288-289, 307, 309
Lennon, John 201
Leno, Jay 219
Lettermen, The 77, 82-85, 226-227, 309
Lewis Family Playhouse (Rancho Cucamonga, CA) 265
"Life in Bloom, A" (celebration of Eddie's life) 290
Lily Ball campaign for Easter Seals 257
Lindsay, Harold 49
Livingstone, Mary (Sadie Marks) 136-137, 156-157, 224, 241, 244, 288
Louisville, KY 257
Lubitsch, Ernst 209
Ludwig von Drake (cartoon character) 175
Lum, Susie 222
Lyme disease 162-163, 177
MacDonald, James 173
Mackinac Island, MI 255
Magnus, Chuck ("TOS") 133, 217, 241
Mahoney, John 235
Marco Polo (Miami, FL) 159
Mark and Clark (Seymour) 150-151, 239
Marshall, Peter 252, 276-277, 290
Martindale, Sandy 116
Martindale, Wink 116
Martinez, Andrew ("The Naked Guy") 198
Marx Brothers 136
Marx, Arthur 206-207, 216
Marx, Groucho 16, 47, 206-208, 210-211, 216, 269
Marx, Minnie 136
Massachusetts Institute of Technology 245
Matthau, Walter 210
Mayfair Theatre (Santa Monica, CA) 146-148
Mayflower II (ship) 161
Mayo, Virginia 266
Mazatlan, Mexico 194
McBain, Ed. *See* Hunter, Evan
McCallum Theatre (Palm Springs, CA) 284
McCann, Chuck 250, 252

McClure, Doug 10, 71
McDowell, Roddy 90
McMillan, Gloria 270-271
Meiseles, Ben 266
Meiseles, Brad 245-246, 266
Meiseles, Brandon 266
Meiseles, Joanna 245-246, 266, 288, 308
Melody Knights (musical group) 73
Menessee, William 93-94, 97
Merv Griffin Theater 164
Metrano, Art 164
M-G-M , 89-90, 92, 107
Michaels, George 161
Michaelson, Gerald, Dr., 275, 285
Mickey Mouse (cartoon character) 73, 173, 180, 205, 229, 243, 307
Miller, Ned 136
Mills, Bob 252
Minnie Mouse (cartoon character) 173, 180, 229, 243, 307
Monroe, Marilyn 150, 165
Monti, Rick 184, 204
Monti, Tina Carroll 9, 16, 105, 109-110, 114-116, 125-129, 133-134, 151, 158, 162, 167-170, 172, 183-184, 193, 199-200, 20, 213, 278, 280-289, 308-310, 311
Morton, Gary 155-158
Motion Picture Health Center 275, 280, 285
Motion Picture Hospital 9, 285-286
MOTION PICTURES:
Blackboard Jungle, The 69-70
Captain Horatio Hornblower 244
Dance, Girl, Dance 153
Dark Corner, The 153
Dead End 32
Duel At Apache Wells 51
E.T.: The Extraterrestrial 170
Essex and Elizabeth 87-88
*Five Came Back,*153
Flight Nurse 51
Fun and Fancy Free 173
Greatest Story Ever Told, The 89-93
Hollywood Revue of 1929, 25
Jiminy Cricket's Christmas 174
Johnny Guitar 51
Jungle Book, The (animated version) 175
Karate Kid, The 79
Kismet 70
Man About Town 245

Mickey and the Beanstalk 173
Mickey's Christmas Carol 173-174
No Time for Sergeants 70
Oh, God! 196
Pinocchio 13, 25-27, 111, 116, 118, 121, 174, 180-181, 259, 269
Rose Tattoo, The 51
Sea of Lost Ships 51
Sunshine Boys, The 195
Taras Bulba 92
Thing, The 69
Thunderbirds 51
To Be or Not to Be 209
Treasure of the Sierra Madre 269
Under Siege, 171-172
Murtha, Jim 254, 261
Music Box Theatre (San Francisco, CA) 165
My Wicked, Wicked Ways (Errol Flynn autobiography) 87
Myrtle Beach, SC 256
Nabors, Jim 101
Nash, Clarence "Ducky", 173
Nathaniel Bartholomew 90
National Fantasy Fan Club (NFFC). See Disneyana Fan Club
NBC (National Broadcasting Company) 43, 46-47, 107, 110, 240
Nederlander Theater Company 212
Nelson, Frank 137-138, 175-176, 209
New Orleans, LA, 228
New Theatre (Overland Park, KS) 210-216
Nicklaus, Jack, 108
Noble, Lawrence 192, 265
North Bay, Ont 261-263
North Georgia University 249, 250, 311
Northridge Earthuake 201-204
Nye, Louis 252
O'Connor, Donald 76
Old Sacramento, CA 256
Olivier, Sir Laurence 60, 87
Olsen, Merlin 107
On Fraternity Row (Eddie Carroll comedy album) 62-63
Once Upon a Time (album, The Lettermen) 84
Oppenheimer, Gregg 153
Oppenheimer, Jess 153-154
Orion Musical Theatre (Edmonton, Alberta) 30, 32-37, 40-44, 230, 265
Orlando, FL 179-181

O'Ross, Ed 257
Owens, Gary 252, 277, 309
Owens, Jim 1151
Ozohan, Mary Lou, Dr., 275
Pacific Pioneer Broadcasters 267, 270, 276
Pacino, Al 156
Page, Patti 76
Panischak, Yurko 19
Parker, Dorothy 148
Pearson, Drew 138
Peck, Gregory 244
Pella Opera House (Pella, IA) 255
Pella, Iowa 255
Perkins, Les 255
Pierce, David Hyde 235
Pike, Jim 82, 84
Pillsbury Doughboy (animated character) 69
Pismo Beach, CA 163
Pitt, Brad 118
PLAYS AND STAGE SHOWS:
A La Carte from Las Vegas (revue) 71, 77-83, 87, 143, 263
Ain't Misbehaving (Horowitz and Maltby musical) 194
Beatlemania 201
Ben Blue's Revue 143
Benny, Monroe, and Cagney 165
Elizabeth the Queen (Anderson) 87
End of a Man 143
Evening with Groucho, An (Ferrante, one-man show) 216
Evening with Jack Benny and Groucho Marx, An 206-207
Finian's Rainbow (Harburg-Saidy-Lane musical) 43
Gigi (Lerner and Loewe musical) 207
Green Grow the Lilacs (Riggs) 42
Jack Benny: Laughter in Bloom (Carroll, one-man show) 16, 176, 185, 192, 219-224, 235-236, 240-254, 261, 264-266, 270, 279, 285, 292-293, 308, 311
Legends in Concert 150, 158, 160-163
Legends of Comedy 219-221, 233
Legends on Broadway 163-165
Life with Father (Russel and Crouse) 49-50, 59
Max 72, 77
Newcomers of 1928 (revue), 82
Odd Couple, The (Simon) 143, 208-216

Oklahoma! (Rodgers and Hammerstein musical) 40-43
Of Mice and Men (Steinbeck) 143
Small Eternity with Jack Benny, A (one-man show) 141, 143, 149-150, 158-167, 206
South Pacific (Rodgers and Hammerstein musical) 277, 341
Spring Awakening (Sheik and Slater musical) 147, 349
Twelve Angry Men (Rose) 143
When Last I Saw the Lemmings 143
Plimouth Village, MA 161-162
Pomona (NJ) 250
Porky Pig (cartoon character) 192
Powers, Bill 192
Poynton, Bobby 82
Presley, Elvis 48, 83, 150
Pylypov, Ivan 19-20
Queen Elizabeth Theatre (Toronto, Ont.) 161
Quinn, Anthony 101
Radio College of Canada (RCC Institute of Technology, Toronto) 37-38, 45
Radio Enthusiasts of Puget Sound (REPS) 269, 308
RADIO PROGRAMS:
FBI in Peace and War, The 50
Great Gildersleeve, The 268
Jack Benny Program, The 107, 136-138, 209, 249, 263, 270
Lone Ranger, The 269
My Favorite Husband 154
Our Miss Brooks 271
Those Were the Days 244, 266
Very Merry Christmas, A 228-229
Wonder Show, The 153
Ramada Express Resort and Casino in Laughlin, Nevada 239-240
Rancho Cucamonga, CA 191-193, 265-266
Randall, Tony 210
Rappaport, John 252, 309
Ray, Nicholas 55
"Red Light, Green Light" (Japanese/English instructional program) 14, 188-189
Reynolds, Burt 10, 71
Reynolds, Gene 114-117
Rialto Square Theater (Joliet, IL) 284
Rickles, Don 68
Riggs, Lynn 42
Riley, Jack 252

Riordan, Richard 250-251
Rogers, Roy 192
Ross, Kerry 252
Rudolph, Maria 245-246, 248, 288
Russell, Talmadge 82
Sacra, Bill 219
Salisbury, Cora 136
Scarvelis, Maria 244
Schaden, Chuck 244, 266
Schaden, Ellen 244
Schaengold, Anita 290, 307
Schaengold, Gary 290, 307
Schell, Ronnie 252
Screen Actors Guild 92, 131, 135
Screenwriters Guild 134
Scrooge McDuck (cartoon character) 173-174
Seagal, Steven 171
Sellersville, PA 261
Shatner, William 37
Shaw and Hitchcock 71-72, 77
Sheldon, Jack 252
Shore, Dinah 47
Shultz, Charles 52
Simon, Danny 210
Simon, Neil 210, 212
Sinatra, Frank 77, 100
Singapore 177
Sixth Army Chorus 52
Skelton, Red 70-72, 89
Smith, Hal 173
Smokey Lake , Alberta (Eddie's birthplace) 22
Snead, Sam 108
Snowdon, Ted 139-140, 143, 149, 158, 164
Song for Young Love, A (album, The Lettermen) 82
SONGS:
"26 Miles," 63
"Actor's Life for Me, An," 111
"Ave Maria," 183
"Bare Necessities, The," 175
"Blueberry Hill," 82
"California, Here I Come," 25
"Give a Little Whistle," 25, 280
"Hard-Hearted Hannah," 25
"Here Comes the Bride," 183
"How is Julie?" 85-87, 226-227
"I Remember It Well," 207-208
"I Whistle a Happy Tune," 280

"I'll Be Seeing You," 82
"In the Still of the Night,"82
"It's Only a Paper Moon," 25
"Kansas City," 42
"Lonely Bull, The," 100
"Love in Bloom," 144-145, 176, 290
"Old Cape Cod," 161
"Paddlin' Madelin' Home," 25
"Rule, Britannia," 245
"Singin' in the Rain," 25
"Smile 82
"Tijuana Taxi," 100
"Way You Look Tonight, The," 82
"When I Fall in Love," 82
"When You Wish Upon a Star," 118-119, 184
"Willie and the Hand Jive," 74
"You Are my Sunshine," 26
"Zorba the Greek," 101
SPERDVAC (Society to Preserve and Encourage Radio Drama, Variety, and Comedy) 267, 269, 308
Spielberg, Stephen 171
Spirit Lake Casino in Devil's Lake, ND 239
Sportsmen's Lodge Coffee Shop 192, 252
Springer, Dorothy "Dot" (Carolyn's mother) 180-181, 183, 193, 231
Springer, Glenn (Carolyn's father) 73, 97, 180-183, 193, 231
Springer, Sandy 228
Squaw Valley 76
St. Catherine's, Ont 261
St. Joseph High School 30-33
St. Jude 90-91
St. Jude's Children's Research Hospital 90
Stadlen, Lewis 148
Starsuk, Rose ("Aunt Rose") 264-265
Stevens, George 89-90
Stevens, Steve 74
Storm, Howard 252
Storness-Bliss, Bjorn 278-279
Stradivarius violins 135, 146
Strange, Billy 83
Strasberg, Lee 37, 61
Strickland, Barbara 250-251, 285, 309, 311
Strickland, Brad 249, 252-253, 285, 309, 311
Strickland, Jonathan 251, 309, 311
Strickland, Rebecca Van Campen 251, 309, 311
Sullivan, Ed 136

Sunday Nights at Seven (biography, Joan Benny and Jack Benny) 147, 195
Sutton, Frank 101-102
Swackhammer, E.W., 115
Sweeney, Amy Strickland 251, 309, 311
Sweeney, Tim, 309, 311
Tai Chi 128, 165
Takei, George 256
Tannen, Herb 13-15, 116, 121
Taylor, Rip 252-254, 256
Taylor, Russi 229, 307
Tea, Donovan 82
TELEVISION PROGRAMS:
Amazing Chan and the Chan Clan, The 111
Andy Griffith Show, The 101-102, 155
Armstrong Circle Theater 51
Bonanza 126
Burns and Allen 140
Constitution, The 158
Courtship of Eddie's Father, The 72
Don Knotts Show, The 106-107, 109-111, 126, 139
Dick Powell's Zane Grey Theater 58
Dick Van Dyke Show, The 155
D-TV 175
Frasier 235-236
F Troop 108, 115
From All of Us to All of You 122
Gary Shandling Show, The 107
Get Smart! 251
Gomer Pyle, U.S.M.C. 101-102
Gunsmoke 58
Hill Street Blues 126
Hollywood Palace, The 100-102, 106
Honeymooners, The 210
House of Mouse 243-244
Howdy Doody Show, The 37
Huckleberry Hound 111
I Love Lucy 153-155
Incredible Hulk, The 72
Jack Benny Show, The 140, 164, 265
Jack Benny's Birthday Special 103, 139, 155
Jeopardy 107
Jerry Lewis Show, The 100
Johnny Otis Show, The 74
Kelsey Grammer Salutes Jack Benny 236
Life With Lucy 155-156
Love that Bob! 140
MASH 115, 123, 134, 212

INDEX

Magician, The 72
Man to Man 107-110
Many Loves of Dobie Gillis, The 72
Mary Tyler Moore Show, The 121-122, 164
Mickey Mouse Club, The 73, 205
Mission: Impossible 155
Mr. Ed 173
My Favorite Martian 72
Our House (pilot episode) 104
Queen for a Day 47
Rebel, The 89
Rocky and Bullwinkle 68
Rowan and Martin's Laugh-In 252
Ruff and Reddy 111
Saturday Night Live 36, 166
Star Trek 58, 155, 265
Steve Allen Show, The 37
Twilight Zone, The 211
Virginian, The 126
Wagon Train 65-66
Yogi Bear 111
You Bet Your Life 270
Thailand 177-178
Thomas, Danny 90
Thorndycroft, Marilyn Dingle 36, 230
Thousand Oaks Civic Arts Plaza (Thousand Oaks, CA) 266
Thurber, James 148
Toledo, OH 69, 90, 115
TOS, *see* Magnus, Chuck
Tower of Power 161
Tower Records 226
Travalena, Fred 116, 256-257
Travalena, Lois 116, 257
Trethewey, Tom 244
Trevor, Claire 32
Tropicana Lounge (Atlantic City, NJ) 152
Tropicana Resort and Casino 237
Trump's Castle (now Trump's Marina, Atlantic City, NJ) 225
Tucker, Forrest 108-109
Twain, Mark (Samuel Clemens) 148
Tweetie Pie (cartoon character) 192
Twentieth Century-Fox , 192
U.S. Armed Forces Radio Service 52, 70
U.S. Army Motion Picture Department 50, 342
"Ugly Duckling, The" (Spanish/English instructional program) 189

Ukraine 19-20, 92
Uminski, Sean 270-271
University of Southern California 148
Valentino, Pat 74
Vallee, Rudy 82
Vaudeville 25, 135-136
Venet, Nick 82-84
Vidor, Jim 252
Vogel, Barry 231, 265
Vogel, Sarah 231
Vogel, Speed 210
Walker, Jimmy 219
Walston, Ray, 72
Walt Disney Studios 119, 121, 124, 158, 173, 188, 222
Walt Disney World 179-183, 221-222, 249
Wang Theatre (Boston, MA) 160
Waring, Fred 76
Warner/Chappell Music, Inc 226-227
Wat Pho (Bangkok) 179
Waukegan, IL 135, 139, 244-248, 284
Wayne, John 60, 192
Weeks, Christopher 165
Weir, Bill 254, 261-262
Western Geophysical Oil 38
Whiteman, Paul 82
Willer, Charlie 244
Williams, Hank 150-151
Wilson, Don 136, 138, 219, 244-245
Windom, William 148
Winter Olympics 76, 280-281
Winters, Jonathan 181
Wisdom of the 90s (Burns and Goldman) 197
Wong, Tom 28-30
Woods, Lyman 136
Yarmy, Dick 251
Yarmy's Army 250-252, 276-277
Yosemite Sam (cartoon character) 192
Young, Alan 173-174

Acknowledgements

Utmost appreciation goes to the remarkable Eddie Carroll for having tremendous talent and being an admirable man. The way he lived and enjoyed life to the fullest made this book possible. Eddie is a model for young talent, showing them how to set goals, stay determined and follow their dreams.

To family, friends and fans…thank you for the many years of memories and adventures that Jiminy and Jack brought into our lives. You are all so special and blessings go out to all of you for taking this spectacular ride with us. Your unwavering support that helped hold up our spirits as we forged through this challenge. The constant support of Anita and Gary Schaengold, President and leaders of The Disneyana Fan Club, and the club members, including Brian (my bear), Darin, and Scarlett, brought much happiness to the Happiest Place, and the same goes for Doug and Jamie Marsh, founders of Friends of The Mouse and their myriad fans, all of whom stood ready to help.

Disney's "Character Voice" Department is the backbone of the vocal side of animation, and the department and its voice actors create a huge part of the Disney family. Thanks Bryan, Renee, Ben, Vanessa, Vicki and of course Rick Dempsey. And deep gratitude goes to the wonderful world of voices: Russi Taylor (Minnie), Bill Farmer (Goofy and Pluto), Tony Anselmo (Donald Duck) and Wayne Allwine (Mickey), who now also is a star in the sky — they are all fantastic, fun and talented personalities who help comprise the close-knit Disney family.

The International Jack Benny Fan Club is an enormous, enthusiastic group of Old Time Radio folks founded by the great enthusiast Laura Leff, a brilliant author and leader of this Club who with her membership has sponsored, organized, and presented wonderful events that keep the legacy of Jack Benny alive. She has done a superb job and has given so much of her life as the number one Jack Benny and Eddie Carroll fan since she was 15.

SPERDVAC (the Society to Preserve and Encourage Radio Drama, Variety and Comedy), REPS, (Radio Enthusiasts of Puget Sound) MARE (Milwaukee Area Radio Enthusiasts) are also among the fan clubs across the country giving tribute to Old Time Radio, and all are made up of great people. Gratitude goes to them all for supporting OTR and Disney not just in the U.S. but all around the world.

Thanks, too, go to all the DJs who are Eddie's fans and who have interviewed him many times over the years and reran the interviews as a tribute after his passing: Walden Hughes, Stuart Shokus, Erskine, Larry and John Gassman, Frank Bresee, and all of you, sincere thanks for the Eddie Carroll interviews you did so well, and I bow to you. So many websites have been so gracious to us over the many years: *LaughingPlace.com*, *micechat.com*, Mark Evanier and *newsfromme.com*, *mouseplanet.com*, *toonzone.net*, Disney D23, voiceactors, and of course *jackbenny.org*.

For the Jack Benny family and their continuing support of Eddie and his "Laughter in Bloom," I send you all hugs and am so proud to have you in our lives and on our team. Thank you to Jack's daughter Joan, with grandchildren Mike, Marie, Joanna, and Bobby, and the great-grandchildren we met: Brandon and Ben. You all made such a difference by coming into Eddie's life.

Deep feelings from our family go to Eddie's doctors, nurses, and therapists because they are our real heroes. The Motion Picture and Television Hospital and the award-winning palliative health care team are treasures. They do "Take care of their own" with dedication, kindness, humor and smiles plus hugs are included.

I will always have special feelings for the support of friends and family. Eddie's brother Bob and his wife Marni, many thanks for helping me put the Tribute Memorial together for Eddie's "Life in Bloom," the celebration of a wonderful man. I include all those 20 friends that spoke or entertained us with reminiscences about Eddie as we remembered him with joy and laughter. They are terrific friends and great talents.

Chuck Magnus (TOS — "the other son"), Erika Eleniak (our niece) and her daughter Indyanna were always nearby with an extra hug and reinforcement to carry on.

My love from deep within for my sister Gloria Birnkrant, and for Jamie and Joy Farr, for their love and their treasured presence throughout our lives and especially for the care we received at the end of the battle that we lost. All those times they gave me a hand to hold on to kept me going onward. Tina Monti and Leland Carroll, our children, you brought so many loving memories of joyous times and silly fun moments to your

Dad and me. You are the fulfillment of our lives together. Bless all of you for coming into and sharing our lives. Thank you!

And to my writing partner, Bradley Strickland, who recalled the memories of laughter and Eddie's stories with me. Brad, we shared many laughs with our tears and somehow got through writing this book. It was a journey we took together.

Thank you all,
Carolyn Carroll

Deepest thanks to all those who consented to interviews or granted permission to quote from their works for the book: Senator Tommy Banks, Joan Benny, Gloria Birnkrant, Tony Butala of the Lettermen, Leland Carroll, Tina Carroll Monti, Bob Elen, Dale Eleniak, Erika Eleniak, Steven Eleniak (Eddie's cousin and the family historian), Mark Evanier, Bill and Jen Farmer, Jamie and Joy Farr, Frank Ferrante, Laura Leff, Chuck "TOS" Magnus, Robert Mills, Gregg Oppenheimer, Gary Owens, and John Rappaport. Your gracious gift of your time and your memories enriched the task immeasurably.

Special heartfelt thanks and love to Carolyn, who shared her feelings, her experiences, and her expertise. Eddie was a lucky man.

And my gratitude goes to my dear wife Barbara, whose support and encouragement are always vital to me, and to our son Jonathan and his wife Rebecca, and to our daughter Amy the puppeteer and her talented husband Tim Sweeney. Though they met Eddie only briefly, Jonathan, Becca, and Amy loved him and valued his wonderful stories.

Thanks to you all,
Brad Strickland

About the Authors

CAROLYN CARROLL was given the wonderful gift of being married to Eddie Carroll for just one day short of 47 years. She was the Program Director for *Jack Benny: Laughter in Bloom* for 17 years, and the adventures and laughter she and Eddie shared and enjoyed together are her warmest memories. She is the mother of Tina Monti and Leland Carroll, Eddie's beloved daughter and son. Carolyn felt writing this book about Eddie was a privilege and his philosophy and way of living his life deserved to be shared with his fans.

BRAD STRICKLAND is the author or coauthor of seventy books. He and his wife Barbara knew Eddie Carroll for nine years, saw him often in shows, and enjoyed his and Carolyn's company. When Eddie called Brad his "number one fan," the title meant more to him than Eddie knew. When not writing, Brad is a Professor of English at the Gainesville campus of the University of North Georgia. He and Barbara have two grown children, Amy (lead puppeteer at the Center for Puppetry Arts in Atlanta and wife of Tim Sweeney), and Jonathan (technical writer and star of the Web series *FW: Thinking*, and husband of Rebecca).

Bear Manor Media

Classic Cinema.
Timeless TV.
Retro Radio.

WWW.BEARMANORMEDIA.COM

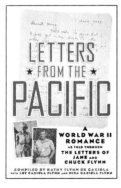

CPSIA information can be obtained at www.ICGtesting.com
Printed in the USA
BVOW010049020413

317043BV00003B/6/P

9 781593 932428